COAL COUNTRY

COAL COUNTRY

RISING UP AGAINST MOUNTAINTOP REMOVAL MINING

Edited by Shirley Stewart Burns, Mari-Lynn Evans, and Silas House

SIERRA CLUB BOOKS
SAN FRANCISCO

The Sierra Club, founded in 1892 by author and conservationist John Muir, is the oldest, largest, and most influential grassroots environmental organization in the United States. With more than a million members and supporters—and some sixty chapters across the country—we are working hard to protect our local communities, ensure an enduring legacy for America's wild places, and find smart energy solutions to stop global warming. To learn how you can participate in the Sierra Club's programs to explore, enjoy, and protect the planet, please address inquiries to Sierra Club, 85 Second Street, San Francisco, California 94105, or visit our Web site at www.sierraclub.org.

The Sierra Club's book publishing division, Sierra Club Books, has been a leading publisher of titles on the natural world and environmental issues for nearly half a century. We offer books to the general public as a nonprofit educational service in the hope that they may enlarge the public's understanding of the Sierra Club's concerns and priorities. The point of view expressed in each book, however, does not necessarily represent that of the Sierra Club. For more information on Sierra Club Books and a complete list of our titles and authors, please visit www.sierraclubbooks.org.

Published by Sierra Club Books,
85 Second Street, San Francisco, CA 94105

Sierra Club Books are published in association with Counterpoint
(www.counterpointpress.com).

SIERRA CLUB, SIERRA CLUB BOOKS, and the Sierra Club design logos are registered trademarks of the Sierra Club.

Interior design concept by Harry Choron, March Tenth, Inc.
Photo editing and layouts by Linda Herman, Glyph Publishing Arts
Composition by David Van Ness

Title page photograph: Hollers in the mist, Boone County, West Virginia.
Photo © Giles Ashford.

Library of Congress Cataloging-in-Publication Data

Coal country : rising up against mountaintop removal mining / edited by Shirley Stewart Burns, Mari-Lynn Evans, and Silas House.
p. cm.
Includes bibliographical references.
ISBN 978-1-57805-168-7 (cloth : alk. paper)
ISBN 978-1-57805-166-3 (pbk. : alk. paper)
1. Mountaintop removal mining—Environmental aspects—Appalachian Region.
2. Coal mines and mining—Appalachian Region. 3. Environmental degradation—Appalachian Region. 4. Environmental awareness—Appalachian Region. 5. Appalachian Region—Environmental conditions. I. Burns, Shirley Stewart. II. Evans, Mari-Lynn. III. House, Silas, 1971-
TD195.C58C614 2009
338.2'7240974—dc22   2009024244

Printed in China on acid-free paper

Distributed by Publishers Group West
13 12 11 10 09
10 9 8 7 6 5 4 3 2 1

To my parents, the late Neely U. Stewart and Cora McKinney Stewart, and
my husband, Matthew Burns, true Appalachians all, whose dedication to family and
whose love of the land and the stories of Appalachia continue to inspire me.
—*Shirley Stewart Burns*

To the people living in the coalfields of Appalachia. May you someday get justice.
—*Mari-Lynn Evans*

To K.H., who loves Appalachia and its people, and in memory of the Widow Combs.
—*Silas House*

Contents

Foreword

Nick Clooney

MOST OF MY ANCESTORS CAME to this country from Ireland during the potato famines. We came floating in on adversity, as did most who found a new home on these shores. I am told that my Irish forebears headed down the Ohio River because they had heard that in spring and summer the land there looked a great deal like Ireland—that it had a hundred shades of green.

They settled on the banks of the Ohio in the little town of Maysville, Kentucky. At first they were laborers, but in time some became professionals. My Grandfather Clooney was a jeweler and gemologist, and he later became the mayor of Maysville. He was also a wonderful writer, with a real Irish flair.

Like all the immigrants to this region, once we got here, we assimilated and became part of Appalachian culture. There's an Appalachian legacy in all of our family, expressed in our love of the land and our love of music. My Grandmother Guilfoyle was a singer, a pianist, and a teacher. She was the one who made sure we had a direct line to the *Grand Ole Opry,* to the WLS *National Barn Dance,* and to the *Ozark Jamboree.* We weren't allowed to miss any of these radio broadcasts. And we never wanted to.

The most difficult thing about describing Appalachia and what it means to the rest of the country is the isolation of

Lower Falls of Hills Creek, Pocahontas County, West Virginia. Photo © Jim Clark.

A collection of objects reflecting the Appalachian heritage of Charles Blevin hangs on the wall of the Red Robin Inn, his local road stop in Borderland, Mingo County, West Virginia, 1971. Photo © Builder Levy.

our culture. Many modern advancements have passed us by, and our land and natural resources have been exploited by outsiders for more than a century. We found ourselves stereotyped as hillbillies; that meant you didn't have shoes or running water. We may not have had those things, but my guess is that out of those negatives, out of the isolation and poverty, came a positive, and that was identity. What we did have was a deep understanding of ourselves and our families, and how important each member of a family was. Our very isolation made us turn inward toward family and friends. We may not have been mobile, but we were centered and grounded. That has been our gift to the rest of the nation.

We learned, however, that Appalachia is in some ways not as isolated as we believed. The rivers connected us to the rest of the world.

My Grandpa Clooney was a very smart man. He had no idea how to talk to children; to him, children were short adults. So he would talk to us about politics and worldly things. When I was five or six years old, he took me down to the Ohio River, pointed to the water's surface, and said, "Put your hand in there." I obeyed. "Now something from your hand is going to go down the great Mississippi River," he said, "and it's going to go past New Orleans, and it's going to go out into the Gulf of Mexico, and it's going to sweep past Florida. It's going to go all the way up to Europe. It's going to touch the places where our forebears came from originally." He looked me in the eye. "You can never think small again. You've got to be part of the big world, and this is part of the big world. You've just touched it."

At the time I didn't want to be bothered with this kind of conversation. I wanted to go get an Eskimo Pie. But of course I heard him, and I understood him. I knew what he meant then, and I know even more what he meant now. I know how important it is to care for Appalachia's waters, and its people, because the effect of abusing them will ripple through the rivers of America.

Even though our business requires that we travel a lot, my wife, Nina, and I have always tried to keep a home in Kentucky. Every time I go away, I feel good about coming back. I feel that I'm returning to something that is quite real, and I know that my heart is still by that muddy river and those stubby hills.

We have become great because of the lavish use of our resources. But the time has come to inquire seriously what will happen when our forests are gone, when the coal, the iron, the oil, and the gas are exhausted, when the soils shall have become still further impoverished and washed into the streams, polluting the rivers, denuding the fields and obstructing navigation.

—Theodore Roosevelt

Editor's Note

Silas House

Coal miner in Jenkins, Kentucky, 1935. Photo by Ben Shahn; courtesy of Library of Congress.

COAL MINING IS A PART OF ME. My grandfather lost his leg in the Kentucky deep mines in the 1940s. After only six months of recuperation, he went back into the mines and worked twenty more years. In the late 1960s, my uncle was in a mining accident that left him branded across his left cheek-bone by a coal tattoo. But he went right back in. My uncles and cousins and brother-in-law all loved their jobs. Mining allowed them to rise out of poverty.

I am proud of my grandfather's lost leg, proud of my uncle's coal tattoo. They are symbols of determination and hard work. Those men helped build this nation.

But slowly, my love for coal mining turned to a love-hate relationship. When I was very small, I stood on a ridge with my father and uncles while they looked down on what had been our family burial ground. The coal company had been required to move all the graves, but it had been discovered that they had left one behind, that of my great-aunt. The company had pushed her grave over the edge of the bank and into the strip mine below. We stood there in complete silence. My father and uncles had never been silent before.

Then, when I was a teenager in the 1980s, there was a strip mine directly across from our house. We breathed the dust and listened to the groan of machinery for the entire two years the mine was in operation. I spent long hours on the ridge above the mines, watching and mourning the loss of the woods and rolling pasture I had played in all my life. It wouldn't have been so bad if the land had been treated respectfully. But it wasn't. Trees were thrown aside like useless things. The good topsoil was buried beneath clay and rock. Still, I knew that coal mining was an important part of our economy.

Just a few years ago, I got my first glimpse of mountaintop removal (MTR)—in which the summit of a mountain is removed to extract coal—while driving along Highway 80 in Perry County, Kentucky. I drove by one of the first mountaintop removal sites that was located alongside the road, where it could be seen. For the longest time these sites had been hidden. The mountain that just the previous spring had been crowded with a thousand redbuds was now a barren plateau dotted by struggling saplings and shoots of brown grass. The land looked as if a nuclear bomb had gone off there.

Silas House hiking in the hills near his home in Eastern Kentucky. Photo © Tim Webb.

Then, in April 2005, I was one of fourteen writers who met on Lower Bad Creek in Leslie County, Kentucky, to view active mountaintop removal. These writers were all Kentuckians, some widely known and some just starting out, and all concerned citizens. We had been invited on the tour by writer and activist Wendell Berry. We walked through a healthy forest near the mining and viewed the wealth of herbs, plants, trees, and water that was being threatened on all sides. We climbed a mountain and looked down on a mountaintop removal mine. We looked down because the mountain was below us now, its head cut off. Discarded. We drove through the valley and saw plateaus that had once been mountains on either side of us.

Later that day we were given flyovers, on which we could look down and see MTR sites that seemed to stretch on forever. We either wept or were completely silent. We were all writers, yet we had no words. There still are no words adequate to describe it, so I don't even try. I don't know how to articulate complete destruction, utter disrespect.

After the flyovers, we drove twenty miles to Hindman, a small town that sits along the banks of Troublesome Creek, where we would attend a town meeting. On the way, I counted eight mountains that had been removed along the road. Gone forever. Some were still dusty, noisy messes of bulldozers and exposed coal seams. Others had been "reclaimed," but I saw no evidence of healthy forests or fertile pastures there. There were sparse patches of grass and a few shrubs, but mostly it was dead land. And these were only the ones by the road. The sites way up in the hollers, where most of them are, don't get as much reclamation attention as the ones out in the public eye—if they get reclaimed at all, since so many companies conveniently file bankruptcy once they've hauled out the last ton of coal, and thereby are not legally required to even attempt to fix the land. Certainly those reclaimed sites won't be the bustling economic centers for malls, golf courses, and subdivisions that MTR proponents are always going on about. At the town meeting, we were greeted by a standing-room-only crowd of people who had come to share the stories of their experiences with mountain-top removal. These people are a part of the land, and they live with mountaintop removal every day. It is their stories that matter.

There were stories of the blasts that went off every two hours throughout the sleepless nights. A man said that his grandchildren wouldn't even come to stay with him because they were afraid of the blasts. "They think the house is going to get swallowed up," he said.

A young woman lives on a road so damaged by coal trucks that ambulances aren't able to reach the older people who live there. Several people spoke of reporting damage to government officials, only to be told that the flooding, damaged foundations, and polluted air were all "acts of God."

There were tales of water that ran red as blood with sulfur. "Our water smells like rotten eggs. I can't drink or cook with it," a young mother said. A man had drilled five wells over the last year because the mining blasts caused every one of them to go dry. Another man stood up, fighting back tears, and articulated the true problem in this whole mess. "We are just throwaway people," he said.

Story after story was told about valley fills, which are created when huge amounts of earth, rock, and unwanted coal and trees are dumped into valleys, causing widespread flash flooding. When mudslides wash out roads, the county's taxpayers pay for the cleanup. Four mothers who all live on the same stretch of road told of their children killed by overloaded, speeding coal trucks.

So many stories that it would take an entire book to record them all. So much pain that an entire library could not contain it.

None of these people at the meeting came with a vendetta against the coal industry. They were there because they wanted their stories taken to a larger audience. They were there because they care about their children and

Brushy Fork coal refuse impoundment, Raleigh County, West Virginia. Photo © Builder Levy.

Spring in Kentucky hills will soon
  awaken;
The sap will run in every vein of
  tree . . .
Spring in Kentucky hills and I
  shall be
A free-soil man to walk beneath
  the trees
And listen to the wind among the
  leaves
And count the stars and do as I
  damn please.

—Jesse Stuart

grandchildren, and because the land is a part of them, too. It is a part of them because it's the land they were raised on, the land their parents and grandparents were raised on, the land their great-grandparents settled. The land is in their blood.

And the land is a part of anyone who is holding this book in his or her hands. Thus, the goal of this book is to bring the bad news to the people with hopes that the people will stand up and do something about it.

That's what I've tried to do, and the only way I've had of fighting back is to write about it. I believe that this is a battle against huge corporations that have unlimited amounts of money. And the people battling them to end this disrespectful form of coal mining? Well, pretty much all they have are their words and music. This is a war of big money versus words and music. I am here to tell you that I believe the songs and stories are winning.

When I first understood what MTR was, I didn't have the words to fight it, but since then I have educated myself on the issue. I've written about it and engaged in debates with those within the coal industry. I've lobbied on Capitol Hill and marched the streets in protest. This is a matter of respect, and I owe it to my ancestors who loved and worked this hard land for generations to stand up for my homeland. I am speaking out in tribute to my grandfather, who worked in the mines for thirty years, to my great-aunt, whose grave was carelessly pushed aside so the company could get to its product. I am fighting back in remembrance of my coal-mining uncles and my farming grandmother, in memory of all the people who have cherished this land. Most of all, I am speaking out for my daughters, who deserve to have these mountains to call their own. The Appalachians are in their blood, after all. They are in all of us.

Preface

Mari-Lynn Evans

I GREW UP IN BULLTOWN, in central West Virginia. It was just a holler off Route 19, and the only people living there were my family. From the time the first William Currence came to America from Ireland in 1672, our family had been farmers on this land. I grew up exploring the rivers and mountains that surrounded us. There were Indian burial grounds just up the hill from our house and Confederate soldiers laid to rest in a small grave near where the cattle fed. We played on the mountains in every season, rode sleighs in the winter, and dug ramps in the spring. The mountain was a part of our family. It was a living testament that stood throughout time, a link to our past and our gift to the future.

William D. and Edward Paul Currence at the Currence family home in Bulltown, West Virginia, 1915. Photographer unknown; Mari-Lynn Evans collection.

In the 1970s our family land, along with thousands of acres of ancestral farmlands, was taken through eminent domain by the U.S. Army Corps of Engineers for the creation of a dam. Water flooded the flatlands, but it could not take the mountains. The pain of losing that land is still raw after almost thirty years. Losing our home place broke my grandfather's heart, tore apart our community, forever separated families, and affected me in ways I could never explain. My family had lived in one place for generations, surrounded by relatives and friends, doing a specific work, and one day it was all taken away.

The last time I went down to where the old house stood, I scooped up some dirt and put it in a little enameled box

Larry Gibson and his dog looking over the moonscape at Kayford Mountain, Kanawha County, West Virginia. Photo © Mark Schmerling.

my grandmother bought me when I was about five. I carry that box with me everywhere I travel in this world. It gives me comfort, but it is also a constant reminder of what I have lost, what my grandparents lost when our land was taken. I want to carry that piece of earth with me, both the joy and the pain, because I learned early what really matters in this life: our family, our community, our way of life.

After our land was taken, we moved to Akron, Ohio, to be with relatives who had gone there in the 1950s to get jobs in the rubber industry. My thick accent made me an obvious transplant from Appalachia, and somehow strangers felt free to tell me embarrassing jokes about incest, outhouses, and moonshine. If you're from West Virginia, a lot of people think that your life is like an episode of *The Beverly Hillbillies*. It wasn't. The negative media stereotypes of people from Appalachia have caused irreparable harm to us: culturally, economically, and socially.

That's why I wanted to make a film about the real Appalachia, the land and the people I knew. We worked for more than five years to produce the three-hour documentary series *The Appalachians,* which aired on PBS in 2005. Working on that film brought me closer to my real self and my heritage. It also introduced me to some truly inspirational people.

One of them was Julia "Judy" Bonds, whom we interviewed for the film about the contribution of women to Appalachian life and her work as an organizer. The subject of mountaintop removal (MTR) mining naturally came up. Judy told me how the coal companies were leveling entire mountains to mine coal and then dumping the soil (and animals and plants) into the hollers. I had seen strip mining, so when she said that mountaintop removal was like "strip mining on steroids," I was shocked. I found that I couldn't stop thinking about what she had said to me that day about the destruction, the exploitation, the genocide of mountain culture—all for cheaper coal.

When *The Appalachians* was completed, I called Judy and asked if I could come down and see MTR for myself. She took me to meet Larry Gibson at Kayford Mountain, less than an hour south of Charleston, West Virginia. Larry is a man with a single mission: to stop the MTR mining that is harming him and the people of Appalachia. After a long hike up a road so damaged you cannot drive it, we reached the top of the mountain where his family had lived for generations. For as far as we could see, everything below his mountain was gone. The once majestic mountain landscape was now a moonscape. It was hard to believe that not so long ago those leveled mountains towered over where we were standing now. Like many who have visited Kayford, I was brought to tears by the devastation.

One of the most vocal opponents of MTR, Larry has paid in many ways for refusing to sell his land to the coal companies. Bullet holes riddle parts of his house. His animals have been killed, and he is regularly threatened by industry supporters who are angry about his activism. Yet he continues to speak out and inspire others.

After meeting at Kayford with Larry Gibson, Judy Bonds, and Vivian Stockman (a photographer who moved from Ohio to West Virginia and dedicated herself to documenting MTR's destruction), I felt compelled to learn more about what was

Julia "Judy" Bonds has been a steadfast defender of the rights of local citizens in coal country. Photo © Mark Schmerling.

Coal

He who spends his days removing
mountains and dropping them
  into streams
is a man of few words. Some are
  numbers:
wages, mortgage, boat, a daughter's
tuition. Some are names,
like "Bob," which he must speed-dial
if he's ever "approached"
by people who mean no good,
  who want
to ask questions. Beyond these
is "the company," strong and wise;
not a friend, more than a friend.
A mass of terms—little mysteries
of working a big machine—fills
his mind and pride. But anyone
would know what having one
  of those
is like. Anyone employed.
Around all other words is the big
  word "job,"
like a wire fence. And if a man
should cross it and elude the guards
and wave, say, a bottle of black
  water,
an x-ray or a bag of dust
at him, the remover of mountains
will think, He looks like someone,
  could be me.
Which doesn't matter because
  he isn't.

    —Frederick Pollack

happening in these mountains and the price being paid by the coalfield residents. To do so, I had to learn more about the entire history of coal in the region. I met with people who had lost their ancestral land because their families had sold off their mineral rights in the early 1900s to out-of-state land companies. The former owners had no idea of the real value of those mineral rights; it was common to sell them for pennies on their dollar value. Entire mountains were sold for as little as the cost of a sewing machine. In some counties, more than 80 percent of the coal rights are still owned by out-of-state corporations. And for more than a century, mineral rights enjoyed precedence over land rights, which means that coal companies have been allowed to mine in any way they choose. Imagine being told that because someone else owned the mineral rights, your own family's land would be destroyed and the mountains leveled.

Coal mining has always been a complex issue and a divisive one, even within my own family. As I was beginning to explore the subject, my brother took a job in the coal industry. He quickly endorsed MTR and believes that the damage it causes is not permanent. He strongly believes that coal companies have every right to mine in any manner they see fit and that coal mining and the jobs it provides are essential to the state's economy. He sees the residents who are trying to stop MTR mining as "tree huggers" who will cost him his job. In Boone County, West Virginia, if he doesn't work for coal, his only other option is to work at a fast-food restaurant or similar low-paying job. It is a real dilemma if you want to live in coal country. And people can't count on their elected officials to help them, since Appalachian politicians are notorious for supporting the mono-economy of coal.

I understand that my brother has a family to support, and certainly he is not responsible for the economic and political pressures that have allowed coal companies to mine in this manner. He is not responsible for the destruction of 500 mountains and more than 1,200 miles of streams in the region. Just like generations of Appalachians before him, he is dependent on King Coal, caught in the middle. Many of those ancestors died of black lung, went years without work in the mines and nearly starved, or had to leave the region. They marched from Matewan to Blair Mountain to demand decent working conditions and pay, and some were murdered by coal company thugs. The federal government then declared martial law and if not for inclement weather would have had the military bomb the striking miners. But, today, my brother is a "Friend of Coal" like most of the other miners. (Friends of Coal is a pro-industry group.)

I, on the other hand, identify myself as a "Friend of the Mountains." (Friends of the Mountains is an alliance of groups working to stop MTR.) Like so many people from coal country, my brother and I are on opposite sides of the most controversial issue in the region today. It has sometimes been difficult for our relationship, because over the three years I've spent on this project, my personal belief has grown ever stronger that MTR is unjust and is in fact a civil rights issue for our society. I understand the need for jobs, but I also understand that short-term employment cannot excuse the devastation of one of the world's oldest ecosystems and the culture in which we were raised.

How could two sets of eyes see things so differently? What brought me to my knees in tears was blessed by my own brother. I wanted to understand how this was happening today in Appalachia, so I slowly began developing a film project that would explore coal mining, especially its impact on Appalachia. My friend and colleague Phyllis Geller agreed to direct; while we were making *The Appalachians*, she too had been moved by the stories about MTR and felt this was a film that needed to be made. The stories needed to be heard.

It was easy to find people who opposed MTR and were willing to talk, but it was almost impossible to find anyone who supported coal, or coal company representatives, to talk on camera. Even my brother refused an interview for fear of reprisal. For more than two years we tried to get interviews with people who support coal and this type of mining. Finally we were given the opportunity, through Randy Maggard, to visit MTR sites and reclaimed sites and to meet some of the

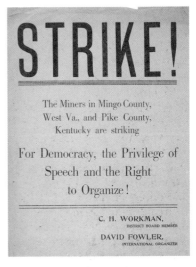

A broadside from the early struggle for unionization in the coal mines. Courtesy of West Virginia State Archives.

miners working with him. Randy heads environmental compliance for an independent coal company based in Kentucky, and he supports the pro-coal position. He values his job and clearly works to do everything in his power to reclaim the mined sites. Randy is quick to point out that what he does for a living is legal and that he is proud of it. A good man caught in a difficult position, he cares about the environment and about the jobs provided by coal.

Someone like Randy makes it impossible to vilify the people working in the coal industry. This project—the film and the book—is not about good guys versus bad guys. It is about the complicated issues of mining, processing, and burning coal effectively and responsibly. It is about the true cost of the energy we use. I owe Randy a debt of gratitude for sharing his time, his experience, and his viewpoints. But while I respect him, I cannot agree with him. The more I saw and the more I heard, the less I could understand how coal companies were allowed to do MTR mining.

Through Randy, we met people like Darcie Vance, who was happy that her family cemetery was now surrounded by a MTR site. The main justification she gave was that now they could four-wheel up to the cemetery to hold Memorial Day services in a small open structure. Before MTR, it had been inaccessible to the family. This lovely, gracious woman fed us lunch while telling us that many people oppose MTR only to get paid off by the coal companies for the inconvenience of subsiding land and other effects of the blasting. She doesn't see any downside to the mining and truly believes that reclamation creates good land for animals and future development.

That trip was quite a contrast to the time we spent filming at Larry Gibson's family graveyard on Kayford Mountain, which overlooks utter destruction as far as the eye can see. One day as we were shooting there, after days of blasting, Larry demanded to see proof that the coal company had not desecrated the cemetery. After almost an hour of unsuccessful talks with the company security guard, Larry called the West Virginia State Police to get permission to enter the site. The police conferred with the guard and told Larry that

Randy Maggard is the head of environmental compliance for Argus Coal. Photo © Marian Steinert.

A nearly forgotten cemetery near a coal operation in southern West Virginia. Photo © Mark Schmerling.

he couldn't go into his own cemetery. The mixture of pain and anger in Larry's face was almost too much to watch. Of course, I had seen it before in my grandfather's eyes. It's hard to lose everything you care about and still fight. Larry is just one among dozens of courageous, inspiring people I've met in the coalfields while producing this project. All are fighting for a common cause: to save their homeland. All are ordinary people who never imagined they would have to learn how to create a movement to save their culture, their very lives. They love the land of Appalachia. So do many of their neighbors and siblings who work for coal.

For this book, we have invited people living in the coalfields, many of whom appear in the film, to tell their *own* stories, alongside essays by established writers and scholars. We hope that the stories in this book and the film it accompanies will help you understand the true cost of coal to the people and the land in this part of America.

Like many of the people you'll meet in our film and this book, I believe that the Appalachians and their people are worth fighting for. Before we lose this land and culture forever, we must take a stand. It's what our ancestors would expect from us. After all, we are proud mountaineers.

Introduction

Shirley Stewart Burns

Barn painting is a traditional advertising tool in rural areas; this barn is located on the border between Pendleton and Randolph Counties in West Virginia. Photo © Jim Clark.

PEOPLE OUTSIDE THE REGION HAVE always been fascinated by the natural beauty and scenic vistas that are Appalachia, and it remains that way to this day. Millions are drawn to this rugged, beautiful landscape, one of the oldest and most biodiverse mountain chains in the world. Some of the earliest writings about the region were from travel writers who entertained their readers with colorful stories of this rough, beautiful land and its people, who were often portrayed as lazy, incestuous drunkards or at least uncultured, uncivilized dullards. These stereotypes set the stage for exploitation that continues to this day, painting a picture of an entire culture that the rest of America feels comfortable discounting and looking down upon.

But this is a distorted picture. The growth and history of the United States are inextricably tied to Appalachia. The American industrial revolution was fueled by the natural resources and working people of central Appalachia. From its timber, gas, and oil to its most known resource, coal, Appalachia's riches have allowed the rest of the country to grow and prosper, even as it has remained one of the poorest parts of the richest country in the world.

The gently rolling curves of Appalachia's mountains have concealed the latest kind of exploitation—the complete obliteration of mountains and streams through mountaintop removal coal mining, an aggressive form of strip mining that literally blows away mountains to gain easy access to the coal seams. What is left of the mountain—called "overburden" by the coal industry—is pushed into the valleys and streams below.

The consequences of this disgraceful practice pervade the region's natural and human landscape. Appalachia is home to thousands of diverse species of flora and fauna, a number of which can be found only there, and their habitats are literally being scraped off the face of the earth. Entire ecosytems are being laid to waste. But the most precious resource being affected is the water. Nearly all of the eastern United States depends on waters that originate in the headwater streams of Appalachia. "We all live downstream," goes a saying in the anti-MTR movement. Hundreds of miles of streams have been covered by overburden, and those not buried are in constant danger of pollution from slurry spills and other wastes that lax governments have allowed to be dumped into the streams. As these headwater streams are destroyed or polluted, the repercussions will be felt throughout the rest of the East Coast.

The impact of mountaintop removal on Appalachian culture and society is equally tragic. It has created a most disturbing chasm between neighbors who are dependent upon coal to earn their living and neighbors whose property has been ruined by mountaintop removal and who believe that their cultural and spiritual connection to the land is being sacrificed for profit. The issue is truly pitting brother against brother and sister against sister. Besides that, an entire way of life is being disrupted. The effects on the region's inhabitants are far-reaching: their native landscape is profoundly altered, the constant assault is leading to a forced migration, and they are made to feel culturally inferior by the coal industry that is making a fortune from them. Even their storytelling tradition is affected.

The vast, untapped coal regions of Appalachia were known to speculators as early as the colonial era. However, since

We who stand against mountaintop removal mining are not doing so arbitrarily. We are not deceived about what is necessary for the good of all. There is no emergency to "maximize coal production." The beauty of Appalachia is that it is free and perfect without us. It is our teacher. That is why these mountains are revered around the world.

—Whitney Baker, from "Getting Quiet"

the coal deposits were located mostly in ruggedly inaccessible areas and were impossible to extract and transport with any efficiency, the resources were not widely exploited until the nineteenth century. Only at the height of the industrial revolution did coal become the prominent economic basis for the region.

From 1880 to 1920, the Appalachian coalfields experienced unparalleled growth. This transition had a huge impact on all aspects of life in the region. An agrarian lifestyle had characterized Appalachia prior to the burgeoning coal economy, and residents witnessed the transformation of nearly every aspect of their lives as the region became another spoke in the industrial wheel. The nation needed coal to fuel expanding industrial centers and to feed people's ever-increasing desire for conveniences, and it looked to regions that possessed abundant supplies of natural resources to satisfy its appetite. Unfortunately, Appalachia became one of those sacrificial places.

At this watershed moment, coal extraction began to flourish. The coming of the railroads in the region signified a point of no return, both environmentally and economically, and enabled the timber and coal industries to expand rapidly. Many of the railroads were owned by the same interests that controlled the unregulated timber and coal industry.

Appalachians who had been living a subsistence/barter existence were forced to turn to wage labor. Broad-form deeds, which allowed coal companies to do basically anything necessary to mine the land, were commonplace. Absentee landownership was pervasive, leading to the neglect of communities, lack of economic development, and a loss of revenue for local governments.

And so Appalachia became ever more dependent on outside forces. No longer did its people grow their own food or make their own clothes; these could be bought cheaper in the stores that stocked goods that were brought in on rail. The once self-sufficient Appalachians now found themselves relying more and more on wage earnings and outside industry to secure their place in the world.

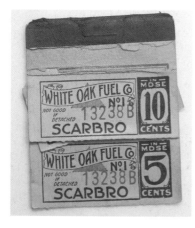

Miners in the early 1900s were usually paid in scrip: metal or paper tokens issued by the coal company. Scrip was used to pay for rent on company-owned homes, goods from the company store, and other services provided by the company. Courtesy of West Virginia State Archives.

Scott's Run Mining Camp near Morgantown, West Virginia, 1935. Photo by Walker Evans; courtesy of Library of Congress.

The emerging coal economy pervaded every aspect of Appalachian life. Because extraction of coal required more people than lived in the coal-producing regions, companies brought in immigrants (who were hugely exploited in the process, being promised far more than they ever received) and outside labor to populate the company towns that sprang up throughout the coalfields. The company supplied a home for the worker and his family and a company store at which to purchase goods. The worker frequently had no say in his own destiny because the company controlled everything. Trapped in the company-town nightmare, many men would have preferred to go back to the farms, hills, and hollers where they had lived for generations, but they now found themselves essentially indentured to the companies.

The old social order in Appalachia was pushed aside and replaced by a new structure based on industrial economics. Before this transition, social status depended upon a person's family. Afterward, a person's stature depended on his or her position in the economic food chain. No longer would family name and family heritage serve as leverage in community matters. The region's new leaders—those who would shape the politics, growth, and economics of the coalfield regions—were tightly linked with interests that wielded economic power. And the type of industrialization that occurred in Appalachia was bad for the region and its people. As leaders and businesses failed to diversify the region's economy, coalfield areas quickly became totally dependent on natural resource extraction.

Over the decades, the coal industry introduced more and more cost-effective machinery in the mines. While extracting more coal, mechanization left more workers without jobs and was soon followed by poverty and out-migration. Exiled from their home to America's large cities, many Appalachians became cogs in the nation's industrial wheels.

The deep mines begat the strip mines, and the strip mines begat mountaintop removal coal mining. Each new process was introduced for one reason only: more money for the companies. Over the last century the industry has spent far more time and effort trying to find cheaper ways of mining coal than it has on securing safer working conditions for its employees.

In the 1960s Appalachians began to rise up in protest against the destruction wreaked by strip mining, so much so that a new piece of federal legislation—the Surface Mining Control and Reclamation Act (SMCRA)—was signed into law in 1977. Unfortunately, a loophole in SMCRA simply opened the door for mountaintop removal coal mining, the latest blow in the history of the mechanization of the coal industry.

With huge multistory draglines (the machines used in MTR), the tops of ancient mountains are systematically decapitated and dumped into nearby mountain valleys and headwater streams. As the size of MTR operations increases, fewer workers are needed, leading to increased unemployment in a region already pervaded by the fear that any job is better than no job at all. Thus, a vicious cycle is allowed to continue. With politicians and lawmakers comfortably in check, and bought-off regulatory agencies that overlook destructive industry practices, coal companies are allowed to run roughshod over anyone who stands in the way of their quest for more profit.

This latest exploitation of the Appalachian coalfields has forever changed the character of the region not only physically but also mentally and spiritually. The ancient, comforting Appalachian Mountains, which bear the scars of past "progress," are now threatened with complete annihilation. Appalachia's people also bear these scars, yet they struggle to regain control of their own destiny and reclaim their heritage. As coal is scraped from the mountains, families are ripped from the land that has sustained them for generations. It is this close connection to the land that leads many residents to take a stand against overwhelming odds in an effort to save their very lives and culture.

In this collection, writings by well-known entertainers, journalists, scholars, and political figures report on how coal country has absorbed and reacted to the practice of mountaintop removal mining and provide important insights into the circumstances that have brought us to a point where the unthinkable has become an everyday occurrence. Powerful images by photographers who have dedicated themselves to documenting the region's landscape and culture and the impact of MTR are set against archival illustrations that evoke past times in the region.

Most important, this book contains the voices of people directly affected by mountaintop removal. These are the words not of a broken people but of strong, proud coalfield citizens who clearly recognize the root cause of their problems and are taking a stand to make a difference. These citizens speak with one voice in demanding better treatment for themselves and their homeland. For too long, what happens in Appalachia has been America's dirty little secret, but these powerful accounts provide a firsthand view of what it takes to light up America. After reading them, you will never again flip on your light switch without remembering the people who offer these testimonies, and the sacrifices they have made.

Mary Miller (left) and Pauline Canterberry, citizen-activists known as "the Dustbusters," pose before a coal preparation plant in their hometown of Sylvester, Boone County, West Virginia. Miller holds the dust rag she uses to demonstrate how much coal dust falls on the town. Photo © Giles Ashford.

Part One

THE COAL-CARVED HISTORY OF APPALACHIA

THE RAVAGING OF MODERN APPALACHIA by the coal-mining industry has deep roots, reaching back to the dawn of the industrial revolution in the 1700s and snaking their way through the mountains over the past three centuries. It was in the early 1900s, however, that the industry began to tighten its grip on the region's economy and the lives of its people. Ever since then, the citizens of the coalfields have been engaged in a love-hate struggle with coal that has mostly resulted in their suffering. Those who questioned King Coal's rule have been painted as disloyal to their region and unpatriotic to their country by the industry and much worse: killed on picket lines, bombed by their own government, and erased from history.

The essays in this part provide some historical context for the current struggle over mountaintop removal, as well as accounts of people's personal experience with the culture of coal. A profile of Grammy Award–winner and country music legend Loretta Lynn focuses on the ties to land and family that anchored the lives of most Appalachians in the early part of the twentieth century. Bryan McNeil's essay explores the role of the United Mine Workers union in the region's coal mining history and its legacy in the current struggles against MTR. Shirley Stewart Burns offers a family history that takes us to West Virginia in the late 1950s, and excerpts from the

In the absence of federal labor laws, children often worked in the mines. "Breaker boys" such as those in this 1911 photograph sorted slate rock from coal as it came out of the shafts. Photo by Lewis Hine; courtesy of Library of Congress.

Page 22: *Men stand in front of a tipple at the Gaston Mine in Fairmont, West Virginia. A tipple is a structure where mine cars were tipped and emptied of their coal—often into railroad cars. Photo by Lewis Hine; courtesy of Library of Congress.*

novels of Denise Giardina and Silas House shed light on the opposition movement of the 1960s.

Also included here are Erik Reece's powerful overview of the century of coal, and former congressman Ken Hechler's firsthand account of his battle in Congress to abolish all forms of strip mining. Hechler, an early leader in this fight, reveals how legislation gone wrong opened the door to mountaintop removal and explains why the fight to stop it must continue. John Hennen analyzes the role of resource extraction in American empire building. Mining engineer Jack Spadaro draws attention to the special risks of coal-waste impoundments—and of being a government whistle-blower. Robert F. Kennedy Jr. continues his father's legacy of standing up for the people of the region, and the part closes with an impassioned speech against the Kentucky state government by the noted writer and environmentalist Wendell Berry, long an eloquent voice on behalf of rural lands and culture. (Readers should bear in mind that the essays here, and throughout the book, were written at different times and therefore may differ in the specific information they provide regarding the impacts of mountaintop removal.)

Taken together, these essays and fictional portraits provide vivid snapshots of Appalachian history and offer insights into how coal has shaped the place and its people.

Loretta Lynn from Butcher Holler

Shirley Stewart Burns and Silas House

Loretta Lynn, one of the most famous Appalachians who has ever lived, was born and raised in Butcher Holler, a small coal-mining community in Johnson County, Kentucky, in the heart of coal country. One of the reasons Lynn became so famous is because she never forgot her Appalachian roots. In fact, she celebrated them in songs like "Coal Miner's Daughter," "You're Looking at Country," and many others that show the complexities of living in a hard country. The film based on Lynn's life, *Coal Miner's Daughter,* features an Academy Award–winning performance by Sissy Spacek and is widely considered a contemporary classic. People throughout the world base what they know about coal mining on this film and on Lynn's music. Perhaps more than any other single person in popular culture, Lynn has helped shape the world's ideas of what coal mining is about, and she has done so in a subtle, natural way, educating people on the real Appalachia without intending to, simply by telling her own story.

Country music superstar and coal miner's daughter Loretta Lynn. Photo © Les Leverette; courtesy of Country Music Hall of Fame and Museum.

Although mining has changed much since Lynn's girl-hood days in Eastern Kentucky, it is still not an easy life for anyone involved. Lynn remembers those days with all their joy and pain. As in many Appalachian communities, coal was central to her family's household, she told this book's editors in a conversation. "We had a family coal bank," she says. "Daddy would pick out some of the coal and leave it

Farmlands in late autumn,
Greenbrier County, West Virginia.
Photo © Jim Clark.

out. The kids would go pick up the coal in little buckets and bring it back to the house. That's what we used for heating and cooking."

The second of eight children born to coal miner Ted Webb and Clara (Ramey) Webb, Lynn was just thirteen when she married the dashing, wild, and charming Doolittle Lynn. The young couple left Butcher Holler in search of new opportunities, and the first of their five children was born shortly thereafter.

Lynn's young husband soon recognized and nurtured Lynn's talents, urging her to share her voice with the world. It wasn't an easy road, but after a few years, she became the most famous woman in country music, known as much for her down-home wit and candid honesty as for her tightly constructed, widely resonating songs. Occasionally she was a lightning rod for controversy. Several of her songs were banned because they were deemed too racy for the times (for example, her song "The Pill" caused a furor because a woman was singing about birth control), and some of her onstage remarks caused audible gasps—for instance, after being criticized for calling President Nixon by his first name, she replied, "They called Jesus Jesus, didn't they?" Despite this, Lynn's popularity never waned but soared even higher. She was the most famous coal miner's daughter in the world, and she was incredibly proud of that fact. People all over the world were inspired by her rags-to-riches story, her honesty, and her willingness to share herself.

Although Lynn left the coalfields at an early age, her sense of place and her heritage remained central in her career and life. No matter where she lived, Lynn identified Butcher Holler as home. "We lived in the last house in the holler," Lynn says of her home place. "It was made out of slab lumber. My parents built it, and the house is still there." Her family has "lived in that holler for generations," she says, and their ties to the land stretch back even farther. "I had no idea how big the world was because we always lived in Butcher Holler." Hearing her speak of it, one is reminded of how the land becomes a part of people, shaping and molding them into who they are.

Lynn remembers Butcher Holler as a place with a strong sense of family and community. "I didn't know where babies came from," she recalls, "but every time another baby came, all the kids got sent to Grandpa's. Mommy told me she found us under a cabbage leaf. We were very poor. Everyone was very poor. But we didn't know it. Sometimes we would feed another family that was worse off than us."

When the coal companies came to Butcher Holler, it left an indelible mark on Lynn's family. "Daddy got a job at the mines for one dollar a day," she says. "His knees bled every night. We couldn't understand why. Then he told us that he was on his knees all day picking coal out. Sometimes he would work in places only three to four feet high for twelve hours a day." Loretta also remembers when the United Mine Workers of America came to Butcher Holler, and how it helped the people of the region: "John L. Lewis came into town with the

A miner stands on the back of a coal car in a mine tunnel in the early 1900s. Photographer unknown; courtesy of Library of Congress.

I've been working in this mine since
  1984
Just like my daddy did and his dad
  did before
Stand in line and ride that train
  down where I can't see
Trying to break down that wall of
  coal in front of me

The preacher tried to teach me what
  was wrong and right
But I learned all my lessons with
  carbide light
Down where air is precious, where
  losers lose it all
Where to stand and be a man you
  have to learn to crawl

(chorus:)
I beat on the mountain
With a hammer keeping time
Way down in the dungeon
Where the sun don't shine
Down in the heart of the darkness
You can hear my hammer ring
I beat on the mountain
But the mountain don't say a thing

—*Arty Hill and Jason Ringenberg,*
from "Beat on the Mountain"

union and better wages. I think people from mountains work harder, and if they want something they'll get it, and if they get a chance to do something they'll do it."

Today the Lynn home place in Johnson County is a tourist attraction run by Lynn's brother Herman Webb. Fans can walk through the four rooms, sit on the porch swing, and see the irises planted by Clara Webb. But the Eastern Kentucky of today is very different than the one Lynn left years ago. Those who travel to pay homage to one of country music's greatest legends find themselves on highways that zoom past mountaintop removal sites that are growing so massive they can no longer be hidden from passersby.

Even Lynn's beloved home place in Butcher Holler is now being encroached upon by mountaintop removal sites. In fact, Johnson County is practically the epicenter of mountaintop removal activity in Eastern Kentucky. New permits are pending to mine still closer to her childhood home. Like so many other places in central Appalachia, Butcher Holler is on the verge of extinction.

Their love of and connection to the land provide a sense of place to many who live in the coalfields. This sense of place and ties to home draw Lynn back to the hills and hollers of the land that sheltered her family and shaped her into the remarkable person she has become. "It's good to have those roots," Lynn says, "to be able to go home again." But just as Butcher Hollow is changing, mountaintop removal changes the landscape of home. Many such homesteads have already been lost to the blades of the bulldozers. "If you forget where you come from," Lynn asks, "where are you going to go?"

The Roving Pickets, 1962

Denise Giardina

RACHEL: I SAW WHAT WAS happening. Dillon would claim later that I was blind to it, but that wasn't so. Who better to see than a nurse?

I knew the machines and strip mines had taken the jobs of the miners, who were getting only one or two days' work a week. Every day I drove past the empty houses they left behind when they moved to Ohio or Michigan. I saw the weed-choked fields where entire camps were torn down to the foundations, saw the boarded-up stores and movie theaters in the smaller towns, the loaded coal trucks from the new strip mines rumbling through Justice like great iron elephants and shaking the buildings, as though the town was being ground to dust. I was sad that Jackie would miss the Italian bakery, the fish market, the tailor shops and little groceries, the dark maroon passenger trains with elegant white window shades. There had been wonderful things in the world, and they were no longer.

And I saw the people. I saw as much as Dillon saw, and more. I talked Arthur Lee into letting the county set up a free clinic one day a week at the Felco company store, now closed and empty save for a row of empty display cases with broken glass. I don't know where Arthur Lee got the money; I suspected it was from some funds he'd skimmed off the county coffers for his own use or taken from the coal companies to

Coal miner's child near Omar, West Virginia, 1935. Photo by Ben Shahn; courtesy of Library of Congress.

George Johnson and his sister on her porch in Myrtle, Mingo County, West Virginia, 1972. Photo © Builder Levy.

do their political bidding. I didn't ask, I just bought the medicines and supplies.

People came to the clinic who had worked all their lives, who had paid their own ways and never taken charity. They came because their children were hungry and sick, because they were hungry and sick, the men in work clothes, the women in shapeless polyester dresses, the children with swollen bellies beneath thin T-shirts. They sat on hard folding chairs or stood against the wall when the chairs ran out, waiting for hours to spend ten minutes with me. They were unused to leaning and they did it awkwardly, as though afraid to trust the wall they rested against.

I saw them in their homes, old people who wheezed and coughed while I laid a cold flat stethoscope on their chests, who slept in camp houses where the wind whistled through the cracks, with coal stoves for heat, only the company no longer provided the house coal, and so they picked up the leavings shed from the fast-moving trains and overloaded trucks. They were men who had worked in the mines until their lungs filled with dust or their backs gave out, women who had cooked and scrubbed the coal dust from kitchen floors and listened for the accident whistle to blow, who finally depended upon their children for food only now their children had nothing to give.

I also watched the television. I heard President Kennedy talk about stamping out poverty in America and I learned for the first time that I lived in a place called Appalachia. It was a strange feeling to think my home had been named without asking anyone who lived here, but I was glad someone was paying attention. Dillon called me naïve. I didn't care. When I finished with my patients they moved to the next line to receive the white, wrapped blocks of commodity butter and cheese sent from Washington. Of course it was demeaning; of course it wasn't enough. Of course Arthur Lee gave cheese and butter to all his buddies, would have given it to me if I'd taken it. But children don't care for all that, and a cheese sandwich would fill a child's stomach.

This is an excerpt from Denise Giardina's novel The Unquiet Earth, *copyright © 1992 by Denise Giardina, reprinted by permission of W. W. Norton & Co.*

Money for a Pepsi

I have been drowning, fighting for a
  breath.
I have watched a coal beltline eat
  my fingertip.
    No, Honey.
        I don't have money
            for you
                a Pepsi.

—Walter Lane

A Family History in Coal Dust

Shirley Stewart Burns

Neely, Cora, and Shirley Stewart at their home in Matheny, Wyoming County, West Virginia, 1974. Photographer unknown; Shirley Stewart Burns collection.

IN THE SPRING OF 1959, MY FATHER left his home in southern West Virginia to look for work. It was his third attempt at securing employment outside the coalfields. He was not doing this by choice. Like everyone else in the southern West Virginia coalfields, he was at the mercy of the coal-mining industry. As the industry mechanized, more and more people lost their jobs, and the population dwindled.

My dad finally landed a job in Chicago, working as a manager for the Zenith Corporation. He and my mom lived there in an economically forced exile, 600 miles away from the family, friends, and land they loved. Dad kept in contact with everyone back home in the hope that job opportunities would increase so that he and Mom could return and raise their children among the family and surroundings of home. In 1964, they returned to West Virginia, where he would work as an underground coal miner for Eastern Associated Coal Company.

For as long as I can remember, coal has been an intimate part of my life. I have never known a time when there was not an underground coal miner in my family. In 1870, at age sixteen, my maternal great-grandfather, Moses McKinney, worked in a coal bank in Meigs County, Ohio. By 1880, he and his family had returned to Wyoming County, West Virginia, to be near other kin, and as soon as he was old enough, my grandfather David McKinney, Moses' son, began to labor as a coal miner in the Wyoming County mines in Stephenson. While his true passion was farming, he depended on mining work to support his growing family. Around the same time, my paternal grandfather, Gillis Stewart, began his lifetime of toil as a coal miner. So did his brother Lacy, who was twenty-two when he died in a mine roof fall in 1930. Grandpaw Gillis had the sad task of breaking this news to their father, and by 1948, Grandpaw himself was dead at age forty-two from black lung disease. My own father, Neely Stewart, was then just shy of his eleventh birthday.

Coal dust blanketed my world in small, often seemingly insignificant ways, too. I have vivid childhood memories of being stopped at railroad crossings hundreds of times while fully loaded coal trains rumbled past. Even today, Appalachians routinely watch as the coal trains haul the riches of their home to faraway places. When I was a child, textbooks were provided to schools "courtesy of" a particular coal company. Today, elementary schools across the coalfields are "partners in education" with coal companies. As a child, I did not give this infiltration a second thought, nor did I ever hear objections from adults. We were oblivious to the very real conflict of interest that happens when any particular industry is allowed to "sponsor" education.

I spent nearly every weekend of my childhood with my best friend up a littler holler not far from my home in Matheny, West Virginia. Behind her house was one of the clearest, cleanest creeks I have ever seen. We spent many days playing in the water and learning where the deep spots were that would go over our heads, testing our courage. Her children will never be able to experience these things. Today my friend and her family still live near the head of this same holler, only now a valley fill from a nearby mountaintop removal site is located there as well. Flooding occurs more frequently and has washed down wood and unidentifiable debris. Nowadays, since the valley fill changed everything, that same creek is off-limits to children because nobody knows what that water contains.

When I was seventeen, I faced what remains the most traumatic, life-altering event I have experienced. At the age

Ode to a Miner
(lines from a song for my father)

When I was a young man
Seems just yesterday
Two choices I had
Were to leave or to stay
My kin lived and died here
Left one choice for me
To go underground
Coal minin' 'twould be

(chorus:)
Black lung, black lung
Black lung took my life
Now I leave behind
My children and wife
I tell all you young ones
Don't go underground
'Cause if the minin' don't kill you
Black lung's still around

I can't walk through the valleys
The mountains are too high
Every breath that I take
Seems to be a goodbye
My life's all but over
And what do I show
But thirty years of hard labor
And this Hell that I've known as . . .
(chorus)

—*Shirley Stewart Burns*

This homestead at Twin Falls State Park in Wyoming County, West Virginia, is typical of dwellings found in the central Appalachian coalfields in the early 1900s. Photo © Matthew H. Burns.

of fifty-one, my father was forced to endure a second open-heart surgery. The surgeons gave him a 95 percent chance of survival. Later, the doctor would dejectedly inform us that, although the heart surgery was a success, my father's lungs, smothered by black lung, had rejected the surgery. Dad would have needed a lung transplant, too. Coal took my father from me, and my life would never be the same. Never again would I have my daddy to provide encouragement, words of wisdom, and unconditional love. In a quick moment, just like that, he was gone.

Even at this juncture, coal still permeated our lives. My daddy had always been concerned that he would not be able to afford to send me to college, but a mere three months after his death, I won a scholarship that was expressly for children of coal miners. I had written the essay for the scholarship proposal on coal mining, my father, and his recent death.

Because he died in 1988, before mountaintop removal became prevalent, I can only imagine what my father would have thought of the practice. I do know that it was his love of the land, as much as love for his family, that brought him back to West Virginia at a time when he was making good money in Chicago. I know that he enjoyed walking the hills behind our home, and I well remember how it pained him when he became so disabled by black lung disease that he could no longer make frequent trips into his beloved mountains. I know that he disdained traditional strip mining and the mess it left behind. And I know that he faithfully visited the family cemetery to pay his respects to his departed loved ones—the same cemetery where he now rests, and that is now separated from an MTR site by only one ridge.

I often wonder what my ancestors, who founded Wyoming County, West Virginia, more than 200 years ago, would think. They left beautiful Augusta County, Virginia, to live in these rugged, challenging hills. I wonder, had they known what devastation lay ahead for the land of Appalachia, if they would have decided to transplant their lives into these hills and valleys. I imagine what they would think if they could see what havoc so-called progress would wreak upon the land that held so much promise for them. If they had known their progeny would become indentured servants to the coal industry, would they still have come to this place? They certainly would have believed that man was intended to have dominion over the land, but I'm far from certain they would have believed it justified the destruction, the obliteration, of the land itself.

I know intimately the love-hate relationship that coalfield residents often have with coal. I have it, too. I am proud of my family's coal-mining heritage—of their strength and fortitude working in the mines and in standing up for their rights. Likewise, I am angry and terribly saddened when I see the environmental degradation and human misery the latest wave of coal mining has left behind. The people, the land, and our heritage deserve better. Every trip home reveals more and more permanent changes to the landscape of the mountains. These changes can be subtle or sometimes quite drastic. As I view them, memories of my daddy and of all my ancestors wash over me, and I am compelled to keep fighting.

Neely Stewart (far right) and kin stand behind the tombstone of Neely's father at the Stewart cemetery in Matheny, West Virginia, 1961. Photographer unknown; Shirley Stewart Burns collection.

Something Ancient

Silas House

The reverse side of a pocket mirror advertises the Harlan Coal Company. Photo © Dave Johnson; Dave Johnson collection.

THEY STOOD ON THE MOUNTAIN with their arms interlocked, their jaws tightening against the cold, their eyes hard and unblinking . . . Anneth, Easter, and Sophie.

The men had already cut down the bigger trees to make way for a road up the mountain. But there was still the brush and the felled trees, and here was a dozer that shook with life as it sat there at the foot of the mountain, waiting for the order to go forward. It would push aside the limbs and pull out the stumps until it reached the summit, where the real work would begin. Behind the dozer was a Mack truck with headlights like big round eyes that looked strangely evil. Easter thought it might have been present simply to suggest a bigger threat. The company had known they would face resistance.

Easter wondered what the driver of the dozer thought of them. Here was Anneth, seven months pregnant. Sophie, who was not more than five feet tall even with her beehive hair. And Easter herself—could he see that the grief of the last few years had thinned and weakened her, had cleaned her completely out? Or could he make out that this same grief had made her stronger, had made her more adamant than ever to fight for what was hers, to keep alive all of her family she could? Did he see in all three of the women's faces that they would not surrender their land? Easter looked at the

The Church family, Thacker Mines, Mingo County, West Virginia, 1970. Photo © Builder Levy.

driver sitting up there—his face dark and unrecognizable because of the morning's new sun behind him—and knew that there was no way he could realize that Sophie had the courage to kill anybody that crossed her family, despite her thin wrists and kind eyes. And there was no way he could fathom the rage that Anneth was able to unloose when the need arose.

It seemed more likely that he saw three women and found this laughable. He tapped the gas, and a metal lid lifted on the exhaust pipe to allow three blasts of black smoke to burst out onto the morning air. The lid closed again and it rattled there atop the pipe, with thin wisps of smoke seeping out around its edges.

"Let's go," Easter said. They moved forward together and climbed into the dozer scoop without difficulty, settling in as if it was a wide, deep porch swing. They sat back against the cold metal. Easter brought her hands up and saw red soil on her palms, like clots of blood. She closed her eyes and started praying: *Lord, keep us in the palm of your hand.* Sophie was between the two sisters now and they both leaned against her, holding hands, unable to speak. There was too much to say. Within the scoop they could feel the vibration of the motor.

The driver hollered but they couldn't make out his words, so he tapped the gas again to startle them. Easter flinched at the sudden jolt but steeled herself against the dozer bucket. There was no way she was going to move now.

More hollering, and the scoop lifted and swung out, dumping them onto the ground in front of the dozer. Easter fell on all fours and saw Sophie tumbling down to land beside her. But Anneth held on to the edges of the scoop, wedging herself in and refusing to let go.

"No!" Easter screamed as the scoop raised higher, the driver pulling the lever back and then forward so that Anneth would fall out. "She's pregnant!" But Easter's voice was lost to the roar, so she prayed into the loudness. She looked back at the mountain, its winter trees black and skeletal. She thought the mountain might rise up and avenge them, but it didn't. She thought of the birds that were usually gathered here and figured they had moved back into the deepest parts of the forest.

The driver brought the scoop down, a great heaviness being released. When it hit the ground, Easter could feel the impact in her ankles and up the backs of her calves. Sophie was beside her, hanging onto her arm, hollering words that were lost on the air. Anneth still had her feet firmly planted against the edge of the scoop, and her back pressed against the metal. There was nothing to read on her face. She had her eyes closed and Easter thought she might be praying, too. The driver swung the scoop in the air and brought it down again, the sound of its striking the ground a dull, wide vibration through the earth.

And then Anneth was tumbling out of the scoop, rolling toward them with her arms out to soften the blow of the ground. Easter pulled her up onto her lap, wiping dirt away from Anneth's face.

"I'm alright," Anneth said, pushing her away. "Get away. Don't let them think they've hurt me."

"But the baby," Easter said. "I want you to go back to the house."

"If you think I'd leave you all now, you're crazy."

Easter took in everything in flashes, as if her eyes closed between images: The dozer rolling toward them now, chunks of dirt caught in the metal tracking that wound about its wheels. The trees, their limbs bending down in a slight breeze as if leaning over to watch the action below. The sky rolling gray and low. And then as the dozer rolled closer and closer, they all knew what they had to do.

They interlocked arms and sat down. The driver didn't stop until he was so close that Easter could smell the soil caked across the bottom of the scoop.

The driver jumped down and came to lean over them. Now she could see that it was Lonzo Morgan. Easter had known him all his life and started to say as much but didn't speak.

"Stop this now, girls. Please. You're going to cause me to lose my job because I can't do this. I won't," he said. His brow was fretted and his eyes were full of frustration. "When I tell them that, they're going to fire me."

"I'm sorry, Lonzo," Easter said. "But this is your mountain, too. Everybody that lives here—it belongs to them as much as it does us. It always has."

"Please," he said, but the foreman grabbed his shoulders and caused him to stand straight up. The foreman talked so close to his face that Easter thought their lips might touch.

The three women lay down as the dozer continued to tremble at their feet. The men all came and stood around them, as if they were women who had fallen from the sky.

Easter closed her eyes and knew that Anneth and Sophie were doing the same. The ground was cold and filled with the hum of the dozer. In an odd way the vibration was comforting. Easter remembered all the times she had walked this old mountain, all the songs they had sung as they climbed its path. All the times she had run in the field of wildflowers that swayed there in spring and summer. Anneth laughing as she fell back in the purple asters. Her mother walking out of the field clutching a handful of jonquils. Her father holding Easter when she was just a baby as he looked out over the view below them.

A bulldozer sits idle on a mountaintop removal site in southern West Virginia. Photo © Giles Ashford.

Yellow stargrass, a native wild-flower, blooms in the open woods of central Appalachia. Photo © Giles Ashford.

There was a flash of whiteness above her, and when she opened her eyes she saw a photographer leaning down with his camera.

And there were hands on her. She pivoted her head back to find the sheriff and his four deputies, their pistols hanging from their sides. Down by the road she saw their police cars, the lights flashing against the mountainside.

"Just go limp," Easter hollered to Anneth and Sophie. "Be still."

They were carrying Sophie away, one man holding on to her ankles and the other with his hands in her armpits, carrying her away like a gut-shot deer. Sophie had followed Easter's advice and simply relaxed as they carried her away. They had tried to grab Anneth but she had gotten to her feet and was backing away as they closed in on her, telling her to just go with them peacefully. But she wouldn't.

Easter saw Lonzo Morgan climbing down from the dozer, hollering. One of the deputies was holding him back, too. "Let go of her, by God!" Lonzo hollered.

Easter let them lift her and felt each flash of the camera as they carried her away, but then she saw a policeman grab Anneth from behind, his forearm caught under her neck in a choke hold as she fought against them. Easter bucked out of their grip, falling to the ground and scrambling to her feet. She ran toward Anneth. As she did, she said a short prayer, asking that God be in her hands.

This is an excerpt from the novel The Coal Tattoo *by Silas House, copyright © 2005 by Silas House, reprinted by permission of Algonquin Books. This scene takes place during the 1960s, when Appalachians—particularly women—rose up to fight back against coal companies who were operating on decades-old broad-form deeds.*

Where the Coal Is Coming From

Robert F. Kennedy Jr.

In 2004, I FLEW OVER THE COALFIELDS of Kentucky and West Virginia, and I saw where the coal is coming from. If the American people could see what I saw, there would be a revolution in this country, because we are cutting down the Appalachian Mountains. These historic landscapes where Daniel Boone and Davy Crockett roamed are the source of our values and our culture, and we're cutting them down with these giant machines called draglines. They're twenty-two stories high, they cost half a billion dollars, and they practically dispense with the need for human labor—and that, of course, is the point.

I remember, when my father was fighting strip mining back in the sixties, a conversation I had with him at the dinner table where he said they are not only destroying the environment, but they are permanently impoverishing these communities because there is no way that you can generate an economy from the moonscapes that they leave behind, and they're doing it so that they can break the unions. And he was right. In 1968 when he told me that, there were 114,000 unionized mine workers taking coal out of tunnels in West Virginia. Today there are only 11,000 miners left in the state, and almost none of them are unionized because the strip industry isn't.

Using these giant machines and twenty-five tons of dynamite that they explode in West Virginia every day—a Hiroshima

Robert F. Kennedy Jr. (left) and mining engineer Jack Spadaro (his essay is on page 88) at a mountaintop removal site in West Virginia. Photo © Vivian Stockman.

bomb every week—they are blowing the tops off the mountains. And then they take these giant machines and they scrape the rubble and debris into the adjacent river valley. Well, it's all illegal. You cannot dump rock and debris and rubble into a waterway in the United States of America without a Clean Water Act permit. So Joe Lovett sued them, and he won in front of a great crusty old West Virginia judge, Judge Charles Haden, who recently died. Charles Haden said the same thing I said; he said, "It's all illegal, all of it," and he enjoined all mountaintop mining.

Two days from when we got that decision, Peabody Coal and Massey Coal, which had given millions of dollars to the Bush administration, met in the White House, and the White House rewrote one word of the Clean Water Act. A new definition of the word "fill" changed thirty years of statutory interpretation to make it legal today, as it is in every state in the United States, to dump rock, debris, rubble, construction debris, garbage, any kind of solid waste into any waterway in this country without a Clean Water Act permit. All you need is a rubber-stamp permit from the Corps of Engineers that, in many cases, you can get through the mail. It has none of the safeguards that the Clean Water Act provides. And this is what we're fighting today. This is not just a battle to save the environment. This is the subversion of our democracy.

The industry and the great big polluters and their indentured servants and our political process have done a great job, and their PR firms and . . . all these think tanks on Capitol Hill, have done a great job over the past couple of decades of marginalizing the environmental movement, of marginalizing us as radicals, as tree huggers, as I heard the other day, pagans who worship trees and sacrifice people. But there is nothing radical about the idea of clean air and clean water for our children. As I said before, we're not protecting the environment for the sake of the fishes and the birds and the trees. We're protecting it for our own sake, because it's the infrastructure of our communities and because it enriches us.

If you talk to these people on Capitol Hill who are promoting these kind of changes and ask them, "Why are you

We have got to learn to respect ourselves and our dwelling places. We need to quit thinking of rural America as a colony. Too much of the economic history of our land has been that of the export of fuel, food, and raw materials that have been destructively and too cheaply produced.

—Wendell Berry, from "Compromise, Hell!"

A beltline transports coal from a mine to a preparation plant in central Appalachia. Photo © Mark Schmerling.

doing this?" what they invariably say is, "Well, the time has come in our nation's history where we have to choose now between economic prosperity on the one hand and environmental protection on the other." And that is a false choice. In 100 percent of the situations, good environmental policy is identical to good economic policy. If we want to measure our economy, this is how we ought to be measuring it, based upon its jobs and the dignity of jobs over the generations, over the long term and how it preserves the value of the assets of our communities.

If, on the other hand, we want to do what they've been urging us to do on Capitol Hill, which is to treat the planet as if it were a business in liquidation—convert our natural resources to cash as quickly as possible, have a few years of pollution-based prosperity—we can generate an instantaneous cash flow and the illusion of a prosperous economy, but our children are going to pay for our joyride. They're going to pay for it with the muted landscapes, poor health, and huge cleanup costs that are going to amplify over time and that they will never, ever be able to pay. Environmental injury is deficit spending. It's a way of loading the cost of our generation's prosperity onto the backs of our children.

A Works Progress Administration Federal Art Project poster, circa 1936, celebrates Pennsylvania miners. Artist unknown; courtesy of Library of Congress.

This [Bush] White House has done a great job of persuading a gullible press and the American public that the big threat to American democracy is big government. Well, yeah, big government is a threat ultimately, but it is dwarfed by the threat of excessive corporate power and the corrosive impact that has on our democracy. And you know, as I said, you look at all the great political leaders in this country and the central theme is that we have to be cautious about, we have to avoid, the domination of our government by corporate power.

Teddy Roosevelt, a Republican, said that America would never be destroyed by a foreign power, but he warned that our political institutions, our democratic institutions, would be subverted by malefactors of great wealth who would erode them from within. Dwight Eisenhower, another Republican, in his most famous speech warned America against domination by the military-industrial complex. Abraham Lincoln, the greatest Republican in our history, said during the height of the Civil War, "I have the South in front of me and I have the bankers behind me. And for my country, I fear the bankers more."

Franklin Roosevelt said during World War II that the domination of government by corporate power is "the essence of fascism," and Benito Mussolini—who had an insider's view of that process—said the same thing. Essentially, he complained that fascism should not be called fascism. It should be called corporatism because it was the merger of state and corporate power. And what we have to understand as Americans is that the domination of business by government is called communism. The domination of government by business is called fascism. And our job is to walk that narrow trail in between, which is free-market capitalism and democracy. And keep big government at bay with our right hand and corporate power at bay with our left.

In order to do that, we need an informed public and an activist public. And we need a vigorous and an independent press that is willing to speak truth to power. And we no longer have that in the United States of America. And that's something that puts all the values we care about in jeopardy,

A church on Cabin Creek Road in Kanawha County, West Virginia, with a coal silo in the background. Photo © Mark Schmerling.

because you cannot have a clean environment if you do not have a functioning democracy. They are intertwined, they go together. There is a direct correlation around the planet between the level of tyranny and the level of environmental destruction. I could talk about that all day, but . . . the only way you can protect the environment is through a true, locally based democracy.

I don't believe that nature is God or that we ought to be worshiping it as God, but I do believe that it's the way that God communicates to us most forcefully. God talks to human beings through many vectors. Through each other, through organized religions, through wise people, and through the great books of those religions. Through art and literature and music and poetry. But nowhere with such force and clarity and detail and texture and grace and joy as through creation.

We don't know Michelangelo by reading his biography. We know him by looking at the ceiling of the Sistine Chapel.

And we know our Creator best by immersing ourselves in creation, particularly wilderness, which is the undiluted work of the Creator. If you look at every one of the great religious traditions throughout the history of mankind, the central epiphany always occurs in the wilderness. Buddha had to go to the wilderness to experience self-realization and nirvana. Mohammed had to go to the wilderness. Moses had to go to the wilderness of Mount Sinai for forty days alone to get the Commandments. The Jews had to spend 40 years wandering the wilderness to purge themselves of 400 years of slavery in Egypt.

Christ had to go into the wilderness for forty days to discover his divinity for the first time. His mentor was John the Baptist, a man who lived in the Jordan valley dressed in the skins of wild beasts and ate locusts and the honey of wild bees, and all of Christ's parables are taken from nature. I am the vine; you are the branches. The mustard seed, the little swallows, the scattering of seeds on the fallow ground, the lilies of the field. He called himself a fisherman, a farmer, a vineyard keeper, a shepherd.

And all the Old Testament prophets, all the Talmudic prophets, all the New Testament prophets came out of the wilderness. Every one of them, and they were all shepherds. That daily connection to nature gave them a special access to the wisdom of the Almighty. Messages that were written into creation at the beginning of time by the Creator. We haven't been able to discern or decipher them until the prophets came along and immersed themselves in wilderness and learned its language and then came back into the cities to tell us about the wisdom of God.

—————◆—————

This essay is excerpted and adapted from Robert F. Kennedy Jr.'s keynote speech at the Sierra Summit convention in September 2005.

Union Legacy and Green Networking

Bryan McNeil

MOUNTAINTOP REMOVAL HAS GENERATED vocal opposition to the coal industry, even in coalfield communities that have lived off coal's bounty for decades. As it spreads across the mountain landscape, scalping forested ridges and filling adjacent valleys, mountaintop removal disrupts natural and social processes on many levels. Coalfield residents live with the direct impacts of blasting, deforestation, flooding, dust, and the loss of access to mountain lands.

A collection of coalfield grassroots groups that emerged in the middle to late 1990s and larger issue-oriented groups such as Greenpeace and the Sierra Club have joined forces to become a noteworthy organization of environmentalists. Working across distance and addressing a range of loosely related issues, the network unites coalfield citizens who have extensive experience as union activists with environmental activists, funding agencies, and professionals.

Mountaintop removal is by design a form of mechanized job loss on an incredible scale. Using mammoth machinery and heavy explosives, mining companies can extract coal with an efficiency and on a scale that dwarfs even the most efficient methods of underground mining. The United Mine Workers of America (UMWA) was designed to protect miners, and though dramatically weakened since the early 1980s, it remains the strongest formal institution for addressing the

An abandoned building in Boone County, West Virginia. Population is dwindling throughout the coalfields. Photo © Mark Schmerling.

Picket line for the United Mine Workers of America, Brookside, Harlan County, Kentucky, on the day after Thanksgiving, 1973. Photo © Builder Levy.

power of the coal industry. But despite the net job losses attributable to the spread of mountaintop removal (numbering in the tens of thousands), and even though most surface mines have been and remain nonunion, opposition to mountaintop removal has developed primarily as an environmental issue rather than a labor issue. Rather than confront the industry over jobs, the UMWA has attempted to preserve the union contracts it does have at mountaintop removal mines.

By contrast, coalitions like Coal River Mountain Watch and Friends of the Mountains put forth a broad organizing platform that blends elements from several activist traditions. Through their rhetoric and actions, activists assert the value of community in a way that espouses a range of interests, many of which are outside the traditional purview of organized labor. Activists in the region recognize that the threats to their communities come directly from the coal industry. Many people resent the fact that the union has not taken up their cause; others are not going to wait for the union to take action.

The history of union organizing in the region stretches back more than a century and is punctuated by legendary and violent events like the 1921 march on Blair Mountain and the Matewan massacre. Such events are part of the lore of the coalfields. Today's coalfield residents have been shaped by more recent events like the Buffalo Creek disaster of 1972 and the rogue wildcat strikes that marked relations between the union and industry throughout the 1970s. The wildcat tradition both drew from and reinforced the deeply valued concept of solidarity that gave rise to the saying "You don't cross picket lines in West Virginia."

Through the turn of the twenty-first century, however, the union's narrow focus on jobs and the workplace was increasingly compromised by political and economic conditions. While the coal industry argued that mountaintop removal provided jobs, these massive, mechanized mines cost the region thousands of jobs that would have been provided by underground mines. A 1997 lawsuit against mountaintop removal mining specifically targeted a union MTR site. As a result, union president Cecil Roberts led the charge to defend those 300 jobs. When the UMWA sided with the coal company against the community and local sentiment, its leaders drove a wedge between themselves and coalfield citizens who opposed MTR.

Divisions between the union and community activists persisted until the two cooperated on several issues from 2001 to 2004. Most notably, the union and activist communities worked together to fight increases in weight limits for coal trucks.

The union's impossible challenge of trying to get along with the coal industry, hold onto dwindling jobs, and maintain the growing grassroots support resurfaced in 2003 during the formal comment hearing on the environmental impact statement on mountaintop removal. A union representative from the Charleston office was among the first to speak and left immediately after delivering a deliberately vague statement about the need to balance jobs against protecting special places like Kayford Mountain and Blair Mountain. The statement offered no critical comment on the environmental impact statement itself.

John L. Lewis was the big deal over at the mines, so Daddy had his picture up, and he has great big fuzzy eyebrows. I asked Mommy who he was, and she said, "John L. Lewis—your daddy was working for a dollar a day in the mines, and he came in and he was with the union, and now they'll make more money." Daddy got off the WPA and got a job back in the mines.

—*Loretta Lynn, from* The Appalachians

A dispute over coal trucks in the community of Prenter, West Virginia, in 1989 epitomized a community invoking the union tradition to take action on its own behalf. Prenter resident Patty Sebok described the community's effort to take its own action against the coal trucks by picketing roads:

> Right below my house, there's a little hollow comes out, and we had all kinda problems with dust, and we had older people with breathing problems and heart conditions. And so, the women decided we were going to do something about it. So we set up our own little picket line. And so, Massey Coal decided he was going to go to court and take an injunction against us. And the judge said, "Are you crazy? You can't take an injunction against community people." And we kept doing it and kept doing it, and we might have had fifteen or twenty ladies and a few older children that were in their older teens. And finally the union got word of it and decided we would have a bigger picket line at a smaller one-lane bridge below there. And we had about 500 people show up, and I think about every trooper in the state of West Virginia. And we all went to jail.

Throughout the history of the coalfields, miners used strikes to win higher wages and better working conditions. Drawing by W. A. Rogers, 1912; courtesy of Library of Congress.

Running to court for an injunction reflects how companies react to unions under labor laws established to regulate the unions in the postwar era of union expansion. Women have always played an important role in labor strikes, at least in part because the labor laws that governed the union did not apply to them. A community setting up its own picket line is an innovative use of the labor tradition to tackle issues that the union would not. And after the initial effort was successful, the union came in to provide support.

While it has proved ineffective at confronting mountaintop removal and, more important, at organizing new mines, the UMWA has led the charge on some social issues that resonate in the coalfields. During 2003, members of the union went to New York to protest the Viacom corporation's plans to create a *Real Beverly Hillbillies* reality television program. Viacom's ABC division was scouring Appalachia looking for a family that was stereotypically "backward" enough for its plans to move them to a Beverly Hills mansion. The union also led the fight against Bush administration efforts to roll

Workers going home from Kayford Mine, owned by the Bethlehem Mining Corporation, Cabin Creek, Kanawha County, West Virginia, 1978. Photo © Builder Levy.

back health and safety regulations inside the mines. As the industry continued to restructure, the union went to court to fight companies that tried to renege on their pension and retirement obligations as a condition of their sale. The union's efforts on cultural politics and retirement benefits should be seen as innovative leadership on behalf of its workforce.

While these positions were popular in the coalfields, the union's inability to take strong stands on critical issues like mountaintop removal and its inability to organize mines have consistently drawn criticism from the rank and file and from coalfield communities more generally. Virtually every activist involved in Coal River Mountain Watch (CRMW) during its formational years had a personal history with the UMWA. They draw on that history, tradition, and experience to frame the issues that confront their communities, from coal trucks to coal dust to flooding.

Across the coalfields, many people want leadership and representation that are neither bound by the political goals of the union nor restricted by labor laws. Community activism, whether impromptu like Prenter's coal truck picket line or more formally organized through groups like Coal River Mountain Watch, fills a void that many coalfield residents perceive. Because community activism does not have an institutionalized role in the carefully structured relationships among labor, capital, and the state, community activists have greater freedom to choose issues and tactics than does the union. Activists like those at CRMW have taken advantage of this freedom to become the leading edge of progressive movements in the coalfields.

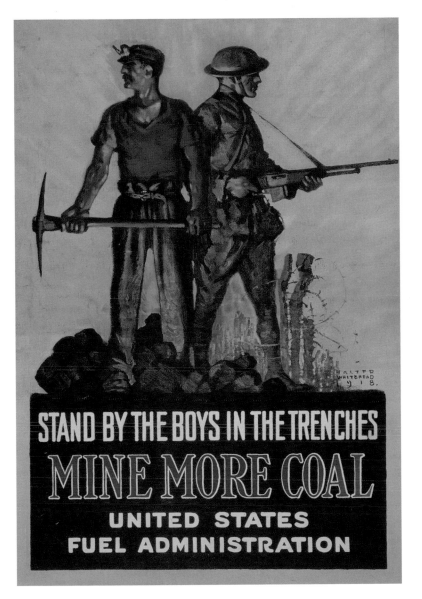

STAND BY THE BOYS IN THE TRENCHES
MINE MORE COAL
UNITED STATES
FUEL ADMINISTRATION

LIGHT CONSUMES COAL
SAVE LIGHT | SAVE COAL
UNITED STATES FUEL ADMINISTRATION

Opposite: A poster for S. J. Patterson Wholesale Coal, circa 1887, contrasts a miner toiling underground with an affluent couple enjoying coal's benefits. *Left:* World War I–era poster issued by the U.S. Fuel Administration. *Above:* A 1917 poster promoting energy conservation. All three courtesy of Library of Congress.

Early spring in Dry Fork Valley,
Randolph County, West Virginia.
Photo © Jim Clark.

Right: Heart Rock in autumn at Dolly Sods, a high, windswept plateau of heath bogs, flagged spruce trees, and boulder fields in Monongahela National Forest, West Virginia. *Below:* Winter in Pendleton County, West Virginia. *Opposite:* A protected view, as seen from Dolly Sods. All three photos © Jim Clark.

How Congress Enabled Mountaintop Removal

Ken Hechler

THE DESTRUCTIVE PRACTICE OF BLASTING off the tops of mountains to harvest the coal seams underneath was made possible not only by more powerful explosives but also by the failure of federal and state regulation to protect those living in the valleys. The judicial system has occasionally slowed this destructive process, though lower-court decisions have all too frequently been overruled on appeal. The well-heeled coal industry has succeeded in buying off legislatures and executive officers whose appointees dictate the membership of supposedly impartial environmental enforcement agencies. In such a political atmosphere, those most affected are powerless. This is a sad commentary on the American system of justice to which we pledge allegiance.

During my more than fifty years as a public servant, one of my main goals was to pass legislation to protect miners and all Appalachians. As a fledgling member of the U.S. House of Representatives in the late 1950s and early 1960s, my concern about the community and environmental damage of strip mining was first sparked by Kentuckian Harry Caudill's landmark book *Night Comes to the Cumberlands*. In 1960, candidate John F. Kennedy visited West Virginia during the presidential primary and was visibly shaken by his firsthand witness of the appalling number of people living in poverty in West Virginia's coal-mining areas. Once elected, he directed

Ken Hechler at Kayford Mountain, Kanawha County, West Virginia. Photo © Mark Schmerling.

Opposite: *Cherry tree and hay bales in autumn, Mineral County, West Virginia. Photo © Jim Clark.*

The Talon coal loadout is located between the Cook Mountain and Twilight Mountain surface mines. Between these two MTR mines also lie the communities of Twilight, Lindytown, and Bandytown, West Virginia. Photo © Jo Syz.

all those personnel working on aid to Appalachia to read Caudill's book. Stewart L. Udall, the able secretary of the interior under both President Kennedy and President Lyndon Johnson, not only wrote a ringing endorsement in his foreword to Caudill's book but also published several revealing studies of the adverse effects of strip mining. President Johnson's War on Poverty and workers from the VISTA program helped to spur the first organized opposition to strip mining in the 1960s.

I was further impressed by the excellent exposés of the harmful effects of strip mining by writers like Ward Sinclair of the *Courier Journal.* A personal letter from the head of the Audubon Society in Louisville brought the problem home graphically. She related having traveled in Europe from Paris eastward to Berlin and Moscow and was pleased to report that the scenes of the war destruction in World War II had been entirely cleaned up and were now lined with flowers. Then, when she returned to this country, the devastation caused by strip mining made the Appalachian area look like it had been the site of the worst bombing of World War II. Upon hearing this story I was even more fired up to do something about it.

The rising social consciousness of the 1960s—including a new kind of attention to environmental protection—helped to spark this flame, too. The burgeoning movement led to the enactment of the Clean Water Act and the Clean Air Act and the establishment of Earth Day in 1970. All these developments assisted me in lining up congressional support for the abolition of the destructive practice of strip mining. I served as the principal architect of the Coal Mine Safety and Health Act of 1969, which put a limit on the amount of respirable coal dust allowed in coal mines, required strict regulations that would protect miners, and would outlaw and phase out strip mining. By the early 1970s I had persuaded ninety House sponsors to indicate their public support for this bill. I believed then and still believe now, however, that regulation could not and does not work because of the tremendous power the coal industry possesses, which enables it to buy off public officials and weaken any efforts at regulation.

The bill called for a six-month phaseout of strip mining, and with my full support, Representative John Seiberling of Ohio, a member of the House Interior and Insular Affairs Committee, amended it to include cash payments and retraining funds for those employed in strip mining when their jobs were eliminated. An important feature placed the administration of the bill with the Environmental Protection Agency, rather than the Bureau of Mines, since it was designed to be enforced by an agency committed to environmental protection rather than production.

In the U.S. Senate, Wisconsin senator Gaylord Nelson and South Dakota senator George McGovern introduced comparable abolition bills. Action was being taken back in West Virginia, too. There, newly elected state senator Si Galperin, who had campaigned in 1970 in Kanawha County on an abolitionist platform, introduced an abolition bill in the state legislature. The VISTA volunteers who were working to abolish strip mining most likely persuaded Secretary of State John D. Rockefeller to come out for state abolition in 1971 and announce that this would be a feature of his 1972 campaign for West Virginia governor. Rockefeller financed an organization called Citizens for the Abolition of Strip Mining (CASM) that pulled together the efforts of nineteen abolition efforts in counties throughout the state. The director of CASM was Richard Cartwright Austin, a Presbyterian minister who lived in the Boone County town of Orgas within sight of a big strip mine. When the funding for CASM dried up, Austin served on my congressional staff.

Two other West Virginians were instrumental in lining up support for abolition. One was state senator Paul Kaufman, who provided legal assistance through the Appalachian Research and Defense Fund (financed by a program of the War on Poverty). The other was Norman Williams, who had been fired as deputy director of the state Department of Natural Resources because he publicly criticized the department for its failure to protect the land and people against destructive strip mining. When he was fired, he joined my staff to bolster the abolition issue.

The mining is also categorically evil in the strictest moral sense: not only is it enormously destructive of men and the earth, but every single element of its destructiveness is unnecessary and preventable. It is now sin—the perversion of good into evil—for the destructiveness is not prevented.

—*Presbyterian minister Richard Cartwright Austin, from* Spoil: A Study of the Strip Mining of Coal

With enough people on board, I scheduled a special briefing for members of Congress and their staff on April 22, 1971. Secretary of State Rockefeller, Representative John Seiberling, West Virginia delegate Ivan White of Boone County, and other abolition advocates were all present. I was pleased that Rockefeller's father-in-law, Illinois senator Charles Percy, stayed for the entire program.

As a result of this briefing, all the cosponsors of my abolition bill, as well as abolition advocates throughout the nation and every environmental organization, joined me in a drumfire of demands that Congress hold hearings on the issue. During the same period, the coal industry spread the word that it would agree to a mild form of regulation to quiet the public uproar for abolition. Finally, the House Committee on Interior and Insular Affairs authorized its Subcommittee on Mines and Mining to open hearings in September 1971. The first witnesses were supporters of regulation, but finally I was scheduled to testify.

I had prepared my testimony carefully to anticipate challenges, and to back up my case I received permission from the committee staff to bring in three experts to sit with me at the witness table: Arnold Miller an experienced deep miner who at that time shared my abolition view and who later would become president of the United Mine Workers; West Virginia University economics professor William Miernyk; and West Virginia University wildlife management professor Robert Smith. On the day of my appearance, however, the subcommittee chairman, Ed Edmondson of Oklahoma, ruled that he would not allow these three to speak even though I had received advance approval from the staff, claiming that he had already turned down similar requests by other witnesses.

When I began my testimony, I was surprised to observe that the chairman of the full committee, Representative Wayne Aspinall of Colorado, who never before had attended subcommittee hearings, was present. Knowing Aspinall's consistent record of support of the coal industry, and noting the dour, disapproving look on his face, I knew I was in for a hard time. I was right.

For more than three hours, I was subjected to the most hostile and vindictive questions and procedural rulings I had ever experienced in my nearly fourteen years of service as a congressman. Most of the time was taken up by humiliating questions as virtually every committee member tried to get me to change my support of abolition. Subcommittee chairman Edmondson was more polished than most of the others in his opposition, hammering away at several central themes: jobs, the safety of surface mining versus the danger of deep mining, and the energy crisis.

This coal camp near Grundy, in Buchanan County, Virginia, photographed in 1971, was later demolished to make way for highway expansion. Photo © Builder Levy.

This massive mountaintop removal site has all but enveloped a once majestic mountain in southern West Virginia; only this lone summit remains. Photo © Giles Ashford.

It came as no surprise when, in 1972, the Interior Committee voted to kill my abolition bill. The scene then shifted to the House floor as the Surface Mine Control and Reclamation Act (SMCRA) was being shaped. Although I tried to mobilize my ninety abolition cosponsors for a vote on the House floor, by 1974, in the face of the Arab oil embargo, the number who voted for abolition had dwindled to sixty-six. The weakened amendments were put forward by congressmen who were responding to coal industry concerns. I tried unsuccessfully to sponsor amendments such as prohibition of strip mining on slopes steeper than twenty degrees, but they were customarily rejected because there just happened to be more congressmen who were subservient to the coal industry than there were genuine environmentalists.

The blackest day in the consideration of SMCRA occurred on July 22, 1974, when Representative Teno Roncalio of Wyoming, the largest coal-producing state in the Union, introduced an amendment to the bill authorizing "mining operations which create a plateau with no highwalls remaining." The language sounded innocent enough to fool many members of Congress, until West Virginia representative John M. Slack, a strong coal industry supporter, offered this explanation:

> This amendment would permit the mountaintop and valley fill type of surface mining presently used at several model mines in West Virginia creating useful plateaus without highwalls. Mountaintop mining produces flat land needed in many hilly regions with minimum damage to the environment. This is a form of mining which should increase, not decline on the basis of its proven results. I urge its adoption.

Of course, many members did not realize that what Slack characterized as "model mines" were a far cry from that. And to refer to "minimum damage to the environment" was a real distortion of the adverse effects of mountaintop removal on the people, the wildlife, and the land itself. In turn, I asked my colleague whether this, indeed, did not weaken, negate, and gut the permanent standards on steep slopes and do great damage to the state.

Slack gave a quick, four-word denial, "Not in my judgment."

And it got worse. In 1974 and 1975, President Gerald Ford vetoed two bills that authorized mountaintop removal. Congress came close in 1975 to overriding Ford's second veto. Because I felt so strongly against mountaintop removal and because I believed that regulation would never work, I defied the urgent pleas of the Sierra Club and others that I swallow my pride and vote to sustain the veto, as a point of principle.

I left Congress at the end of 1976. The next year, the new Congress sent the Surface Mining Control and Reclamation Act to newly elected president Jimmy Carter. As an early activist on the subject, I was invited to the Rose Garden in August 1977 for the signing of the bill. I told President Carter that the bill would never work unless it was enforced in such a way as to overcome the pressures of the coal industry. Carter assured me that he would alert Secretary of the Interior Cecil Andrus to our concerns.

Despite President Carter's optimism, the Surface Mining Control and Reclamation Act of 1977 has failed to protect the land and the people against the ravages of mountaintop removal. For the first year or so, the best and the brightest staff members of the federal Office of Surface Mining won some temporary victories, but gradually the pressure of the coal industry resulted in the weakening of enforcement. With these developments, especially at the state level, the inspectors and dedicated staff members became disillusioned, and many of them resigned. President Ronald Reagan's secretary of the interior, James Watt, abruptly removed environmentalists from the leadership and staff of the Office of Surface Mining, leading to more firings and resignations. In West Virginia, the toothless Department of Environmental Protection never lived up to its title, inasmuch as every governor proclaims himself a "friend of coal."

Why haven't the Clean Water Act and the Clean Air Act helped to outlaw some of the outrageous practices of mountaintop removal? Legal challenges have occurred. Attorney Joe Lovett has established an effective organization, the

Almost level, West Virginia
Scalped-off mountains
Dumped into our rivers
Dark and dusty, blasting toward
  the sky
Murdering our mountains
Teardrops in our eyes

(chorus:)
Digging coal
Blasting rocks
In the place I belong
West Virginia, mountain mama
Please help save
What is left

—Ken Hechler, from "Almost
Level, West Virginia" (to the
tune of "Country Roads")

During the administration of George W. Bush, a sticker on a guardrail in southern West Virginia proclaims "Bush [hearts] Coal." Photo © Vivian Stockman.

Appalachian Center for the Economy and the Environment. In his first case, he went before conservative Republican circuit judge Charles Haden and logged his first victory in 1999. The decision in this case, *Bragg v. Robertson,* declared that the plaintiffs' rights had been violated and that mountaintop removal clearly violated provisions of the federal Clean Water Act. Robert C. Byrd, U.S. senator from West Virginia, denounced Haden's decision and attempted unsuccessfully to overrule it through congressional legislation. But the victory for the land and residents was short-lived. In 2001, the Fourth Circuit Court of Appeals overturned Haden's decision.

During his eight years in office, President George W. Bush's administration repeatedly threw wrenches into the mix, the most recent of which happened at the end of August 2007. The Office of Surface Mining proposed new regulations to insulate mountaintop removal from legal challenges under the Clean Water Act. The central aim of the new regulation is to make it no longer a violation of the Clean Water Act to dump material in such a way as to block streams. This effort to circumvent the act bypasses the 2002 rewrite of clean water regulations by the Environmental Protection Agency (EPA) to add "mine waste" to the list of materials that can be used to fill in streams for development. Then there was the EPA's 2004 ruling that the legal requirement prohibiting any mining activity within a buffer zone of 300 feet from the stream should be followed only "to the extent practicable."

The struggles that began in the 1960s continue. Many of the flawed arguments that previous generations used to advocate for strip mining are being repeated, and the destruction goes on. Still, there are no real solutions for the people of Appalachia, the waters of the United States, or the air that we breathe. It is left to a new generation to complete the groundwork that we began and to continue to demand more from their elected officials and the agencies that are supposed to work to protect the people and the environment from the devastating consequences of such practices as mountaintop removal.

Empire Building,
One Chunk of Coal
at a Time

John Hennen

A DOCUMENT PRODUCED IN 2000 BY a veteran coal industry attorney affirms that population decline in West Virginia coalfields is a positive by-product of mountaintop removal operations. Depopulation is a good thing, says the lawyer, since "the people most affected" by MTR will be removed to "a better life." The costs of relocation should be absorbed by the state, not directly by coal companies, with renewable assistance grants, education benefits, and the condemnation of land occupied by "stubborn people in the way of a permitted surface mine project." The depopulation plan is part of a broad strategy to liberate coal properties while removing the causes of poverty in the region—that is, people.

As face-slapping as this guileless plan is, its themes are not completely removed from past assumptions by local-color writers, philanthropists, well-meaning public reformers, idealistic volunteers, visiting playwrights, and others who have attributed the problems of Appalachian coal country to two general factors: (1) extraordinary greed and venality of the coal industry and/or (2) cultural pathology of mountain residents who, either voluntarily or as helpless victims, have "devolved" into states of dependence, despair, and belligerent suspicion. What is missing from these generalizations is any hint of what is really at the heart of coal country's historical,

Harry, a young driver for the Maryland Coal Company mine, and his mule, Sallie, near Sand Lick, Grafton, West Virginia. The boy was reluctant to be photographed, thinking it might result in his being sent back to school. Photo by Lewis Hine; courtesy of Library of Congress.

Child laborers in the coal mines, 1911. Photo by Lewis Hine; courtesy of Library of Congress.

systemic exploitation: our national faith in the righteousness of profit, expansion, and accumulation.

When corporate bodies embrace the ecologically and socially destructive core of accumulation *too* aggressively, they become an embarrassment to believers in self-regulating free markets. When residents of the coalfields question or resist the sacrament, they, too, are an embarrassment. So, all parties must then adapt, causing the polluters and destroyers to develop methods like "clean coal technologies." Common folks must internalize the values of acquisition. Once they do, they will want to relocate to Lexington, Charlotte, Washington, or Atlanta to function as, in Orwell's elegant phrase, "clerks for the empire."

There is nothing new about the idea of American empire, and nothing extraordinary about the life-giving role of natural resources in securing and sustaining imperial power. Thomas Jefferson remarked in 1780 that the American "Empire of Liberty" rested upon access to "extensive and fertile country" and later listed "mineral productions of every kind, more particularly metals, limestone, pit coal & saltpeter," as necessities for national expansion. Not long after, President Andrew Jackson decided that the removal of another group of Appalachians, the Cherokee, would be in the best interest of the tribe. It did not hurt matters that the removal was also for the greater good of white settlers who needed Cherokee land and gold.

By the 1890s, the nation's coal regions were closely tied to a new imperial phase that historian Charles S. Morris called the "Empire of Production." American polemicists linked the country's economic health and social stability with military strength, advocating the protection of the country's growing coal-fired merchant fleet with an expanding coal-fired navy. Capital was courted by Appalachian boosters such as West Virginia governor and coal operator Aretas B. Fleming, who in 1891 welcomed investors to tap into the state's "inexhaustible wealth of vast mineral deposits."

Periodic uprisings by the subjects of King Coal between 1900 and 1938 usually included miners' protestations that they were being denied their rights as Americans: companies were routinely able to marshal legal, political, and extralegal power to repress dissent, whether peaceful or violent. When striking miners threatened to win, state authorities and sometimes— as during the West Virginia Mine War of 1920–1921—federal forces arrived to end the strike and maybe help bust a union local. During World War II, the Empire of Production mobilized to defeat external threats and then to construct a cold war national security framework. For a generation or so, there was a coal boom during which thousands of Appalachian miners dug coal to produce electricity and cars for consumers, as well as ships, tanks, aircraft carriers, destroyers, and bombers for the United States and its cold war dependents.

In this World War I propaganda poster from 1917, the U.S. government encourages citizens to conserve coal. Artist unknown; courtesy of Library of Congress.

By the late 1950s, intensive mechanization and expanded strip mining steadily eroded the demand for miners. By the mid-1980s, the economic security of the once densely unionized coalfields had vanished. The heretofore unimaginable destructive capacity of modern mining operations was enabled by giant loopholes in the Surface Mining Control and Reclamation Act of 1977, encouraging the permanent destruction of mountains if done for a "higher and better use" (never clearly defined).

Coal has, until now, played a supporting role to oil in the "Empire of Consumption." Not long after the end of World War II, the United States was producing more than 60 percent of the world's oil. But even in the 1950s, the United States was beginning to import oil. By 1972, domestic oil production had peaked, and the Organization of Petroleum Exporting Countries (OPEC) dominated both production and pricing. America became more dependent on other countries for its oil. Some commentators—including President Jimmy Carter—warned that the country was threatened by reckless consumption that, if not checked, would weaken America in the long term.

Americans rejected the nay-saying Carter in favor of Ronald Reagan's militant consumerism. During his two terms, Reagan cut taxes and public services, expanded military spending, drove up budget deficits, dramatically militarized America's global profile, and generally whooped through an era of self-indulgence and unparalleled (at that time) arrogance. Reagan embraced America's gluttonous ingestion of energy, especially oil, and laughed off any cockeyed notion that there was anything untoward about it. Reagan retired in 1989, leaving behind a cabal of think-tank true believers who foresaw an unchallenged global Pax Americana, relying on awesome military power to project American might and culture throughout the world—all nourished by Persian Gulf oil.

The most passionate of these Reaganite *übermenschen* called their plans the Project for a New American Century (PNAC). Long before the attacks of September 11, 2001, they lobbied for the conquest of Iraq as a first step toward

Overlooking the destruction at the Edwight mountaintop removal site, Raleigh County, West Virginia. Photo © Denny Tyler.

Americanizing the Middle East and locking up distribution rights for Iraqi and Iranian oil reserves. The problem was, as fortuitous as the September 11 attacks turned out to be for the PNAC's big thinkers, the Pax Americana did not get much traction beyond Georgetown. The implosion of the neocons' Middle East fantasy—the predictable outcome of a thousand lies and delusions—has, however, sparked a new imperial quest. Since we can't get our oil out from under their sand, let's get our gasoline out of Appalachian coal! The mantra is "reducing our dependence on foreign oil." The legacy will be the obliteration of Appalachian mountains and communities.

The American empire includes, give or take, about 800 military bases in 130 countries and some 6,000 domestic military installations. The U.S. Air Force spends about $4.5 billion annually on aviation fuel—and for years its strategists have dreamed of a massive conversion to synthetic fuels,

Down in the Coal Mine

Down in the coal mine
Underneath the ground,
Where a beam of sunshine
Never can be found.
Digging dusky diamonds
All the season round
Down in the coal mine
Underneath the ground

—J. B. Geoghegan,
recorded in 1908

projecting the consumption of about 400 million gallons of domestic coal-to-liquid fuel in air force jets by 2016. The November 25, 2008, *Seattle Times* reports that "the Air Force is converting its gas-guzzling fleet of aircraft to synthetic fuels and encouraging the creation of a liquefied coal industry that could tap the nation's vast coal reserves." The chair of the National Coal Council's Coal Policy Committee claims that private and public support for coal-to-liquid technologies is a "national security imperative to provide an adequate fuel source for our military and civilian aviation industries." A network of corporate, labor, political, academic, and media representatives is beating the drum for "clean coal technology," "carbon sequestration," and "coal liquefaction," all dependent on technologies that would unleash potentially disastrous side effects and may never be practicable on a wide scale.

The developing narrative surrounding the holy grail of "clean coal" delegitimizes any challenge to the flawed logic of consumption. The promotional narrative never—repeat, *never*—acknowledges the devastation caused by the extraction of coal but focuses only on the technical challenges to coal's infinite and, of course, "green" applications. It is an imperial narrative, based on the global projection of military power, rationalizing the voracious consumption of natural resources and mountain communities in the name of "national security."

Whether the 2008 economic collapse, the elections of that same year, and a growing popular mobilization will nurture a broad-based renunciation of our national obsession with profit, expansion, accumulation, and consumption, whatever the long-term costs, remains to be seen. Without that renunciation, much of what we know and cherish about Appalachia, and our own humanity, will not long endure.

Moving Mountains

Erik Reece

NOT SINCE THE GLACIERS PUSHED toward these ridgelines a million years ago have the Appalachian Mountains been as threatened as they are today. But the coal extraction process decimating this landscape has generated little press beyond the region. The problem, in many ways, is one of perspective. From interstates and lowlands, where most communities are clustered, one simply doesn't see what is happening up there. Only from the air can you fully grasp the magnitude of the devastation. If you were to board, say, a small prop plane at Zeb Mountain, Tennessee, and follow the spine of the Appalachian Mountains up through Kentucky, Virginia, and West Virginia, you would be struck not by the beauty of a densely forested range older than the Himalayas but rather by inescapable images of ecological violence. Near Pine Mountain, Kentucky, you'd see an unfolding series of staggered green hills quickly give way to a wide expanse of gray plateaus pocked with dark craters and huge black ponds filled with a toxic by-product called coal slurry. The desolation stretches like a long scar up the Kentucky-Virginia line, before eating its way across southern West Virginia.

Central Appalachia provides much of the country's coal, second only to Wyoming's Powder River Basin. In the United States, 100 tons of coal are extracted every two seconds. Around 70 percent of that coal comes from strip mines, and

A blast goes off at a mountaintop removal site in central Appalachia. Photo © Giles Ashford.

The Twilight MTR surface mine, a Massey Energy Company operation in Boone County, West Virginia. Photo © Jo Syz.

over the past twenty years, an increasing amount has come from mountaintop removal sites. In the name of corporate expedience, coal companies have turned from excavation to simply blasting away the tops of the mountains. To achieve this, they use the same mixture of ammonium nitrate and diesel fuel that Timothy McVeigh employed to level the Murrow Building in Oklahoma City—except each detonation is ten times as powerful, and thousands of blasts go off each day across central Appalachia. Hundreds of feet of forest, topsoil, and sandstone—the coal industry calls all of this "overburden"—are unearthed so bulldozers and front-end loaders can more easily extract the thin seams of rich, bituminous coal that stretch in horizontal layers throughout these mountains. Almost everything that isn't coal is pushed down into the valleys below. As a result, 6,700 "valley fills" were approved in central Appalachia between 1985 and 2001. The Environmental Protection Agency estimates that more than 700 miles of healthy streams have been completely buried by mountaintop removal, and thousands more have been damaged. Where there once flowed a highly braided system of headwater streams, now a vast circuitry of haul roads winds through the rubble. From the air, it looks like someone had tried to plot a highway system on the moon.

Serious coal mining has been going on in Appalachia since the turn of the twentieth century. But from the time World War II veterans climbed down from tanks and up onto bulldozers, the extractive industries in America have grown more mechanized and more destructive. Ironically, here in Kentucky where I live, coal-related employment has dropped 60 percent in the past fifteen years; it takes very few men to run a strip mine operation, with giant machines doing most of the clear-cutting, excavating, loading, and bulldozing of rubble. And all strip mining—from the most basic truck mine to mountaintop removal—results in deforestation, flooding, mudslides, and the fouling of headwater streams.

Alongside this ecological devastation lies an even more ominous human dimension: an Eastern Kentucky University study found that children in Letcher County, Kentucky, suffer from an alarmingly high rate of nausea, diarrhea, vomiting, and shortness of breath—symptoms of something called blue baby syndrome—that can all be traced back to sedimentation and dissolved minerals that have drained from mine sites into nearby streams. Long-term effects may include liver, kidney, and spleen failure, bone damage, and cancers of the digestive track. Erica Urias, who lives on Island Creek in Grapevine, Kentucky, told me she has to bathe her two-year-old daughter in contaminated water because of the mining around her home. In McRoberts, Kentucky, the problem is flooding. In 1998, Tampa Energy Company (TECO) started blasting along the ridgetops above McRoberts. Homes shook and foundations cracked. Then TECO sheared off all the vegetation at the head of Chopping Block Hollow and replaced it with the compacted rubble of a valley fill. In a region prone to flash floods, nothing was left to hold back the rain; this once forested watershed had been turned into an enormous funnel. In 2002, three so-called hundred-year floods happened in ten days. Between the blasting and the flooding, the people of McRoberts have been nearly flushed out of their homes.

A sign near the Hobet Mining sediment pond in southern West Virginia. Photo © Giles Ashford.

Consider the story of Debra and Granville Burke. First the blasting above their house wrecked its foundation. Then the floods came, four times wiping out the Burkes' garden, which the family depended on to get through the winter. Finally, on Christmas morning 2002, Debra Burke took her life. In a letter published in a local paper, her husband wrote: "She left eight letters describing how she loved us all but that our burdens were just getting too much to bear. She had begged for TECO to at least replace our garden, but they just turned their back on her. I look back now and think of all the things I wish I had done differently so that she might still be with us, but mostly I wish that TECO had never started mining above our home."

In the language of economics, Debra Burke's death was an externality—a cost that simply is not factored into the price Americans pay for coal. And that is precisely the problem. In 2005, American power plants burned more than a billion tons of coal, accounting for more than 50 percent of this country's

Unemployment in the Coal Mine Industry

My morning paper route will soon
  be done forever
and all these ghost porches of
  company houses
can go on breathing up the valley
  air alone.
Their white painted sides as painted
  as the snow
falling across the road a flake at a
  time
till everything is covered with quiet.
We too are moving on, back home
  to grandma's
where the trees are still too thick
  to climb
and school's an hour away by bus
  at dawn,
and the rides there are as dark and
  deep
as the lines in daddy's face.

—Larry Smith

electricity use. In Kentucky, 80 percent of the harvested coal is sold and shipped to twenty-two other states. Yet it is the people of Appalachia who pay the highest price for the rest of the country's cheap energy—through contaminated water, flooding, cracked foundations and wells, bronchial problems related to breathing coal dust, and roads that have been torn up and turned deadly by speeding coal trucks. Why should large cities like Phoenix and Detroit get the coal but be held accountable for none of the environmental consequences of its extraction? And why is a Tampa-based energy company—or Peabody Coal in St. Louis or Massey Energy in Richmond, Virginia—allowed to destroy communities throughout Appalachia? As my friend and teacher the late Guy Davenport once wrote, "Distance negates responsibility."

Another violent death was that of three-year-old Jeremy Davidson. At two-thirty in the morning on August 30, 2004, a bulldozer, operating without a permit above the Davidsons' home, dislodged a thousand-pound boulder from a mountaintop removal site in the town of Appalachia, Virginia. The boulder rolled 200 feet down the mountain before it crushed to death the sleeping child.

But Jeremy Davidson's death is hardly an isolated incident. In West Virginia, 14 people drowned in the past three years because of floods and mudslides caused by mountaintop removal; in Kentucky, 50 people have been killed and more than 500 injured in the past five years by coal trucks, almost all of which were illegally overloaded.

In the town of Rock Creek, West Virginia, stands the Marsh Fork Elementary School. Back in 2004, Ed Wiley, a forty-seven-year-old West Virginian who spent years working on strip mines, was called by the school to come pick up his granddaughter Kayla because she was sick. "She had a real bad color to her," Wiley told me. The next day, and the day after that, the school called again because Kayla was ill. Wiley started flipping through the school's sign-out book and found that fifteen to twenty students went home sick every day because of asthma problems, severe headaches, blisters in their mouths, constant runny noses, and nausea. In May

Playground at Marsh Fork Elementary School, Raleigh County, West Virginia. In addition to the looming coal silo, an impoundment capable of holding 2.9 billion gallons of coal slurry lies directly behind the school. Photo © Giles Ashford.

2005, when volunteers with Mountain Justice (a grassroots organization of young people devoted to educating people regarding MTR) started going door-to-door in an effort to identify citizens' concerns and possibly locate cancer clusters, West Virginia activist Bo Webb found that 80 percent of parents said their children came home from school with a variety of illnesses. The school, a small brick building, sits almost directly beneath a Massey Energy subsidiary's processing plant where coal is washed and stored. Coal dust settles like pollen over the playground. Nearly three billion gallons of coal slurry, which contains extremely high levels of mercury, cadmium, and nickel, are stored behind a 385-foot-high earthen dam right above the school.

In 1972, a similar coal impoundment dam collapsed at Buffalo Creek, West Virginia, killing 125 people. Two hundred eighty children attend the Marsh Fork Elementary School. It is unnerving to imagine what damage a minor earthquake, a heavy flash flood, or a structural failure might do to this small community. And according to documents that long-time activist Julia "Judy" Bonds obtained under the Freedom of Information Act, the pond is leaking into the creek and groundwater around the school. Students often cannot drink from the water fountains. When they return from recess, their tennis shoes are covered with black coal dust.

Massey responded to complaints about the plant by applying for a permit to enlarge it, with a new silo to be built even closer to the school. It was this callousness that led to the first major Mountain Justice direct action on the last day of May. About a hundred out-of-state activists, alongside another hundred local citizens, gathered at the school and marched next door to the Massey plant.

Inez Gallimore, an eighty-two-year-old woman whose granddaughter attended the elementary school, walked up to the security guard and asked for the plant superintendent to come down and accept a copy of the group's demands that Massey shut down the plant. When the superintendent refused, Gallimore sat down in the middle of the road, blocking trucks from entering or leaving the facility. When police came to arrest her, they had to help Gallimore to her feet, but not before TV cameras recorded her calling Massey Energy a "terrorist organization."

Three other protesters took the woman's place and were arrested. Three more followed.

In the end, the media coverage at the Marsh Fork rally prompted West Virginia governor Joe Manchin to promise he would put together an investigative team to look into the citizens' concerns. But seven days after that promise, on June 30, Massey received its permit to expand the plant.

The history of resource exploitation in Appalachia, like the history of racial oppression in the South, follows a sinister logic—keep people poor and scared so that they remain powerless. In the nineteenth century, mountain families were actually doing fairly well farming rich bottomlands. But populations grew, farms were subdivided, and then northern coal and steel companies started buying up much of the land, hungry for the resources that lay beneath. By the time the railroads reached headwater hollows like McRoberts, Kentucky, men had little choice but to sell their labor cheaply, live in company towns, and shop in overpriced company

Miners buying groceries in a coal company store, Pursglove, West Virginia, 1938. Photo by Marion Post Wolcott; courtesy of Library of Congress.

stores. "Though he might revert on occasion to his ancestral agriculture," wrote coalfield historian Harry Caudill, "he would never again free himself from dependence upon his new overlords." In nearly every county across central Appalachia, King Coal had gained control of the economy, the local government, and the land.

In the decades that followed, less obvious tactics kept Harlan County, Kentucky, one of the poorest places in Appalachia. Activist Teri Blanton, whose father and brother were Harlan County miners, has spent many years trying to understand the patterns of oppression that hold the Harlan County high school graduation rate at 59 percent and the median household income at $18,665. "We were fueling the whole United States with coal," she said of the past hundred years in Eastern Kentucky. "And yet our pay was lousy, our education was lousy, and they destroyed our environment. As long as you have a polluted community, no other industry is going to locate there. Did they keep us uneducated because it was easier to control us then? Did they keep other industries out because then they can keep our wages low? Was it all by design?" Whether one detects motive or not, this much is clear—forty-one years after Lyndon Johnson stood on a miner's porch in adjacent Martin County and announced his War on Poverty, the poverty rate in central and southern Appalachia stands at 30 percent, right where it did in 1964. What's more, maps generated by the Appalachian Regional Commission show that the poorest counties—those colored deep red for "distressed"—are those that have seen the most severe strip mining and the most intense mountaintop removal.

There is a galling irony in the fact that the Fourteenth Amendment, which was designed to protect the civil liberties of recently freed African slaves, was later interpreted in such a way as to give corporations like Massey all the rights of "legal persons," while requiring little of the accountability that we expect of individuals. Because coal companies are not individuals, they often operate without the moral compass that would prevent a person from contaminating a neighbor's well, poisoning the town's drinking water, or covering the

This 1903 cover of Puck *magazine illustrates the coal industry's fear of strikes. Artist unknown; courtesy of Library of Congress.*

A lined slurry pond typical of those found throughout central Appalachia. Photo © Giles Ashford.

local school with coal dust. This situation is compounded by federal officials who often appear more loyal to corporations than to citizens. Consider the case of Jack Spadaro, a whistle-blower who was forced out of his job at the U.S. Department of Labor's Mine Safety and Health Administration (MSHA) precisely because he tried to do his job—protecting the public from mining disasters.

When the Buffalo Creek dam in West Virginia broke in 1972, Spadaro, a young mining engineer at the time, was brought in to investigate. He found that the flood could have been prevented by better dam construction, and he spent the next thirty years of his career at MSHA investigating impoundment dams. So when a 300-million-gallon slurry pond collapsed in Martin County, Kentucky, in 2000, causing one of the worst environmental disasters east of the Mississippi, Spadaro was again named to the investigating team. He found that Massey had known for ten years that the pond was going to break. Spadaro wanted to charge Massey with criminal negligence, but circumstances were arrayed against him. Elaine

Chao, Spadaro's boss at the Department of Labor, is also the wife of Kentucky Republican senator Mitch McConnell. And Massey had donated $100,000 to a campaign committee headed by McConnell. Spadaro got nowhere with his charges. Instead, someone changed the lock on his office door, and he was placed on administrative leave.

Spadaro's story seems to validate what many coalfield residents have been contending for years—that the very agencies that should be regulating corporations are instead ignoring, breaking, and at times even rewriting the law in their favor, as when Department of the Interior deputy secretary (and former coal lobbyist) Stephen Griles instructed his staff to rewrite a key provision of the Clean Water Act to reclassify all waste associated with strip mining as merely benign "fill material." A federal judge rejected that change, arguing that "only the United States Congress can rewrite the Act to allow fills with no purpose or use but the deposit of waste," but the change was upheld in 2003 by the U.S. Fourth Circuit Court—on which sat John Roberts, the then recently appointed chief justice of the Supreme Court.

On July 8, 2005, I was standing in Monroe Park in Richmond, Virginia, next to a pretty girl with pierced lips and colorful yarn braided into her blonde hair, as Mountain Justice activists prepared to march ten blocks to the headquarters of Massey Energy to demand the closure of the prep plant behind Marsh Fork Elementary School.

Short, gray-haired Judy Bonds stepped to the mike and told the crowd, "I'm honored to be here with you. We're an endangered species, we hillbillies. Massey Energy is terrorizing us in Appalachia. Little old ladies in their seventies can't even sit on their porches. They have to cut their grass wearing respirators. That's how these people have to live. The coal companies are the real terrorists in America. And we're going to expose them for the murdering, lying thieves that they are."

With that, the marchers started down Franklin Avenue, behind a long banner stretching across the street that read Industrial Capitalism Kills Our Land and People. They

In an opinion handed down on June 21, 1968, by the Kentucky Court of Appeals . . . the majority held that the owner of underlying minerals may totally ruin the surface of the earth without the consent of the man who owns and tills it—and without paying him anything for his loss!

—Harry Caudill, from
My Land Is Dying

marched on past blooming crepe myrtle trees and exclusive clubs. Then they hung a right, and suddenly we were all standing in front of a granite-and-concrete monolith that had been cordoned off with yellow tape.

Don Blankenship is the CEO of Massey, a man that many feel had dubious access to the Bush administration. Records show that from 2000 to 2004, when MSHA assistant secretary David Lauriski weakened a mine safety standard, it usually followed a meeting with Blankenship.

The stated goal of the Richmond march was to get Blankenship to personally accept Mountain Justice's demand that Massey shut down the prep plant next to the Marsh Fork Elementary School. Of course, everyone knew that was not going to happen.

On April 9, 1963, snarling police dogs pinned a black protester to the ground on a street in Birmingham, Alabama; the *New York Times* was there to report it. Martin Luther King Jr. and the Southern Christian Leadership Conference (SCLC) were ecstatic. "We've got a movement, we've got a movement!" one member exclaimed. "They brought out the dogs." Without the arrests in Birmingham, and the press coverage that followed, John Kennedy would not have pushed for the Civil Rights Act, and without daily attempts to register black voters in Selma, and the violence that followed, Lyndon Johnson would have dragged his feet for years on the Voting Rights Act. King and the SCLC knew they needed numbers, and they needed confrontation. They needed Bull Connor's dogs and Selma sheriff James Clark's police batons coming down on the heads of older African Americans. They needed to call out, for all to see, the men who enforced brutal oppression every day in the South.

In their own way, Mountain Justice activists worked hard to expose the injustice spreading across the coalfields of Appalachia. Through nonviolent actions and demonstrations, they attempted to show the nation how coal companies break the law with a pathological consistency and operate with little regard for the human consequences of their actions. But on the national stage, in 2005, Mountain Justice Summer

Citizen-activist Judy Bonds speaks out at a public meeting. Photo © Giles Ashford.

could not compete with high gas prices and a foreign war, even though it is precisely that war over oil that is driving coal demands higher and laying mountains lower faster—that plus the fact that U.S. energy consumption increased 42 percent over the past thirty years. Urban affluence and this country's shortsighted energy policy are making Appalachia a poorer place—poorer in beauty, poorer in health, poorer in resources, and poorer in spirit.

"This wouldn't go on in New England," Jack Spadaro once told me. It wouldn't go on in California or Florida or along the East Coast. After the sixties, America and the mainstream media seemed to lose interest in the problems of Appalachia. Although the Martin County slurry pond disaster was twenty times larger than the *Exxon Valdez* oil spill, the *New York Times* ignored it for months. But the seeming invisibility of the people in Appalachia does not make their plight any less real.

That the civil rights movement happened so recently in our country's history can seem dumbfounding, but not to the people who still live in the shadow of oppression. Those who live in the path of the coal industry—beneath sheared-off mountains, amid unnatural, treeless landscapes, drinking poisoned water and breathing dirty air—are fighting their own civil rights battle. And, as in the past, justice may be slow in coming to the mountains of Appalachia. But justice delayed could mean the ruin of a place that has sacrificed much for this nation, and has received next to nothing in return.

Oh, the rich they get richer
And the poor mine the coal
And the lights must keep burning
In the cities, we're told
But where will we turn to
When the boom turns to bust
And the once-verdant mountains
To rock piles and dust

—Anne Shelby, from
"All That We Have"

———※·※———

This essay is excerpted and adapted from an article originally published in Orion *magazine in 2006.*

The Problem in Appalachia

Jack Spadaro

Jack Spadaro stands in a West Virginia forest. Photo © Mark Schmerling.

In October 2000, I was asked by the assistant secretary of labor under President Bill Clinton to participate in an investigation of a coal slurry spill that occurred on October 11, 2000, in Martin County, Kentucky. What I saw there shocked me, and I could not be quiet about it.

My only purpose in raising the alarm about this investigation as I did was to make certain that the mining company and the agencies responsible for enforcing mine health and safety and environmental laws be held accountable for their failure to do so. More than 100 miles of streams were polluted by the Martin County spill. All life-forms in and along the streams and rivers were obliterated. About 1.6 million fish were killed. The water supply for more than 27,000 people was contaminated. When I objected to weakened investigation reports and less than appropriate enforcement actions, I was immediately attacked by administrators in the Labor Department appointed by the Bush administration. They tried to fire me but failed because of the public uproar.

The fact remains, however, that Massey Energy, the company responsible for the spill, which has one of the poorest environmental records in Appalachia and a less than desirable mine health and safety record, has gotten away with what the Environmental Protection Agency called the worst environmental disaster in the southeastern United States. Massey

Flooding takes its toll in a Wyoming County community in the heart of the coalfields. Photo © Vivian Stockman.

has been able to do this because corporate executives have had direct access to and influence with top officials of the Mine Safety and Health Administration and other government agencies. According to Common Cause, a nonpartisan group that holds political leaders accountable to the public interest, Massey Energy contributed $100,000 to the National Republican Senatorial Committee while the company was being investigated for the slurry spill. Massey Energy was ultimately fined just $5,600 for the Martin County spill.

There are about 650 coal-waste dams in the United States, most of them located in central Appalachia. About 225 of the coal slurry impoundments sit on top of abandoned underground mine workings where the potential exists for additional breakthroughs like the one that happened in Martin County.

These dangers lurk throughout the region, one of the most biologically diverse parts of North America. Its woodlands constitute the largest unbroken forest east of the Mississippi River and are home to approximately 250 bird species, 150 tree species, and countless animal, plant, and aquatic species.

The ecological wealth of this land is being devastated by coal mining. Since the early 1970s, about 380,000 acres in West Virginia, 320,000 acres in Kentucky, and 90,000 acres in Virginia have been strip-mined for coal. Mountaintop removal operations have become the predominant form of strip mining

Buffalo Creek

The river belches out its dead, and
   they flood
the banks with dragging feet asking
   What happened to us?
*What happened? It was morning
   and time*
for breakfast. They gather in puddles
   outside your window
and listen closely for the *hmm-click*
   of the burner
as you cook your morning eggs. They
   gather in the yard
behind the church and in the
   Foodland parking lot. They gather
in the fog and rockdust and orange
   pall of tipple lights.
They gather on the banks from Kistler
   to Chapmanville
to Salt Rock and the Ohio and ask
   What happened?
It was morning and time for breakfast.

   —Jason Frye

in this region, and their accompanying valley fills contain millions of tons of soil and rock that are dumped with little regard for the effects upon any kind of life—animal, plant, or human—that exists downstream. Some valley fills contain more than 300 million tons of mining debris and extend downstream from their headwaters as far as six miles.

Appalachia's people, as well as its land, are suffering because of mountaintop removal. One example is Jeremy Davidson, whose story is recounted in Erik Reece's "Moving Mountains" essay in this book, but there are many others who suffer in silence.

The region's water—our most precious resource—is suffering, too, as it is being tainted in the process. Sediment loading of streams, particularly in the Kentucky, Cumberland, and Big Sandy river basins in Kentucky, and the Guyandotte, Coal, and Tug river basins in West Virginia, has accelerated at an alarming rate in the past twenty-five years. This is due to increased runoff from the unstable, eroding slopes of valley fills and poorly graded mountaintop removal areas. The sediment load in areas downstream from mountaintop removal operations can now be measured in the millions of tons. It is estimated that about 1,200 miles of streams downstream from mountaintop removal operations have been severely damaged by sedimentation and heavy metal deposition.

Flooding of the main stem rivers and the Ohio River itself can be attributed to this sediment increase, which reduces stream and flood control reservoir capacities. It is estimated that some flood control reservoirs in Eastern Kentucky, particularly Fishtrap Lake on the Levisa Fork of the Big Sandy River, have lost as much as 60 percent of their storage capacities.

More than 1,900 miles of streams have been buried or severely degraded—or, to be more accurate, they have been completely obliterated—by the valley fills. These mine waste fills are the largest earth structures in North America.

Since 2001, there have been at least seven periods of severe flash flooding in the region that can be directly attributed to increased runoff from mountaintop removal operations and other types of strip-mining operations. Flash flooding

James Gauze, a disabled former miner, rests on his porch after cleaning up debris left by the flooding creek behind his home in June 2004; with him are his granddaughters Tyshira Joplin (in chair) and Alysa Estep and neighbor Josh McCoy. Photo © Builder Levy.

occurred on July 8, 26, 28, and 29, 2001, in southern West Virginia and Eastern Kentucky. Flash flooding occurred again on May 2 and July 19, 2002, and still again on June 16, 2003.

There have been fatalities. As far back as June 1, 1997, two people died in the Clear Creek area of Raleigh County as a result of flash flooding caused by runoff from a mountaintop removal operation. On July 8, 2001, three people drowned in flash flooding related to strip-mining operations, and on May 2, 2002, at least seven people died as a result of rapid runoff and flooding caused by mountaintop removal.

Unless the mining practices I have described are controlled far more strenuously or curtailed, by the year 2012 more than 2,500 square miles of Appalachian mountains, forests, and streams will have been utterly destroyed. At least 3,500 miles of streams will have been covered up completely. One of the most precious ecosystems in the world will be lost forever, and the people living immediately downstream from these massive mining operations will be forced to leave their homes and communities just to survive.

Speech against the Kentucky State Government

Wendell Berry

Mountaintop removal site at Oven Fork, near Whitesburg, Letcher County, Kentucky. Photo courtesy of Mountaintop Removal Road Show.

In 1996, when Ellen Davis, a scholar of the Bible at Duke Divinity School, was taken to a mountaintop removal site in Kentucky, she remembered Jeremiah:

> I have seen the mountains, and here, they are wavering,
>   and all the hills palpitate.
> I have seen, and here, there is no human being,
>   and all the birds of the heavens have fled.
> I have seen, and here, the garden-land is now the wasteland.

If you take seriously the knowledge that humans are capable of neighborliness and caretaking, are capable of caring well for the earth for the earth's own sake and for the sake of their neighbors now and yet to come, and if you know that according to our greatest teachers this neighborliness is *expected* of us, then you will grieve in knowing that we humans are destroying the earth. You will be offended in knowing that we are doing so with governmental approval and with governmental encouragement. If you are at all a normal human, you will find that hard to swallow. You may find it, in fact, a putrid lump that will gag you somewhat before you can get it down.

And yet to the Kentucky state government, a wholly owned subsidiary of the coal corporations and of any other corporations that bid high enough, earth destruction is a

Poet, essayist, farmer, and activist Wendell Berry at his farm in Eastern Kentucky. Photo © Trevor Humphries.

normal economic enterprise. Earth destruction by strip mining has been an officially accepted practice in the Eastern Kentucky coalfields for nearly half a century. In the Knott County courtroom on the night of July, 15, 1965, confronting, as he had and would, the already catastrophic damage of strip mining that was going to get worse, Harry Caudill spoke of "the gleeful yahoos who are destroying the world, and the mindless oafs who abet them."

Forty-three years later, bad has come to worse, and worse has come to worst; the gleeful yahoos still reign supreme in the coalfields, and the mindless oafs who abet them still hold dominion in Frankfort. This is not because money talks, as Senator Mitch McConnell seems to think. It is because money votes, and money buys people who vote. It is because might, with enough money, does not have to worry about right. It is because, in the magnetic field of money, the flags and crosses on certain political lapels turn into price tags.

I must hurry to say that I am not talking about all Kentucky politicians. There has always been in this capitol a "saving remnant" of women and men who are not for sale. It is because of those people that we, the powerless, have never yielded to despair, but have continued to come here with the hope that at last this government will see the truth and do its duty.

Abandoned coal trestle near Chavies, Kentucky, 1940. Photo by Marion Post Wolcott; courtesy of Library of Congress.

Paradise

When I was a child my family would travel
Down to Western Kentucky where my parents were born
And there's a backwards old town that's often remembered
So many times that my memories are worn.

(chorus:)
And Daddy, won't you take me back to Muhlenberg County
Down by the Green River where Paradise lay
Well, I'm sorry, my son, but you're too late in asking
Mister Peabody's coal train has hauled it away.

Well, sometimes we'd travel right down the Green River
To the abandoned old prison down by Adrie Hill
Where the air smelled like snakes and we'd shoot with our pistols
But empty pop bottles was all we would kill.
(chorus)

Then the coal company came with the world's largest shovel
And they tortured the timber and stripped all the land
Well, they dug for their coal till the land was forsaken
Then they wrote it all down as the progress of man.
(chorus)

When I die let my ashes float down the Green River
Let my soul roll on up to the Rochester dam
I'll be halfway to Heaven with Paradise waitin'
Just five miles away from wherever I am.
(chorus)

—John Prine

Over the past forty years, with other powerless people, I have been here many times. We have come, moneyless, into the magnetic field of money, trying to stop the mindless destruction of the land and people of our state. We have made our protests and our arguments, presented our facts, appeared before committees, spoken to those willing to speak to us. And virtually always we have failed. The destruction has continued. Nothing has changed.

Newly reminded of our political nonentity, we have gone home to await another chance to try again. Meanwhile, the destruction has gone on. When I return from one of these tours of the capitol, if the Kentucky River is raised and running, I can see the land of our mountain counties flowing past my house. And I know that that river, vital to the future of our state and its economy, is seriously impaired at its headwaters and degraded in all its length by pollutants, and that the most powerful among us simply do not care.

What are we to do? Well, to begin with, there is no "we" that I can confidently speak for. I have been speaking for myself so far, and I will continue to do so.

Human nature, which I fully share, tells me that in the face of great violence it is easy to think of retaliatory violence. I reject that entirely. I do not believe in violence as in any sense a solution to any problem. I am willing also to take the further step into scripture and say that we should love our enemies—or at least act toward them as if we love them.

The next temptation is to do as our enemies do, to say, "If they do it, so must we." And I have in fact spent some time on the argument, which can be logically made, that Kentucky conservationists ought to start a fund drive and apply for grants in order to *buy* our fair share of state government. I reject that also. Even a good cause cannot justify dirty politics.

But thinking of that argument, I convinced myself of a proposition that is more difficult: if current governmental practice affords no apparent recourse but to become as corrupt as your opponents, you have got to become more radical.

Kentucky conservationists are not the first people to have to confront their own helplessness before an alien government. Others have done so, and you know some of their names. Mahatma Gandhi and Martin Luther King are two of them; there have been many others. Their solution to the problem of powerlessness is to make of powerlessness a

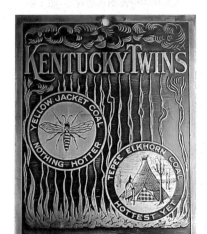

Advertisement for two Kentucky coal companies, Yellow Jacket Coal and Tepee Elkhorn Coal, in metal relief. Photo © Dave Johnson; Dave Johnson collection.

power. The name of this solution is nonviolent resistance or insistence, including civil disobedience. If your government will not rise to the level of common decency, if it will not deal fairly, if it will not protect the land and the people, if it will not fully and openly debate the issues, then you have to get in the government's way. You have to forbid it to ignore you. You have to provide it with two new choices: either it must grant you the consideration that it rightfully owes you, or it must expose itself openly as a government not representative of the people but owned by the privileged few.

And here yet another temptation asserts itself. Why not wait until our cause becomes vivid and urgent enough, and our side numerous enough, to vote our opponents out of office? Why not be patient?

My own answer is that while we are being patient, more mountains, forests, and streams, more people's homes and lives, will be destroyed in the Appalachian coalfields. Are 400,000 acres of devastated land and 1,200 miles of obliterated streams not enough? This needs to be stopped. It does not need to be "regulated." As both federal and state governments have amply shown, you cannot regulate an abomination. You have got to stop it.

Speaking for myself still, I will say that I don't like the idea of resorting to nonviolent obstruction, and I don't feel very brave about it. It involves more time and trouble than I want to donate; the penalties can be unpleasant, and they can be much worse than that. Furthermore, as I am now out of patience with useless protesting and lobbying, I have no interest in useless civil disobedience. You are not going to catch me making a merely symbolic gesture. But I began my opposition to strip mining on that July night in the Knott County courtroom in 1965. I have been patient for forty-three years. And there are now enough of us who are concerned—there are enough of us here today—to require our government either to accept its responsibility or, publicly and to its everlasting disgrace, refuse to do so. Surely the members of this government who represent coal corporations will be impressed by the tenfold increase in our numbers from

It would be no small advantage if every college were . . . located at the base of a mountain. . . . It were as well to be educated in the shadow of a mountain as in more classical shades. Some will remember, no doubt, not only that they went to the college, but that they went to the mountain.

—*Henry David Thoreau*

Protesters rally against MTR at the Kentucky state capitol in Frankfort. Photo © Richard X. Moore.

February 14, 2007. Surely they will notice, more to their dismay, that many of this increased number are young people.

If this general assembly and this administration give notice as usual that they are blind by policy to the ongoing destruction of the land and the people they are sworn to protect—and if you, my friends, all other recourse having failed, are ready to stand in the way of this destruction until it is stopped—then I too am ready.

—◦≫∙◦∙≪◦—

This speech was given by Wendell Berry at a large rally on the steps of the Kentucky state capitol in February 2007.

Part Two

DRAWING A LINE IN THE COAL SEAM

Even as the anti-strip-mining movement of the 1970s gained momentum, technological advances in surface mining were laying the groundwork for the horrific devastation of mountaintop removal and all its attendant ills: job losses due to mechanization, flood damage from stripped hillsides and breached impoundments, and poisoned air and water in many a once-pristine hollow. But as traditional strip mining gave way to MTR, the twin threads of exploitation and resistance continued to intertwine.

In this part, we examine the scourge of mountaintop removal and the way people are standing up in opposition to this devastating form of coal mining. Beginning with actress Ashley Judd's emotional journey back home to witness the scalped mountains, we travel the winding roads of Appalachia as residents join together to rescue their homelands from abuse abetted by political neglect or corruption. The essays in this part show how residents have been aided by investigative journalists like Michael Shnayerson and Jeff Biggers, who helped bring the issue to the national stage; by creative attorneys like Joe Lovett, who have found ways to take coal companies to court for their misdeeds; by dedicated researchers like Michael Hendryx, who compile evidence of the harm done to human and ecological health; by organizers like community activist Shannon Bell and the Sierra Club's Mary

A drill stands idle at the Jupiter Mine MTR site in Boone County, West Virginia. Photo © Denny Tyler.

Page 98: Coal trucks amid the devastation of Kayford Mountain. Photo © Mark Schmerling.

The song of mountain-streams,
  unheard by day,
Now hardly heard, beguiles my
  homeward way.
Air listens, like the sleeping water,
  still,
To catch the spiritual music of the
  hill, . . .

*—William Wordsworth,
  from "An Evening Walk"*

Anne Hitt; and even by an occasional courageous politician, as seen in Jon Blair Hunter's "confession" before the West Virginia legislature.

Along the way, we encounter David Orr's analysis of where our craving for buried carbon has led, a Jonathan Swift–inspired satire on the logical outcome of such a thirst, an excerpt from the acclaimed novel *Strange as This Weather Has Been,* and other keen insights into the problem of mountaintop removal—including some possible clean-energy solutions. Rounding out this part is a spiritual accounting by Father John Rausch of how destructive mining flouts God's charge to humans to steward the earth, with his thoughts on the role of religion in the anti-MTR struggle.

The writings here show that even though local citizens welcome outside help—and realize that they cannot win this war against big industry alone—they are still on the front lines of battles that are largely invisible to the rest of the world. They are fighting with the most powerful combination of weapons: words, music, and the rising, converging voices of people who are tired of their land being destroyed in the name of greed. And in the current turning tide, it appears that the people just might win before all is said and done.

The Last Patch of Green Earth

Ashley Judd

Buttermilk, IN ADDITION TO BEING a very fine staple in a meal (at cow temperature, preferably, with cornbread crumbled in it to accompany a bowl of soup beans), is also the name of my hound. He looks just like it, the most beautiful creamy yellow color, with soft curls that remind me of the foamy bubbles that collect at the edges of a milk pail.

Buttermilk has been with me a decade, my constant companion. I know him better than I have known any human, and he surely knows me better than anyone. I call him my thighbone; we sleep alongside one another and we don't like to be apart, not one bit. So, as he goes wherever I go, he went home with me to Eastern Kentucky in September for a visit.

A mixed visit, since we did happy, poignant stuff, like reopen the Paramount, a glamorous old movie palace in Ashland, for movie showings (I chose *It Happened One Night* for the kickoff film). We walked around my beloved Bellefonte Country Club, where my Ciminella grandparents were long-time members, and reminisced about the glorious, carefree fun of those childhood days I spent with them (I would do daredevil dives into the deep end for my Papaw to watch from the seventeenth hole). My Mamaw Ciminella took me to the club every day, and what a contrast it was from her raising on Black Log in Martin County (later the site of the

Ashley Judd has long been active in opposing mountaintop removal. Photo courtesy of Ashley Judd.

Drawdy Falls near Peytona, West Virginia. Photo © Mark Schmerling.

disastrous spill that loosed 306 million gallons of toxic sludge into the Tug Fork River).

Buttermilk and I went to Inez, too, where we visited my great-grandparents' house. I had never been there before, yet I drove straight to it without any directions, guided by something strongly intuitive inside me. Perhaps I was oriented flawlessly by the loving descriptions spoken over the years by my dad and cousins. My photographs of the creek bottom and the mountain behind their small house have diaphanous, milky orbs all over them; my sister says these are signs of angel activity.

Then we went over to Pike County, and it was there that I was glad I know my dog so well. We had been enjoying a long day's worth of poking around the hills, stopping with my heart full to bursting in front of the Dalton mailbox (which still bore Mamaw's maiden name), and sometimes just pausing to weep at the beauty and the ineffable connection I feel with those sacred mountains. I long ago stopped trying to explain why I, or any hillbilly, love them so. I just do. We just do. Stop asking. It does not need to be, nor can it be, explained.

So when we got to Island Creek in Pike County to look at a typical (although rather small-scale) mountaintop removal coal-mining site, I was prepared to use my nasal, piercing call to bring my baby back home to me. Surely he'd be off, as he invariably is, exploring and scouting.

Buttermilk is a runner; that dog can cover thirty miles in a half day, easily, if I let him. He is sure and swift and has never met a vertical ridge he couldn't scale in fleet-footed, gravity-defying style. In 2007 I was crawling to summit a slippery outcropping in British Columbia, the culmination of a long and viciously difficult hike, and there was my Buttermilk, standing at the top looking down at me. I had seen him splinter off left to use a deep crevasse, one impassable to me, to bound to the windy top. "What took you so long, Ma?" his waving tail asked, as he watched me heave myself up before he ran off again.

Yet at Island Creek, when we got out of the car, he didn't move. He didn't run. He didn't explore. He didn't sniff. I swear, he didn't even hike his leg. He didn't even look at me to ask my permission to take off. He sat at my right ankle, looking with me at a desolate graveyard that had been, only weeks before, a pristine, breathtaking vision of ancient biodiversity, wildlife habitat, and mountains so old that geologists have settled for calling their age "deep time." We were at a funeral, and he knew it, perhaps even better than I, and his incorrigible need for running was instinctively curbed by sorrow.

I know full well that animals experience grief. And Buttermilk did that day. Why would he want to run over the empty spaces, corpses of what once were hills? There is nothing to celebrate there, to sniff joyously, no wee creatures to gleefully harass. They are all dead, everything is dead, either blown to bits of rubble or lying in chaotic shambles, such as old-growth hardwood trees unceremoniously strewn in loose piles or simply gone, gone, gone.

When all the trees have been
  cut down,
when all the animals have been
  hunted,
when all the waters are polluted,
when all the air is unsafe to breathe,
only then will you discover you
  cannot eat money.

—Cree prophecy

It reminded me of the first time my husband took me to Culloden, Scotland, where English forces crushed the Highlanders and Bonnie Prince Charlie in 1746. I was memorizing a Blake poem, but as we approached Culloden I sensed that Dario was becoming irritated with me and didn't want to help me retrieve verses that still eluded me. I set aside the poem, tuned in to where we were, and felt the horrible, solemn grief that comes when visiting places where massacres have occurred, places where things so unspeakably unfair have occurred that they stifle life even today. I was as yet unfamiliar with the events of April 16, 1746, but I knew I was in a wordless, sad place that drained my own spirit.

This, I know, is what happened to Buttermilk on Island Creek. He may not have known about twenty-story draglines or explosives so volatile they must be trucked in separately; about busted unions and exploited workers, collapsed wells and contaminated water, overloaded coal trucks and eroding roads. But he knew desolation and he knew death. He knew what he needed to know.

There is environmental genocide in our mountains. It is happening on a scale that is unfathomable, that is difficult to overstate and scary to try to portray. I just got off the phone with my mother, telling her that I have to read Silas House and Erik Reece, Wendell Berry (whom I nag Governor Beshear to nominate for the Nobel Prize in Literature, which he should have won two decades ago) and Van Jones. If I don't, the denial in our society can make me feel crazy. I know what is happening. I know how shockingly outrageous it is. And yet one is made to feel like a lunatic for speaking of it: out of touch with reality like a fringe conspiracy theorist, because such things "are simply not possible" and "no one would really let that happen" and "the companies would never do that" and "our government would stop it."

Um, I say, actually the government is, um, complicit. Um, Chief Justice Roberts? Yeah, the one on the Supreme Court? He overturned everything that came in front of him in favor of the coal companies. Um, President Clinton, who is my pal and whom I overall like very much, was a total nightmare on

A mountaintop removal operation near Whitesburg, Kentucky. Photo courtesy of Mountaintop Removal Road Show.

this issue and screwed Appalachia mightily. And, yeah, this fragile little thing called Section 404 of the Clean Water Act is all, and I mean *all*, that stands between ancient mountains and their annihilation in less than three years. One is made to feel mentally unstable for describing such things.

Yet they are true, all too true. Bill Clinton has repeatedly said that doing nothing during the Rwanda genocide in 1994 is the single greatest regret of his presidency. Yet here at home, full-blown environmental genocide and collapse are happening, and we are doing nothing. Naturally I accept that I set myself up for ridicule for using such strong terms, or perhaps outrage from human victims of slaughter, but I do believe in the profound interconnectedness of all life, and I agree with Einstein's assertion that "you cannot pick a flower that you do not disturb a star." Is it not genocide when millions of acres of 280-million-year-old mountains in the most biodiverse ecosystem in North America—a forest that seeded our continent after that last ice age and contains genetic material that is beyond any value humans can ascribe to it—is completely destroyed, and all the animals therein? If it isn't, then what is it? Bare minimum, we should not be doing this to the mountains, much less to the people of Appalachia ravaged by this murderous practice.

Native hardwood forests are being clear-cut prior to mountaintop removal mining. Photo © Giles Ashford.

After looking around Island Creek a good long while, Buttermilk and I got in the car and went to the last patch of green earth left in that hollow. We had Sunday dinner on the ground, and my soul felt the commingling of mirth and despair. A proper dinner on the ground: I love it when I live out the words of my favorite bluegrass songs. As I ate, I remembered my Great-Aunt Pauline of Little Cat Creek, over in Lawrence County, and her cooking. If I could magically have any meal in the world, it would be her fried chicken dinner with buttermilk biscuits and blackberry jam. And I remembered conversations during these meals, conversations I didn't really understand at the time, about coal mining, a really scary kind of coal mining where they just strip everything God made off the surface and discard it like it's trash, and then they leave and the earth is raw and rain falls and

Stripped

I was humming "Mist on the
  Mountain"
and shelling peas
I was figuring board feet
I was carting off stones
and quilting lettuce
and thinking about a baby growing
  ripe inside
I was voting
I was lifting pain out by the roots
the bread indoors
breathing beneath a thin towel,
when the D-10 dozer came
and rolled me off the front porch

       —George Ella Lyon

everything erodes and slides around dangerously because the rocks and roots and all the clever design of nature are messed up so nothing holds and people are buried in their homes. And then I remembered Aunt Pauline and Uncle Landon agonizing over her decision to sell a bit of her land. She loved her home, loved her mountains. I'll have to talk to my Great-Aunt Toddie, her sister, to get more of the story of what all happened. I fear what I may learn (or remember), but I know my people are not immune to the poverty my home is unfortunately famous for. After all, the War on Poverty was declared not far from Mamaw's own front porch.

This particular day's story drew to a close. Buttermilk and I drove home to Ashland, stopping for a milkshake in Paintsville and then taking the long way, via small two-lane roads with numbers, not names. At least not names printed on any map. But folks around here, they know their names . . . of roads, of mountains, of trees, of fascinating wildflowers that grow only here. They know because it's home, a home that is under siege.

They know because it's disappearing in apocalyptic destruction while we just cut our lights on and off, or stand in front of the open fridge debating between yogurt and cottage cheese, having no idea that our electricity comes at such a price, a price that is simply incalculable—as incalculable as 280 million years of natural forces that birthed the mountains.

When Buttermilk and I got back to my godmother's house, he promptly ran off on a wild tear. I assumed my mountain-woman stance, in a dress and barefoot, a hand on one hip, a way of being as natural to me as breathing. I hollered mightily for him so my voice could carry across the creek bottoms, up the ridges, and out over the mountaintops. I was sure the alarm of my voice would wake every neighbor, and I knew that my voice must carry beyond my beloved home and ring out past these ancient hills to the entire world if these mountains are to nurture and comfort another generation.

"Coal Is All West Virginia's Got"

Shannon Elizabeth Bell

DRIVING THROUGH THE COALFIELDS OF southern West Virginia, drivers often find themselves behind vehicles plastered with one of the many bumper-sticker proclamations of loyalty to the state's unofficial king: "I [Heart] Coal," "Coal Keeps the Lights On," "Friend of Coal," or "Coal Makes WV Go!" Signs with the same slogans can often be seen staked in residents' yards, much like campaign posters or sports team flags. Because of special coal education materials and curricula created by the West Virginia Coal Association, schoolchildren throughout the southern coalfields are taught the "many benefits the coal industry provides in daily lives." Students of all ages are encouraged to enter projects in the Coal Regional Fair, which awards cash prizes in the categories of science, math, English/literature, art, music, technology/multimedia, and social studies. As Maria Gunnoe, an organizer for the Ohio Valley Environmental Coalition and a lifelong coalfield resident, expressed in a 2007 interview, "The coal companies here *recruit* in the schools just same as the military does." Coal companies not only are recruiting future employees but are in effect "recruiting" a future citizenry socialized to believe that the coal industry is indispensable to the life, culture, and economic future of its communities and state.

The coal industry has effectively promoted and sustained an ideology that has kept entire communities from realizing that coal is not exactly the lifeblood of the state. With the help

Miner Andrew Kosto, Sycamore Mining Company, Cinderella, Mingo County, West Virginia, 1971. Photo © Builder Levy.

of various government officials, the industry has also perpetuated the myth that there are no alternative industries that can, or should, be promoted in the state's southern coalfields.

However, a closer look at West Virginia's economy makes it clear that the coal industry is not as significant as it would have the citizenry believe. While it is true that coal is important to the state's economy, it is certainly not the only industry, or even the main industry, in West Virginia. According to the U.S. Department of Commerce, the $3.5 billion that coal contributed to the state's gross product in 2004 represented only 7 percent of the total gross product. Furthermore, a 2005 report on tourism and the West Virginia economy reveals that mining's contributions to the West Virginia state product declined from 1998 to 2002; according to a 2007 tourism report, coal's contributions to the state product are forecast to continue declining over the next thirty years.

The tax revenue generated from coal severance tax represents less than 7 percent of the general revenue fund for the state, and the West Virginia Executive Budget for 2007 forecasts a 9 percent decline in severance tax revenues by 2010. Even more disheartening is the fact that very little of this coal severance tax actually goes to the coalfield towns, which must bear the brunt of the numerous social, economic, and environmental injustices related to coal-mining practices. The town of Sylvester is situated in close proximity to a mountaintop removal coal mine, next to the enormous Elk Run Coal Preparation Plant, and beneath an enormous sludge dam. Still, it received only $701.42 in coal severance tax during the 2006–7 fiscal year, according to the West Virginia State Treasurer's Office.

Coal employment data follow a similar trend. As the West Virginia Coal Association and the West Virginia Bureau of Employment Programs reported in 2005, the 40,924 individuals the coal industry employs make up only 5 percent of the total employed civilian labor force in the state. Health care, hospitality services, retail trade, professional and business services, and local, state, and federal government are each far more significant employers within the state than is coal.

This drawing of a runaway coal car, published in Harper's Young People *in July 1887, was titled "It seemed like a thunder bolt to the awe struck spectators." Drawing by W. A. Rogers; courtesy of Library of Congress.*

If so many other industries have a greater impact on the state's economy and people, why is coal still viewed as the backbone of West Virginia? If other industries in the state provide more jobs and contribute more to the state's economy, why does coal boast such faithful followers and staunch supporters, who go so far as to place signs in their yards that proudly proclaim "Friend of Coal" or who support bills in the legislature that are obviously detrimental to West Virginia communities? While coal does represent a significant portion of the West Virginia economy, it is not significant enough to be what, as the bumper stickers declare, "Makes West Virginia Go"; there is some other invisible force behind such unwavering loyalty.

Although the population of West Virginia skyrocketed during the first half of the twentieth century, this trend was short-lived. The West Virginia Health Statistics Center reports that

Kermit, a railroad and coal town in Mingo County, West Virginia, at dusk, 1968. Photo © Builder Levy.

Retired mine operator Horace Robinson filled a room of his home with photographs documenting the history of Dorothy, Boone County, West Virginia, the coal town in which he lived nearly all his life. Detail of photo © Builder Levy.

since 1950, the state has experienced a net out-migration of 40 percent of its population. This loss in population over the last fifty years has been due primarily to increased mechanization in the coal mines and the advent of mountaintop removal, which has continued to reduce the number of mining jobs throughout the state.

As Shirley Stewart Burns reveals in her book *Bringing Down the Mountains,* during the 1950s, there were 120,000 coal miners in West Virginia, compared with today's 16,037. Coal *was* central to building West Virginia's economy; entire towns were formed practically overnight because of this industry. But with the advent of the longwall mining machine, the continuous mining machine, and, most recently, mountaintop removal, a vast workforce of coal miners is no longer needed. In the hope that Appalachians won't notice this, the coal industry has launched massive propaganda campaigns to ensure that people believe that coal—and little else—is still putting food on their tables.

To boost this way of thinking, the industry has created the aforementioned Friends of Coal, an entire "grassroots movement" (launched by the West Virginia Coal Association) to indoctrinate citizens with the "Coal Is All West Virginia's Got" ideology. According to the WVCA, the Friends of Coal is made up of "thousands" of West Virginians "who consider coal to be the lifeblood of the state's economy." Furthermore, the Friends' Web site asserts, these "grassroots" citizens are "dedicated to informing and educating West Virginia citizens about the coal industry and its vital role in the state's future."

Don Nehlen, popular retired football coach of the West Virginia University Mountaineers, is the official spokesperson for the organization. Coach Nehlen travels around the state making public appearances, giving speeches, and passing out stickers and yard signs that declare Friends of Coal. Through this campaign, the coal industry spreads the message that being a good West Virginian means being loyal to the coal industry.

Friends of Coal is just the latest coal industry propaganda. For decades, the industry has devoted millions of dollars to highway billboards, television and radio campaigns, and high-profile "community improvement projects," such as playgrounds, health fairs, and Little League teams (named after the sponsoring coal company, of course). Any public project that can display how "necessary" the coal companies are for the social and economic well-being of West Virginia communities provides an opportunity to spread coal propaganda.

While conducting random household interviews in Boone County, West Virginia (the top coal-producing county in the state) during the summer of 2006, I repeatedly encountered residents who mentioned how critical they believed Massey Energy (the local coal company) was to the well-being of their town. One resident said:

> This town wouldn't even have what it has if it wasn't for Massey. . . . They bought all the computers for schools around here. . . . They buy gifts and things for nursing homes. . . . [The elementary] school had Mr. and Mrs. Santa Claus that was sponsored this year by Massey. And all these kids in the area that don't get gifts—they bought Barbies and trucks for them.

Another, who also happens to be the human resources director at a Massey Energy mine, explained:

> What I will say is that if these three companies of Massey weren't here, you might as well close the doors on this little place. This is it. We are it. You know, and just in the taxes that we pay, the payroll that we have—and I know, a lot of employees don't live here, but they come through here. You know, they stop at the gas stations, they stop at the little convenience stores, all of which would go out of business if we weren't on the river. So, we think there is a big impact. The schools would suffer. You wouldn't have the money coming from us to go to them.

New computers, presents for needy children, a new roof on a church, Thanksgiving dinners for nursing home residents—all serve to distract citizens from recognizing the truth: that the coal industry is the *reason* towns in southern West Virginia are in need of such "charity." The facts speak for themselves: the Appalachian Regional Commission reports

In mountaintop mining, the topsoil, or what we in the industry refer to as "non-coal material" is not lost or buried or washed away, as some overly emotional environmental extremists like to claim, because nothing in Nature is ever really lost or destroyed. The topsoil is simply relocated to areas under the mountain, where it is protected by many layers of rock and other natural materials, or it is transferred further downstream by means of rainfall events to rivers, lakes, oceans and other pleasant places.

—Anne Shelby, *parody of pro-industry propaganda disseminated on the Web site of the Kentucky Coal Association*

Resting after cleanup from flooding at the Phillips home in Rutherford Hollow, North Matewan, West Virginia. Photo © Builder Levy.

that in 2000, more than 75 percent of Appalachian coal counties were classified as "economically distressed." Moreover, McDowell County, which, according to the West Virginia Office of Miners' Health, Safety and Training, has produced the most coal of any county in West Virginia, not only is the poorest county in the state but, with a per capita income of $10,174, is ranked as the twenty-eighth poorest county in the entire United States by the U.S. Census Bureau.

Coal companies not only have impoverished coalfield residents but have taken away their sense of self-worth. Many coalfield towns have seen a decline in community-based civic organizations, which used to fill the needs of the town from within, instead of in the top-down manner in which the coal companies operate. Another interview respondent articulated this deeper problem associated with "charity" from coal companies: "I feel like [Massey] took away the pride in the town. Because now everything that's done for the town, Massey does it."

Some residents do recognize the hand that the coal industry has played in the high unemployment rate and the decline in the economy of coalfield towns. Interview respondents in Boone County are particularly aware of Massey Energy's manipulative hiring practices, wherein the company employs out-of-town, and even out-of-state, miners and contractors at the expense of local citizens in need of jobs. As one said: "We've got plenty of people that needs a job, but all these other guys comes in and gets the jobs. . . . I believe a lot of it was because this valley was union. They was union workers, and Massey's not. And [they are] afraid to hire people from around here because it was always a union valley."

Another noted:

> Massey won't hire [local people]. They won't hire a lot of them, and most of them head out of here, you know, they leave. They've got to find work somewhere. So somebody else gets a share of what we should be gettin' here. See, when Armco was here and Peabody [coal companies], they hired people around here. The money stayed right around here. Now they drive all the way to Charleston or Beckley to go to K-Mart.

The abandoned meeting place of the United Mine Workers of America, Local 8377, in Boone County, West Virginia. Photo © Mark Schmerling.

The reality is that the coal industry is, and historically has been, an oppressive tyrant that has impoverished and debilitated an entire region of Appalachia. The citizens of West Virginia deserve the option for a future apart from the destitution King Coal has decreed.

Even while it wields immense political power and influence, it is clear that coal is no longer the center of the West Virginia economy or the main employer. However, it is also true that if any of the industries that contribute millions of dollars to West Virginia's economy, including coal, were to collapse overnight, there would be serious consequences for the state, especially in the southern coalfield counties, where the coal industry has fought to maintain a mono-economy so that no other industry can compete with its influence and domination.

Most organizations in central Appalachia that are fighting unjust mining practices recognize that coal production cannot be stopped tomorrow. What they do believe should be stopped immediately are irresponsible mining practices—and mountaintop removal mining is at the core of irresponsible mining. These groups advocate for serious planning for a more sustainable future, one that eventually phases out coal mining.

It is clear that economic diversification of the southern coalfields is critical to the survival of this region of the state. One of the first steps, however, must be convincing the local citizens, and the politicians, that coal is not—and *cannot* be—the future of West Virginia. The future of West Virginia, and of southern West Virginia in particular, rests on the ability of local citizens to dethrone King Coal and demand a sustainable economy.

Blood and Coal (a Swiftian Proposal)

George Ella Lyon

SOMEONE IN THIS COUNTRY NEEDS blood every two seconds.

A total of 43,000 pints are used in the United States each day.

It takes forever to get that much blood a pint at a time. First, you have to wait for volunteers. Then, when they show up, you have to ask a lot of questions, do a brief physical and some tests, to make sure taking that blood is safe—safe for them to give and you to use.

You have to be good to them, treat them with respect. Apologize for asking about their sex lives. Give them a magazine to read while they wait. Then, if they qualify and sign the permit, you have to have a nice room they can lie down in with a clean, comfortable bed, like an examining table, for each donor. You have to get each person settled in gently and make sure the history and the plastic pouch waiting to be filled match before the extraction can begin.

You must employ lots of workers to attend to various parts of this removal and keep the line moving. One comes and paints the inner elbow with sterilizer, ties the tourniquet, finds a good vein, breaks skin with that needle, and taps the flow at last. Red wealth rolls out drop by drop, a rope of life leaving the body, filling the bag.

Some folks' blood rushes out; the sap of low-pressure people takes longer. (If the pressure is too low, you turn them

Contaminated water flows from a garden hose near Lick Creek, between Williamson and Rawl, West Virginia. Photo © Mark Schmerling.

"Hard Coal for the Poor," which appeared in Harper's Weekly, *January 1874, depicts children collecting "hard coal," or anthracite, which was sometimes given to the poor in northeastern cities for use in heating and lighting. Wood engraving after a drawing by Sol Eytinge; courtesy of Library of Congress.*

back with a joke at the gate. You say, "We appreciate the offer but we just don't have time.") Whatever the flow rate, you take only a pint from each donor. You leave them plenty to live on until their marrow makes more.

Throughout this process, workers check on the blood source, making sure all is safe and healthy, and when that flat bag has swelled to a bright ruby of life, they withdraw the needle carefully. Then they must wait for the mouth of the wound to clot, have the donor lie quietly, get up slowly, sit a while before leaving the donation room.

Even after all this, there's more to be done. The last stop is the canteen, where a worker provides cookies and peanut butter crackers, soft drinks and juice to replenish some of the energy that has been taken and to guard against a blood sugar drop. After fifteen minutes, when they're pretty sure the donor isn't going to pass out at the wheel on the way home, the canteen worker hands out a tract about how to care for yourself after giving blood: drink plenty of fluids, avoid strenuous work in the next twelve hours, rest as much as possible for the next twenty-four. Be alert for dizziness or bleeding. And if you remember that you have a disease you forgot to mention, call this number.

Though they say donation takes an hour, in my experience it takes a good hour and a half. Per person. Per unit. Think of all the workers. The cubicles. Equipment. Tests. All that space and time and care—not to mention niceness—for one pint of blood.

Wouldn't it be a lot more cost-efficient, much less labor-intensive, and a hell of a lot faster to find prime candidates, screen them by hacking their health records, then murder them and drain the blood fast? Two people could do it.

Then instead of a pint you'd have 5.5 quarts from a 154-pound male or 3.5 from a woman weighing 110 pounds. (Most American adults weigh considerably more than that, so this is a case where obesity may work for us.) There's no need for chitchat or snacks, and you could probably sell their organs, too, if you did it discreetly.

Oh, I know people would protest, but people always protest. Progress has its price. Nobody likes to lose family members, but let's be realistic. We've got to get blood from somewhere. You can't run this nation without blood.

And if the person who is removed has life insurance, that'll be a bonus to the family. Not to mention the extra room created in the home. Room for recreation or perhaps a small business. Room to grow and keep this economy rolling.

The fact is, we just can't afford this donation mentality anymore. It's outmoded, inefficient, and requires way too much overhead. Families can recover. With all that new room and new money, they may not even miss their loved one. And, anyway, some losses just have to be absorbed.

Here's how we see it: the world is full of people, and the people are full of blood. God didn't fill people full of blood for nothing. For the good of all, some of them have to go. Blood is money. That's the bottom line. Blood keeps the lights on.

When you defile the pleasant streams
And the wild bird's abiding place,
You massacre a million dreams
And cast your spittle in God's face.

—John Drinkwater

Joe Lovett Takes King Coal to Court

Michael Shnayerson

Advertisement for King Coal Cigars, circa 1911. Photo © Dave Johnson; Dave Johnson collection.

To see yet another ridgetop of southern West Virginia scraped clean of its trees and underbrush, the underlying earth obliterated by blasts, and then the whole ridgetop reduced, blast after blast, by hundreds of feet to a wide gash of rubble in the surrounding green, is to be led, inexorably, to a question: How can this be legal?

The short answer is: it's not.

Why it happens anyway is an American story of politics and power, at both the state and the federal level. It's a story of the coal industry, as well as the West Virginia lawmakers whose campaigns it funds and whose votes it controls. It's a story about state judges who owe the industry and about federal judges who don't but who get appointed for their pro-business, conservative leanings. Above all, it's a story about coal's influence on the White House, which appoints those federal judges and, when that doesn't suffice, rewrites the laws. From 2000 to 2008, those lines of influence led to the administration of George W. Bush, but Republicans don't merit *all* the blame. Mountaintop coal removal took hold and metastasized in the 1990s under President Bill Clinton. And West Virginia's two U.S. senators of long standing—Democrats Robert Byrd and Jay Rockefeller—both endorse the practice. The truth is that King Coal never has much cared which party is in power, as long as it can subvert that power to serve its needs.

The law that mountaintop removal violates, as a young environmental lawyer named Joe Lovett realized in a eureka moment one evening in the early fall of 1997, is Section 404 of the federal Clean Water Act. Other laws are broken, too, Joe soon came to believe, both in MTR's concept and in its practice where it tends to pollute streams and deserves all the violations that get slapped upon it by state mining inspectors. But Section 404 is the big one, the invocation of which by Joe in various lawsuits would lead the Bush administration to do the remarkable things it did.

What Joe saw that night was that while the Clean Water Act forbids pollution of American rivers, lakes, and streams, it does make pragmatic exceptions. One is Section 404, by which a permit can be granted to place "fill material" in U.S. waters. But, Joe read, the "fill" must have a beneficial purpose. A farmer might apply to put fill in a stream for some agricultural purpose; a contractor might hope to place fill in a marshy area so as to construct a building on it. Under no circumstances, Joe read, can sheer waste be dumped into a stream and called fill, just so the dumper can get rid of his waste.

But that was exactly what the coal industry had been doing in Appalachia since the first small mountaintop removal operations of the 1970s. And every time it had applied to the U.S. Army Corps of Engineers for a Section 404 permit to do that, the corps had granted the permit. Now that the industry had ramped up to far larger operations—often five or six square miles, with twenty-story dragline steam shovels moving from one stretch of ridge to the next like grazing dinosaurs—it was still applying for Section 404 permits to dump waste into valley streams as fill, and the corps was still granting those permits.

Bragg v. Robertson, Joe's first, landmark suit challenging the legality of those permits, was argued in 1999 before a federal district judge in West Virginia—a Republican appointee who nevertheless ruled in Joe's favor. To its credit, the Clinton administration saw that Joe was right, and that if he was right in that one case, he would win a systemic ruling that stopped the mining industry cold. So federal lawyers sat

Amendments to the [Clean Water Act] should be considered and accomplished in the sunlight of open congressional debates and resolution, not within the murky administrative after-the-fact ratification of questionable regulatory practices.

—*U.S. District Judge Charles Haden II, ruling against the Bush administration's attempt to modify federal law to allow dumping mining waste in streams*

A demolition crew prepares the Red Fox mountaintop removal site at Keystone, McDowell County, West Virginia, for blasting. Photo © Builder Levy.

down with Joe and his cocounsel, Jim Hecker. They started clarifying the definition of fill such that the practical effect would be an end to big mountaintop operations, though perhaps not all of the small ones. Joe and Jim insisted that the government also enforce the "buffer-zone rule," by which mountaintop waste be kept not only out of valley streams but 100 feet away from them on either side. The industry had ignored the rule ever since it was written. How could it control the waste it shoved off the mountaintop? Impossible, the industry declared. On January 20, 2001, when George W. Bush was inaugurated, the work of redefining fill remained undone—the legal hairsplitting had taken more time than anyone had expected—and the buffer-zone rule was still a point of contention.

In due time, the new president turned his attention to both of those issues.

The coal industry had come out big for Bush—Al Gore, after all, was an *environmentalist*—and delivered. Historically, West Virginia with its union miners had voted Democratic, but not in 2000. Whether the state's five electoral votes had tipped the balance could be argued, but the fact was that Bush had won by exactly that many: 271 to 266. In gratitude, Bush appointed one of the industry's favorite lobbyists, J. Steven Griles, as deputy secretary of the Interior Department:

the number two position, but the power behind the throne in regard to overseeing coal.

Griles was a big, broad-shouldered, blustery Virginian with a deep southern bass voice and a ruddy face that turned even ruddier when he lost his temper, which was fairly often. He knew all about mountaintop removal. As a rising bureaucrat in the Reagan White House before his lobbying days, he had helped gut one of the few rules that governed it. Griles took up residence in a big corner office of the vast Interior building and placed a full-grown, stuffed Alaskan grizzly bear outside his door, upright, with its long teeth bared and front claws extended, ready to pounce. No one missed the joke.

Joe Lovett, in his sit-downs with the Clinton lawyers, had persuaded the government to conduct a years-long study of damage done by mountaintop removal across a broad swath of Appalachia—no one knew exactly how many ridges had been destroyed, how many valley streams buried. This, too, had remained undone when Bush came into office. Griles, in one of his first assists to the coal industry, redirected the environmental impact statement, or EIS, as it was called. Now, instead of suggesting ways to mitigate the damage, its purpose was to "streamline" coal mine permitting. Griles could not entirely squelch the EIS's scientific studies, but they were put in mice type at the end. Even so, the numbers were devastating, and they came to define the destruction. Between 1985 and 2001, some 380,000 acres of rich and uniquely diverse temperate Appalachian forest had been destroyed; some 1,200 miles of valley streams had been impacted or buried.

Despite its distaste for that EIS, the Bush administration commissioned an EIS of its own—on the buffer-zone rule. Predictably, this one concluded that the rule could be changed. Now, if coal operators merely *tried* to keep waste 100 feet from valley streams, they were in compliance.

A word here, a word there—by 2003, the administration's lawyers had become adept at small clarifications of existing laws that turned the laws on their head. So it was with their redefinition of fill. That spring, Joe won another victory in

This stripped tree is all that remains of the native hardwood forest that has been clear-cut in preparing a site for mountaintop removal. Photo © Giles Ashford.

Massey got his eye on a mountain
And he knew he just had to have her
He always got what he wanted
So what came next amounted to
    murder

Old Massey had his way with our
    sweet girl
He just tore down all her great big
    trees
Ripped her dark flesh, cut her pretty
    face
He didn't care, he did just what he
    pleased

(chorus:)
Oh, she was a beauty, Lord God, she
    was a sight
But now she's gone, honey she's
    gone
She never will be back again, and it
Didn't take much more than a night

    —from "The Ballad of Massey
    and the Mountain,"
    words and music by Silas
    House and Jason Howard

federal district court affirming that the Clean Water Act forbade fill that was waste, and that the "overburden" dumped by mountaintop mining was waste—period. The government would appeal, as it always did with Joe's victories, to the Fourth Circuit Court of Appeals—the most conservative appeals court in the land. But this time, Joe might win even there. As a safeguard, the Bush lawyers simply broadened the legal definition of fill. Now it was anything except garbage. Mining waste? That was fine.

As the administration conducted these parries at the federal level, West Virginia's most notorious coal king set out to fix what he saw as bias at the state level against his own company, publicly traded Massey Energy, and the industry in general. Never mind that even Don Blankenship's own peers thought the playing field already was pretty well tilted their way. Massey's chairman and CEO professed to be shocked—shocked—by the frequency with which the West Virginia State Supreme Court ruled in favor of maimed and mangled coal miners seeking workmen's compensation from their erstwhile employers. And he could hardly help but note that, in a most unusual lower state court ruling, a small rival put out of business by Massey had won a settlement of $50 million. Soon, if Massey's lawyers failed to quash it on procedural grounds, that settlement, amplified with interest to $70 million or more, would come up for appeal to the West Virginia State Supreme Court. And Don didn't like what he saw when he surveyed that court's five justices.

Unlike federal judges, who are appointed for life, supreme court justices in West Virginia—and many other states—are elected by popular vote. For this reason alone, Joe Lovett rarely bothered to bring a case to the state courts: judges who would soon have to run for reelection were too vulnerable, he felt, to coal industry influence. But to Don, two if not three of the five supreme court justices who would soon hear Massey's appeal of that $70 million settlement were unacceptably liberal. One of those, Warren McGraw, was up for reelection to a twelve-year term in the fall of 2004, and Don decided to do something about that.

Bear Rocks, in the Dolly Sods Wilderness, Monongahela National Forest, West Virginia. Photo © Jim Clark.

Don didn't go out and find Brent Benjamin to run against McGraw; if he had chosen his own candidate, he probably would have found one with more impressive credentials. Benjamin was a corporate lawyer who had never argued a case before the state supreme court and, with his generous girth, looked like a barrister out of Gilbert and Sullivan. But Benjamin was McGraw's opponent, and so Don supported him—to the tune of $3.5 million, a whopping figure in a state judicial race. To comply with federal election laws, Don didn't give the money directly to Benjamin: he set up a so-called 527 political action group, which spent the money on ads smearing McGraw. But the effect was the same: Benjamin won. And for all his postelection protestations that he would "call 'em as he saw 'em," Benjamin provided the swing vote in the eventual three-to-two state supreme court ruling in Massey's favor, setting aside the entire $70 million settlement.

By then, at least, the political winds were changing. Steve Griles had resigned amid charges that he had failed to cut ties with his lobbying firm while in office and done all he could to help his pals in the coal industry. The charges went unproved, but in the summer of 2007, another one stuck. Under oath before a congressional subcommittee, Griles claimed he had had only insignificant ties with disgraced lobbyist Jack Abramoff. When that was found to be a lie, Griles was convicted of perjury and sent off to a ten-month jail term.

In West Virginia, Joe Lovett won federal court victories stopping each of the two ways the Army Corps of Engineers permitted mountaintop removal. While those were pending appeal, the industry was blocked from pursuing new permits. Unfortunately for residents of the coalfields, Massey and its peers could keep blasting away at sites approved by their existing permits—work that could go on for years. But now there was hope, and hope had a name: Barack Obama.

The end of the Bush years and the quashing of the Republican machine by Barack Obama's historic victory in November 2008 stirred hopes that the scourge of mountaintop removal may at last be stopped as the crime against nature that it is. But that won't happen overnight, and for this story to have even a halfway happy ending, a few plot twists need to turn just so.

For starters, the Fourth Circuit Court of Appeals must uphold Joe's latest lower-court victory against the Army Corps of Engineers and its permitting of mountaintop removal—a ruling the court is weighing even now. Three times it has struck down Joe's victories on technical grounds, fashioning pretzel-like logic to dismiss his clear, straightforward reading of the Clean Water Act. If the court rules for Joe, that will mark the beginning of the end of mountaintop removal—because the Obama administration is hardly likely to appeal to the U.S. Supreme Court. If the court finds a new pretext, Joe will bring a new case at the federal district level, where he's won four times in a row. If he wins again, he won't face Bush government lawyers set to appeal. Those lawyers are *gone*.

Burying Our Future

Jeff Goodell

According to NASA climatologist James Hansen, there is still time to avert a climate crisis. All we need to do, he said in a June 2008 speech in Washington, D.C., is "phase out coal as quickly as possible." Of course, given that coal generates more than half the electricity in America, and is even more vital in the developing world, this is easier said than done. But if we can't kick the coal habit, can we at least burn coal in a way that doesn't cook the planet?

The key to coal's future—and our own—is a technology called carbon capture and storage (CCS). At first glance, the idea seems straightforward: as coal is burned, remove the carbon dioxide, pressurize it into a supercritical liquid that's roughly the consistency of oil, then pump it underground. Depleted oil and gas wells make good storage sites, say the proponents of CCS, as do deep saline aquifers 2,000 feet or so underground. You can even pipe the CO_2 offshore and inject it under the ocean floor. In theory, the CO_2 will stay buried in these spots for hundreds, if not thousands, of years, thereby allowing us to continue burning coal without trashing the earth's climate.

Politically, CCS is a godsend. During the 2008 election, both Barack Obama and John McCain courted Big Coal (swing) states like Pennsylvania, West Virginia, Indiana, and Ohio, where the promise of "clean coal" is the easy answer

Train crossing at the company town of Thurmond, a thriving coal town in its heyday in the early 1900s; the Thurmond Historic District, located in the New River Gorge National River, is now a center for wilderness tourism. Photo © Jo Syz.

to every hard question about energy security, global warming, and the economy. The promise of CCS is also a central ingredient in the American Coalition for Clean Coal Electricity's "clean coal" campaign. The coal industry trade group is spending $35 million on slick TV ads to reposition coal as an indispensable fuel for the twenty-first century—a task not unlike repositioning Barry Manilow as a hip-hop star.

Unfortunately, CCS is more fantasy than reality at the moment. Squirting CO_2 into old oil wells is simple enough—the oil and gas industry does it all the time to help push out stubborn reserves. But capturing billions of tons of CO_2 from power plants and pumping it underground—and doing it safely and cheaply, on a global scale, both in the West and in the developing world—is another thing altogether. Even the Bush administration had doubts. In January 2008, the Department of Energy (DOE) canceled FutureGen, a next-generation coal plant that was being funded by the DOE and a consortium of big coal and electric power companies, citing cost overruns. Just two months earlier, administration officials had called FutureGen the "centerpiece" of their strategy for clean coal technologies.

To understand the problems with CCS, let's start with the mechanics of capturing and storing CO_2 from the stack of a coal plant. For pollutants like sulfur dioxide and nitrogen oxides, a scrubber can be bolted on the stack and be done with it. But CO_2 billows out in such a diffuse stream, and in such huge volumes, that nobody has yet figured out a good way to capture it from a stack that is not prohibitively expensive and does not reduce the efficiency of the plant by as much as 30 percent. Other possibilities, such as burning coal in pure oxygen, may someday make the job of capturing CO_2 from a pulverized coal plant easier, but this technology is nowhere near ready for commercial deployment.

It may turn out that capturing CO_2 will require shifting to an entirely new kind of process, called integrated gasification combined cycle (IGCC), which uses heat and pressure to transform coal into a gas that is then burned to generate electricity. IGCC has many advantages, but most important is

A coal-burning power plant belching out CO_2 and other pollutants. Photo © iStockphoto.com/ Bronswerk.

the fact that CO_2 can be removed during the gasification process, when the volume of the gas is much smaller than it is when it is released up the stack of a conventional coal plant. The disadvantage of IGCC is that it is new and different and expensive, and this industry has a long history of fighting anything new and different and expensive. In any case, the important point is that the ability to capture CO_2 is likely to apply only to *new* coal plants. Retrofitting the thousands of existing coal plants is, at the moment, a pipe dream.

For the sake of argument, however, let's assume a smart engineer invents a cheap, efficient way to capture CO_2 from existing coal plants (many people are throwing money at the problem). The big question is, Can we bury enough to make a difference? Right now, there are three carbon capture and storage projects in operation in the world (all are used to enhance oil and gas recovery; storing the CO_2 is secondary). The most significant is in Sleipner, Norway, where StatoilHydro, a big

Caterpillar 988G wheel loaders, like this one in Marmet, West Virginia, work night and day moving coal to conveyor belts that take it to waiting trucks and barges. Photo © Giles Ashford.

Norwegian oil and gas company, has been pumping a million tons of CO_2 into a reservoir beneath the North Sea each year since 1996. It is an enormous engineering project, deploying one of the largest offshore platforms in the world. But compared with the engineering effort that would be required to stabilize the climate, it's nothing. It would take ten Sleipner-size CO_2 storage projects to offset the annual emissions of *a single big coal plant.*

David Hawkins, head of the climate change program at the Natural Resources Defense Council and a forceful advocate of CCS, is undaunted by such facts. He explained, "Yes, burying billions of tons of CO_2 is a huge job, but that is not necessarily an argument against CCS. You can't solve a big problem without a big effort." But Vaclav Smil, an energy expert at the University of Manitoba, Canada, has argued that "carbon sequestration is irresponsibly portrayed as an imminently useful option for solving the challenge [of global warming]." Smil pointed out that to sequester just 25 percent of the CO_2 emitted by stationary sources (mostly coal plants), we would have to create a system whose annual volume of fluid would be slightly more than twice that of the world's crude-oil industry.

Then there are questions about what happens to all that CO_2 once it is pumped underground. "We have confidence that large-scale CO_2 injection projects can be operated safely," a study on the future of coal by the Massachusetts Institute of Technology concluded. But because our experience with large-scale injection is so limited, no one knows for sure what the risks are. CO_2, which is buoyant underground, can migrate through cracks in the earth and around old wellheads, pooling in unexpected places. This is troublesome because CO_2 is an asphyxiant—in concentrations above 20 percent it can cause a person to lose consciousness in a breath or two. In theory, you could enter a basement flooded with CO_2, and, because it's an invisible, odorless gas, you would never know it's there.

Liability is also a large and unresolved problem. If a microseep of CO_2 asphyxiates five girls in a basement during a slumber party in Illinois, who is going to be held accountable? Injecting CO_2 can also push briny salt water from deep aquifers up toward the surface, potentially ruining drinking water supplies. If a town's water is ruined, who pays? One solution that is frequently discussed is a version of the Price-Anderson Nuclear Indemnities Act, which assures power companies that if their nukes melt down, they won't be liable for the full cost of the disaster. That might be a good deal for Big Coal but not such a good deal for the rest of us, who will essentially end up holding the bag if something goes wrong.

Finally, there is the all-important question of cost. The era of cheap power from coal is over—today, the capital cost of building a new coal plant is more than double what it was just a decade ago, and if you factor in the cost of capturing and burying CO_2, the cost of a coal plant rivals that of a nuclear plant. Most studies show that until the price of CO_2 reaches about forty dollars a ton, power companies will find it cheaper to keep dumping the CO_2 into the air rather than capturing and burying it underground. However, given the political realities in the United States, that kind of disposal won't happen anytime before 2020, even if climate legislation is passed during the Obama administration. Add to this the technical issues that still need to be sorted out with CCS, and you can see why Greenpeace argues that it is unlikely that CCS will be commercially deployed before the year 2030. Indeed, given how quickly the price of renewable energy is falling (wind and large-scale concentrated solar power are already competitive with coal in many parts of the country), it is a mystery why anyone would go to the trouble of building a coal plant at all.

I don't mean to be entirely dismissive of coal's future in a world that takes global warming seriously. Clearly, every ton of CO_2 that is safely buried underground is a step in the right direction. But betting our future on an expensive, unproved technology like CCS is, at best, reckless. We don't need to bury our problems. We need to reinvent our world.

Coal on its way to being stored and then exported. Photo © iStockphoto.com/Pamspix.

Blowing Away
King Coal

Jeff Biggers

A wind farm in Tucker County, West Virginia. Photo © Mark Schmerling.

ON JANUARY 16, 2009, AS Barack Obama visited a wind turbine factory in Ohio, Rory McIlmoil snaked along a muddy mountain road in West Virginia on a similar mission. He was headed up Coal River Mountain, the last mountain left untouched in a historic range ravaged by strip mining.

On a ridge, the twenty-eight-year-old activist brought his four-wheeler to a skidding stop. He could not believe what he saw. Bulldozers had begun clearing the site for the first phase of a mountaintop removal operation, a radical strip-mining process that would clear-cut 6,600 acres of hardwood trees, detonate thousands of tons of explosives, and topple the mountain range into the valley. A hundred-foot swath of forest just below the ridge lay like an open wound.

To McIlmoil's way of thinking, this should have been ground zero in Obama's green recovery plan. Not a future wasteland. Just the spring before, McIlmoil had climbed this same ridge, looked out over a breathtaking quilt of lush forests, and envisioned an industrial wind farm. With his boundless enthusiasm for alternative energy, he soon began to draft a proposal. As the year wore on, he showed in his proposal, here in the deep heart of coal country, that a row of whirling wind turbines could produce enough megawatts to serve the entire region, provide hundreds of clean-energy jobs, and generate significantly more tax revenues than the mountaintop removal operation. With his ruddy good looks and the deep voice of a young Johnny Cash, McIlmoil has emerged as a champion of clean energy and green jobs in West Virginia and around the country. Joining forces with the Coal River Mountain Watch, a tenacious group of coal-mining families and environmentalists, he helped launch the Coal River Wind Project, a breakthrough initiative to transcend the century-old stranglehold on the region by the state's politically powerful coal industry.

"The benefits of economic diversification, new safe jobs, and reducing CO_2 emissions are important," McIlmoil says. "But for most residents, if a wind farm is what it takes to save their mountain, then they're all for it."

After witnessing 470 mountains in central Appalachia get blown to bits by strip mining, the Coal River wind proponents were drawing a line in the sand. The verdict was in on mountaintop removal, which had been launched as a quick-and-dirty option to procure coal cheaply. Thirty-eight years and a million and a half acres of destroyed hardwood forests later, mountaintop removal had had its way with the region, with appalling effects. It not only had destroyed the mountains' natural heritage but also had ripped out the roots of the Appalachian culture and depopulated historic mountain communities in the process.

More than 1,200 miles of waterways had been sullied and jammed with mining fill. Blasting and coal dust had made life unbearable for anyone in the strip-mined areas. Wells had been busted and polluted with toxic waste. Due to the mechanization of aboveground mountaintop removal, and its shakedown of a diversified economy, coal-mining jobs had plummeted as poverty rates rose in strip-mining areas.

West Virginians saw what happened at a Tennessee power plant in December 2008. A restraining wall burst, and a billion gallons of coal ash poured out of a pond and deluged 400 acres of land in six feet of sludge. The proposed mountaintop removal site on Coal River Mountain lay beside a six-billion-gallon toxic coal-waste sludge dam above underground mines. If the proposed blasting took place, a fracture

They've knocked me down, all right—
but I always got back up on my feet.
And I swear I won't fall again.
These mountains can't
protect themselves.
We got to do it.
I got to do it.

—*Wayne Bernard*

The Clark Branch coal refuse impoundment in Keystone, McDowell County, West Virginia, has permits to hold more than one billion gallons of coal slurry. Photo © Builder Levy.

along the sludge lake could be catastrophic for the communities downstream.

For many West Virginia residents, questioning the 200-year-old colossus King Coal is tantamount to blasphemy. West Virginia produced 158 million tons of coal in 2007, second only to the state of Wyoming, and generated $338 million in severance taxes. In a nation that still depends on coal for more than 50 percent of our electricity, West Virginia plays a key role in keeping on the lights. The Marfork Coal Company, a subsidiary of the Virginia-based Massey Energy, the largest coal company in West Virginia and fourth largest in the nation, remains a major force in the state's economy and politics.

"When you look into the climate implications of coal, you realize that Rory and the Coal River group are at the forefront of an important struggle," says filmmaker Adams Wood, who has been following the events at Coal River Mountain for a documentary, *On Coal River*. "He is taking on an enormously powerful industry and doing it with extremely limited resources and mostly on-the-job training."

McIlmoil's scrawny frame suggests a David in comparison to the coal companies' Goliath. He grew up in suburban Atlanta and Charlotte, North Carolina, raised by a single mother, and dreamed of playing professional baseball. During his freshman year in college, an eye-opening trip to Mount Saint Helens shifted his studies to earth and environmental science. After a postcollege stint in Ecuador, studying environmental issues in indigenous mountain communities, McIlmoil moved to Washington, D.C., to study at American University. One day, after hearing a bluegrass jam about the effects of mountaintop removal in Appalachia, he was done for. He never looked back, throwing himself into the nitty-gritty of coal-mining analysis.

"The more I learn about the state and coal economy, and the people living in the communities around the mountain, the harder I work," McIlmoil says. "Without a strong legal and political push to upset the status quo, the whole area is doomed to destruction and contamination."

While writing his master's thesis on the impacts of mountaintop removal, McIlmoil jumped at the opportunity for an internship at the North Carolina–based Appalachian Voices, an environmental organization that dealt with mountaintop removal. Soon he began imagining how wind energy could replace coalfields. According to J. W. Randolph, the Washington legislative aide for Appalachian Voices, McIlmoil's timing was impeccable, as the anti–mountaintop removal movement was growing.

"What the movement needed was someone who could speak to the future beyond the coal status quo," Randolph writes in an e-mail. "Legislators, investors and those who work on strip mines wanted to know what's next. Rory provided that much-needed voice that can explain, in excruciating detail, how much benefit we could bring to our region from wind power and alternative energy. He can show people our new Appalachian future and back it up with data three miles long."

Within months of his landing at the Whitesville, West Virginia, office of Coal River Mountain Watch, whose mission is to "stop the destruction of our communities and environment by mountaintop removal mining," McIlmoil's sleep-deprived passion for wind energy became famous. Hunched for hours

An eighty-ton-capacity Caterpillar 777D rolls down into the Kayford Mountain mine. Photo © Giles Ashford.

Azrael on the Mountain

the crane used in mountaintop removal coal mining

Azrael spoke
The angel of one wing, featherless
Come from the sun where God, effortless
lavishes heat and light
and demands the soul
whom Azrael has come to fetch
but fell clumsily
a wing torn loose and lost
a feathery sea-swell, glistening black
gloriously iridescent on the horizon

and Azrael, winged like a maple seed
whirled and fell
his feathers wrenched away
lingering like fiery cirrus in the twilight
his gray down the darkness coming on

and Azrael fell, skeletal and gigantic
a shambling scandal to the glory of God
who is forever radiant, forever the light of now
and Azrael woke to the scaffolding of his single wing
girded against the sky
and cried out—
Majesty, where am I?

over permit maps and satellite imagery, he meticulously analyzed wind farm models and traced the outlines of old strip and mountaintop removal mines on the computer. He slept a few nights a week on the couch at the Coal River Mountain Watch office.

"His technical knowledge fits with our local knowledge of the mountains and strip mining like hands folded in prayer," declares Julia Bonds, codirector of Coal River Mountain Watch, whose longtime advocacy for social justice in the coalfields was recognized with a Goldman Environmental Prize in 2003.

What is Thy will?
but God, who cannot abide a fault or flaw
shuddered and turned away
gazing, instead, at the galaxy
intent on the milky hymn
the swirl and spiraling of eternity.

Azrael looked about, bewildered—
where was the soul he was to sunder from its self
where the standers-by at the bedside
where the silent grief, the choked sobs
the watery sorrow on the face

And how was he to pause
great, gray-winged and magnificent
his talons poised above the soul
to seize it and soar—
the lamentation of the living
the chaos of wind and wing-beats
rising toward God.

Azrael, bereft of duty
one-winged, plucked, absurd, ignored by God
drags himself in his grandeur
grotesque, insanely on the mountain top
back and forth

—Victor Depta

Maria Gunnoe's family cemetery, dating from the late 1800s, lies on a wooded knoll just a few hundred yards from mining activities in Boone County, West Virginia. Photo © Giles Ashford.

McIlmoil quickly found a partner and codirector of the wind project in Lorelei Scarbro, a coal miner's widow and grandmother whose back fence literally demarcated the front lines of the impending mountaintop removal site. Hired as a community organizer for Coal River Mountain Watch in the fall of 2007, Scarbro has seen hundreds of well-meaning young activists trundle through the area. In her eyes, what McIlmoil lacked in mountain heritage, he made up for in his willingness to listen to and understand the local residents in rural Appalachia.

Worried locals listen to speakers at a permit meeting in Boone County, West Virginia. Photo © Giles Ashford.

"What we need most are people to stand beside us, not in front of us or behind us," Scarbro says. "My husband, who spent thirty-five years as an underground union coal miner and died of black lung in 1999, is buried in the family cemetery next door. There is no price you can put on the memories we have here. We have a sense of place here that many people don't know and can't begin to understand. There are many Appalachians who know this sense of place."

McIlmoil has come to love the people of the mountains as well as the place. "Everybody should know the people living around Coal River Mountain," he says. "They're good, beautiful people, and they have a greater connection to the mountain and their history than I could ever hope to have."

Working with other energy analysts and mining experts, including Appalachian Voices director Matt Wasson and Alliance for Appalachia coordinator Dana Kuhnline, McIlmoil, Scarbro, and Coal River Mountain Watch team member Matt Noerpel drew up a virtual plan for a wind farm on Coal River Mountain. As McIlmoil envisioned it, the wind potential on the mountain blew away the short-lived economic benefits of the proposed mountaintop removal sites. It's clear that the state can use all the economic activity it can get. In a recent listing of the best states in which to do business, *Forbes* ranked West Virginia fiftieth.

McIlmoil concluded that on fewer than ten cleared acres across the same mountain range the wind farm would create 200 local jobs during construction, and 50 permanent jobs during the life of the wind farm. In the process, it would provide enough energy for 150,000 homes, and allow for sustainable forestry and mountain tourism projects. The plan also called for a limited amount of underground coal mining.

After the April 2008 launch of the Coal River Wind Web site and its virtual plan for the valley, McIlmoil and Scarbro, along with Noerpel and other members of the Coal River Mountain Watch, spent the next six months going to battle in the community for their plan.

At the wind partners' first local presentation in the Marsh Fork area, only five people showed up. Undaunted, Scarbro

A home on Mud River, in Lincoln County, West Virginia, is dwarfed by the MTR site behind it. Photo © Vivian Stockman.

and McIlmoil held meetings there for several weeks and noted that crowds kept getting bigger and more welcoming. By the third meeting, McIlmoil realized the wind plan had taken root in the community when a Massey coal miner listened quietly to the presentation, left the meeting, and then, already halfway home, came back and asked for materials to pass around.

For filmmaker Catherine Pancake, at work on a study chronicling the rise of clean energy in the United States, the Coal River Wind Project emerged as a bellwether for renewable energy. "They are showing what happens when citizens with a viable green energy plan come into brutal contact with a multibillion-dollar industry," she says. "Rory and Lorelei are effectively killing the popular and bogus 'jobs vs. the environment' argument used ad infinitum in local and state politics."

Despite the positive reception of their proposal by several county and state agencies and public officials, McIlmoil soon learned that the viselike grip of the coal industry locked down any governmental or legislative support for the wind farm. Marfork Coal Company simply had no intention of halting its demolition plans on Cold River Mountain. With nineteen Appalachian mining operations valued at $2.6 billion in 2008, parent company Massey had demonstrated a merciless coveting for coal at any expense.

In a haunting parallel to the Tennessee coal ash disaster, a Massey subsidiary in Eastern Kentucky had been responsible for the Martin County spill. By 2008, it had been forced to pay $20 million in penalties for dumping toxic mine waste into the region's waterways; before the year was out, Massey shelled out a record $4.2 million for civil and criminal fines in the death of two coal miners in West Virginia.

So far the coal giant's public comments on the new competition have been relatively innocuous. In a statement e-mailed to the media in late 2008, Massey spokesman Jeff Gillenwater declared that his company "supports many forms of energy, including wind energy." However, Massey was perplexed, Gillenwater added, "by the Coal River Mountain Watch's focus on this particular site, to the exclusion of any other."

In the dog days of summer 2008, McIlmoil and Scarbro kept the pressure on. After receiving a grant from the Sierra Club for an in-depth economic study of the wind proposal, McIlmoil and Scarbro made their first presentation to representatives of Governor Joe Manchin's office. The polite indifference from the pro-coal governor's office did not surprise them, so they launched a national campaign. They were soon overwhelmed by supportive calls, national media attention, and an online petition, which topped 10,000 signatures, calling for the halt of the proposed strip mine and the creation of the wind farm. The Coal River wind advocates also received the Building Economic Alternatives Award from Co-op America (now Green America), a nonprofit group devoted to sustainability.

There was no celebration, however. Days earlier, McIlmoil and Scarbro had read in the local *Beckley Register-Herald* of Massey's intention to begin blasting on the first area of the strip mine. The company had taken out a classified ad in the newspaper to alert the community. The activists' concern at the bold move by Massey turned to outrage when they discovered the coal company lacked certain blasting permits and state agency approval of the mining plan revision.

Drawing from their growing support across the country, McIlmoil and Scarbro managed to flood Governor Manchin's and state agency offices with thousands of e-mails and phone calls, resulting in a suspension of any blasting. All eyes were now on the governor to reconsider the economic ramifications of mountaintop removal and form a commission to investigate and promote renewable energy sources, such as the Coal River wind proposal. It didn't happen. "It would be inappropriate for the governor to interfere in the regulatory process," Manchin's communications director, Lara Ramsburg, said in an e-mail statement to the *Charleston Gazette* in September 2008.

Costumed activists portray King Coal and Death at an anti–mountaintop removal rally in Charleston, West Virginia. Photo © Vivian Stockman; courtesy of Ohio Valley Environmental Coalition.

On November 20, 2008, at the same time newly elected President Obama announced a forthcoming economic recovery package and clean-energy job programs, the West Virginia Department of Environmental Protection, with the approval of Manchin, granted Massey the surface-mining permit revision for the initial part of its proposed mountaintop removal of Coal River Mountain. In a further blow to coalfield citizens against mountaintop removal, the Bush administration's Environmental Protection Agency passed an eleventh-hour ruling in early December that did away with a twenty-five-year tradition of regulating the dumping of coal-mining waste into waterways. The ruling effectively cleared the way for Massey, like other coal companies, to accelerate its assault on the Appalachian Mountains.

"Once the demolition begins," Scarbro declared at a local hearing, "it will be very difficult to stop it, and once the mountain is removed, it won't grow back. The potential for wind energy and good jobs will be gone forever, along with our renewable water and forest resources."

Disheartened but not stymied by the news, the Coal River wind advocates released the results of a four-month economic study by West Virginia–based Downstream Strategies. According to the report, the first of its kind in coal country, the proposed wind farm on Coal River Mountain, consisting of 164 wind turbines and generating 328 megawatts of electricity, would provide more than $1.74 million in annual property taxes to Raleigh County. By comparison, the coal severance taxes related to the mountaintop removal mining would provide the county with only $36,000 per year. Moreover, the report noted that the coal reserves in the area would last only seventeen years at best, in contrast to the eternal supply of wind.

In support of Coal River Mountain residents who staged a protest against the coal companies, James Hansen, head of NASA's Goddard Institute for Space Studies and the nation's foremost expert on climate change, has declared: "President Obama, please look at Coal River Mountain. Your strongest supporters are counting on you to stop this madness."

"When I first came here," says McIlmoil, "I was all about just beating Massey and driving a wind turbine into the heart of their territory. But now there are hands and hearts, lives and histories, all holding onto that turbine, and I dream of a day when one of the community folks gets to hit the 'On' switch that turns on the first turbine."

How seriously the nation appreciates the vanguard role of clean-energy advocates like McIlmoil will, ultimately, decide whether Coal River Mountain will be the first peak in Appalachia literally saved from mountaintop removal—or the 471st mountain to be eliminated from American maps.

⟞◦⟝

This essay first appeared in slightly different form in Salon, a Web site located at www.salon.com.

Making Their Own Future

Penny Loeb

In April 1997, I gazed across the town of Blair in Logan County, West Virginia, and saw dump trucks as big as houses rumbling across chopped-off mountains. A twenty-story-high dragline shovel hovered over a nearby home. Even worse, the charred remains of homes—their owners bought out by Arch Coal's land company—scarred a once pretty place. Blair and its troubles opened my investigative article for *U.S. News & World Report* in August 1997, the first on mountaintop removal in a national publication. A month later, James Weekley from Blair walked into attorney Joe Lovett's office with my article. Lovett, then in his first week of practicing as an attorney, soon launched a decade-long battle against mountaintop removal, highlighted by the *Bragg v. Robertson* case over valley fills.

The *Bragg* case became the focal point of my book *Moving Mountains: How One Woman and Her Community Won Justice from Big Coal,* which I wrote while watching struggles unfold over the next decade. Early on, I realized that coal mining dominates life in southern West Virginia and that residents there are concerned with bettering their educational and economic opportunities. As I watched activism and lawsuits evolve, I became more curious about how mining battles affected the social fabric of the southern coalfields.

The *Bragg* case was named for plaintiff Patricia "Trish" Bragg, whose first struggle with the industry arose because

James Weekley near his home in Pigeonroost Hollow, West Virginia. Photo © Mark Schmerling.

Alysa Estep walks across debris left by flooding in the creek bed behind her grandfather's house in Litton Hollow, Chattaroy, Mingo County, West Virginia. Photo © Builder Levy.

of deep mining. In 1994, a large Arch Coal deep mine had dried up water wells at two dozen neighbors' homes in her hometown of Pie. Trying to find help, Trish discovered the West Virginia Organizing Project and organizer Elaine Purkey. Over the next half dozen years, Trish, Elaine, and other project members waged several successful campaigns for better mining practices. Her work with the project (founded on the organizing principles of Saul Alinsky) also helped Trish empower herself, going to college in her later years and graduating with a bachelor's degree summa cum laude.

When Trish began her activism, no lawyers would go near the coalfields, but that changed due to the pioneering efforts of Joe Lovett and Jim Hecker of Public Justice, a public interest law firm. These days, environmental cases are nearly a given when a mountaintop removal mine is proposed. The fortuitous entrance of attorneys Ben Bailey and Brian Glasser into the *Bragg* case led to a series of successful nuisance cases over water loss and dust. Crusading attorney Kevin Thompson has won settlements in blasting cases and is the first to tackle environmental illness lawsuits, starting in Rawl.

The *Bragg* case yielded important, yet less recognized, improvements in mining practices. A new valley-fill design has shortened the fills and made them more stable. Most companies now plan to restore mine sites to their approximate original contours. Most plan to replant native hardwood forests as well. The uproar over the case in 1999 helped jump-start economic development in Mingo and neighboring counties. Government officials are encouraging other kinds of industry to replace coal when it is gone. A giant wood flooring plant and tourism from the Hatfield-McCoy ATV trail in southwest West Virginia are the biggest successes.

However, coal mines are still expanding at the fastest rate ever, spurred by emphasis on homegrown energy. The most controversial mine is a deep one near East Lynn Lake, a popular recreation area owned by the U.S. Army Corps of Engineers. Despite a decade of battles against the industry, many don't realize that only about 40 years' worth of easy coal remains atop mountains in West Virginia, while at least

130 years' worth of coal remain deep in the ground—a more dangerous place for miners.

The future of both mountaintop removal and deep mining is tied to larger questions about how the Obama administration will respond to global warming. Thanks to the Internet and national environmental groups, the struggle against mountaintop removal has mushroomed. But, at least for now, the struggle for safer and better-controlled mining will probably continue, as will the journey toward a stronger economy in southern West Virginia. Proposals for wind generators atop mountains and a manufacturing plant for wind or solar equipment are hopeful signs.

Despite national activism, those who can bring about the most change are people like Trish Bragg, who live in the coalfields and can police mining practices vigilantly. Ironically, Arch Coal itself took an important step when it set up a citizens' oversight committee for its vast new deep mine next to Blair. Already the group has brought in a new public water line and has embarked on a war against drugs. Perhaps someday, citizens and the coal companies can work together for the betterment of the region.

The mountains, rivers, earth, grasses, trees, and forests are always emanating a subtle, precious light, day and night, always emanating a subtle, precious sound, demonstrating and expounding to all people the unsurpassed ultimate truth.

—*Yuan-Sou*

The Children of Twilight

Michael Hendryx

Signs warn of blasting danger from the Argus Energy mine near the Lincoln–Wayne County line in West Virginia. Photo © Marian Steinert.

INSIDE A COMFORTABLE LIVING ROOM is not where you typically expect to hear an explosion. But Twilight is not a typical place, unless you're a resident of southern West Virginia. The explosion comes from one of the nearby mountaintop removal mining sites, blasting away the rock and soil that cover the seams of coal beneath. My host and I stop our conversation and step outside to watch.

That explosion is only one example of the personal evidence I've accumulated that coal mining in Appalachia poses serious risks to public health. Coal mining is a highly destructive practice, and it results in local air and water pollution that can be devastating to community residents. I've sat at a kitchen table and listened to a husband and wife tell stories of water running black into their kitchen sinks and bathtubs. "Black water events," they're called; it means that their well water has become contaminated with coal slurry. I've stood in a man's workshop as he talked about all the cancer cases in the neighborhood, one after another up and down both sides of the street. Most cancer mortality around the country is from lung or colon cancer. You see these here, too, but residents in these areas often talk of unusual types, stomach cancer in this house, brain cancer in the next.

I've watched a woman who lives near a coal-processing facility wipe a thick film of coal dust off her porch furniture, and gone back two weeks later and watched her do it again. The dust rises from the crushing, mixing, and transporting activities of the facility located only a few blocks away. Coal dust from processing plants contains not only coal but all the other impurities that are present in coal: arsenic, nickel, beryllium, cadmium, and other carcinogens and toxicants. Some of these dust particles are small enough to be inhaled and can lead to cancer and heart and lung disease. The contaminated water, too, contains impurities that can cause cancer or kidney disease. I've heard government officials claim there's nothing wrong, or, when that excuse fails, say there's nothing they can do to protect the health of their own citizens.

The research I do concerns numbers, statistics, columns of figures, charts, and graphs: X number of deaths every year in the coalfields, over and above what one would expect in some other part of the country. For example, compare the per capita death rates of Appalachian coal-mining counties to other counties outside Appalachia, and $X = 10,923$, based on death rates from 1997 through 2005. (This number was found by converting the excess age-adjusted death rate in mining areas to number of deaths, based on the size of the population living there.) That's 10,923 lives lost every year to our national addiction to coal. Those lives become real, become more than figures on a page, when I hear the stories people tell me, and when I see the fading towns, the defiant faces, the dusty stockpiles by the roads, when I stand in the heat at the edge of a pit where the coal is ripped from the earth and feel the dust in my own throat.

I watched the airborne dust from that explosion near the town of Twilight settle over the neighborhood as children played barefoot in the yard next door. My host looked on quietly; he's seen it many times.

Government officials throw up their hands. It's not our responsibility, they say. We can't do anything, they say.

Preposterous.

There are many lies connected with the coal-mining industry: that coal can be "clean"; that West Virginia has

B. I. Simmons holds a tray containing some of the medications he must take daily; he attributes his poor health to the contaminated water found throughout his Mingo County community. Photo © Mark Schmerling.

enough coal to last hundreds of years even though estimates indicate that coal production in the state will peak in about twenty years; and that the coal industry doesn't pose a grave threat to public health in either the production or the consumption of its product. But perhaps the biggest lie is that coal mining is good for the economy of West Virginia. Yes, there are some jobs in the mining industry, although far fewer than there used to be before the advent of mechanized mountaintop mining. And yes, the industry does provide tax revenue to the state. But consider that, year after year after year, the economy of West Virginia, so heavily dependent on coal, is weak compared with the national economy. Compared with the rest of the country, West Virginia has higher unemployment, higher poverty rates, and lower income levels. Then consider that, *within* West Virginia, coal-mining counties are weaker economically than nonmining parts of the state—higher unemployment, higher poverty rates, and lower income levels. Yet almost invariably, as economic development for the state is discussed by government officials, *more* coal mining is proposed as the answer.

Once again, preposterous.

As Einstein said, insanity is doing the same thing over and over again and expecting a different result.

Clearly, more coal mining is not the answer. It is not the solution that will create a strong economy and a healthy population. When coal reserves in West Virginia peak and then enter permanent decline in about twenty years, the number of jobs will be even fewer than currently exist. Better alternatives are available that are diametrically opposed to coal mining, such as an economy based on renewable energy rather than fossil fuels. West Virginia has tremendous potential in the areas of wind, hydropower, and biofuels. The region could serve as a carbon sink rather than the source of atmospheric carbon emissions. The forests of Appalachia, if left intact and nurtured rather than destroyed to reach the coal seams, would provide unequaled service in efforts to mitigate climate change. Reforestation of areas that have been destroyed by mountaintop mining could create jobs, contribute to local

Kenny Stroud and his son look at discolored well water in their home in Rawl, Mingo County, West Virginia. Residents say that the local well water, once clear and good-tasting, changed when companies began injecting coal slurry into abandoned underground mines. Photo © Vivian Stockman.

economies, and help reduce levels of carbon dioxide. We could begin to implement all these ideas today.

Instead, we have chosen to allow clouds of toxic dust to fall upon the heads of children so that our laptops run cheaply. We allow literally thousands of our fellow citizens to die every year so the rest of us can enjoy electricity without giving a thought to its origins or its true costs. This is the choice that we have collectively made. But it could be different.

America and the world have a tremendous appetite for energy, and we may not stop mining coal until the day when the last black rock is torn from the ground, washed with chemicals, transported to a power plant, pulverized into powder, and blown into a furnace. For the sake of the children of Twilight, I hope we'll be prepared for what we'll do *after* the day when the last profitable rock is burned, when the coal companies pack their bags, leaving the empty towns and the toxic ponds and the naked mountains behind.

Sometimes when I'm driving through southern West Virginia, on my way to meet someone to hear their stories of what the coal industry has done to their home, or their community, or their health, I will suddenly come across a place of incredible beauty. It might be a view from the top of a hill, down into a green valley where the rays of the sun pass through a morning mist, or a stream running quietly among the trees, or the autumn hilltops rolling away forever into the horizon. And I will catch my breath and, for a moment, appreciate these sacred places, and wonder at whether they will be spared, or how long they might last, or how it is that the parallel of this beautiful place is unknown in the world, and yet we feel we must destroy it. I hope that we will not.

It is also vandalism wantonly to destroy or to permit the destruction of what is beautiful in nature, whether it be a cliff, a forest, or a species of mammal or bird. Here in the United States we turn our rivers and streams into sewers and dumping-grounds, we pollute the air, we destroy forests, and exterminate fishes, birds and mammals—not to speak of vulgarizing charming landscapes with hideous advertisements. But at last it looks as if our people were awakening.

—*Theodore Roosevelt*

A Sin of Omission

Jon Blair Hunter

Mount Olive Baptist Church and, behind it, the Wheeling Steel preparation plant in Stirrat, Logan County, West Virginia, 1970. Photo © Builder Levy.

I STAND HERE TODAY TO OFFER my confession. God created our mountains. God created our clear mountain streams and rivers. God created our lush, green forests. God created our hardy mountaineer ancestors who settled in these hills because of our mountains, our clear, clean streams, and our lush green forests. And, yes, God also put the coal in those mountains. But I fervently believe that he did not intend for us to destroy the mountains, the streams, the forests, and his people to mine it. Coal can be mined without mountaintop removal.

Mr. President, God, through his son, Jesus, has taught us about the sins of commission and the sins of omission. To intentionally destroy God's creation, be it human or a mountain, I fervently believe is a sin of commission. To stand by and do nothing is a sin of omission. On this holy day, Ash Wednesday, I wish to confess my sin of omission, and I promise to sin no more. That is why today I have introduced Senate Bill No. 588 (Preventing Excess Spoil or Overburden Near Certain Streams), a bill designed to stop this unholy destruction of our mountains, of our streams, of our forests, and of our people.

Mr. President, let me document the sin of destruction of our magnificent mountains and forests. To mine the coal seams, up to 800 feet of a mountaintop is blasted away, using a million tons of explosives. In fact, every two weeks

Blasting at the Premium Energy/ Mingo Logan surface mine in Gilbert, Mingo County, West Virginia. Photo © Builder Levy.

the amount of explosives used in this process is equal to the amount of explosives in the atomic bomb that was used over Hiroshima. According to the Office of Surface Mining, 1.4 million acres, or 2,200 square miles, of mountains and forests have been destroyed.

What about our clear, clean streams? One thousand two hundred miles of streams have been destroyed, Mr. President. Seven hundred twenty-four miles have been completely buried. And in just the last six years alone, 600 miles of streams have been damaged and about 275 of those completely buried. This is about the same distance as between here and Florida, or it's about the same distance to North Carolina and back, Mr. President.

What about our people? First, we have lost jobs. Since 1980, when about 60,000 of us worked in the coal mines, that number has dropped to about 17,000 in 2006. That is 43,000 lost jobs. Southern West Virginia has seen a massive loss of both jobs and population. Those left behind have seen increased flooding, blasting damage to their homes and wells, air pollution and dust all over everything, water pollution, loss of timber jobs, and loss of hunting and fishing habitats as well as wildlife.

I am here to tell you that these floods are not an act of God. This destruction is an act of an outlaw coal industry. I have lived in this same location for thirty years, and this never happened before. It did not happen until the coal company stripped our mountains, filled our headwater streams, and allowed their silt ponds to leak, break, and rupture.

—Pauline Stacy, from
"Personal Statement"

Our communities and our way of life have disappeared. Our health has been severely impacted by the dust, the chemicals, the heavy metals polluting our air and our water, resulting in skin rashes, respiratory problems, cancer, and kidney and liver problems. Our children in these areas are twice as likely to have autism.

Mr. President, I have just received an article from the *New England Journal of Medicine* that relates that selenium has recently been linked to Type II diabetes. Mr. President, selenium is one of the major metals that comes out of this process, and, Mr. President, our citizens lead the nation in Type II diabetes. A coincidence? I think not!

Some recent polls of West Virginia citizens have indicated that about 60 percent of them are opposed to this type of process—mountaintop removal. I only wish 60 percent of our legislators were. In truth, I suspect you are. But, like gamblers, we are addicted to the revenue, and, as addicts, we are committing the Sin of Omission. I know we will not pass Senate Bill No. 588, but, as one of my last confessions, I wanted to present that bill to you.

Thank you, Mr. President, for hearing my confession.

⟫⟪

These remarks by the Honorable Jon Blair Hunter, state senator of West Virginia, were delivered in Charleston, West Virginia, on February 6, 2008. Senator Hunter is addressing Earl Ray Tomblin, president of the West Virginia Senate.

Not Just an Appalachian Problem

David W. Orr

SEEING PICTURES OF THE DEVASTATION did not prepare me for the reality of New Orleans. Mile after mile of wrecked houses, demolished cars, piles of debris, twisted and downed trees, and dried mud everywhere. We stopped every so often to look into abandoned houses in the Ninth Ward and along the shore of Lake Pontchartrain to see things close up: mud lines on the walls, overturned furniture, moldy clothes still hanging in closets, broken toys, a lens from a pair of glasses, each house with a red circle painted on the front to indicate results of the search for bodies. Despair hung like Spanish moss in the dank, hot July air.

Ninety miles to the south, the Louisiana delta is rapidly sinking below the rising waters of the Gulf. This is no "natural" process, but rather the result of decades of mismanagement of the lower Mississippi that became federal policy after the great flood of 1927. Sediment that built the richest and most fecund wetlands in the world is now deposited off the continental shelf—part of an ill-conceived effort to tame the river. The result is that the remaining wetlands, starved for sediment, are both eroding and compacting, sinking below the water and perilously close to no return. Oil extraction has done most of the rest by cutting channels that crisscross the marshlands, allowing the intrusion of salt water and storm surges. Wakes from boats have widened the original channels

Jamie Wolford's single wide mobile home was moved off its foundation by rampant flood waters in Pie, Mingo County, West Virginia, 2004. Detail of photo © Builder Levy.

Turtle on a dirt road bordering Kanawha State Forest. Photo © Mark Schmerling.

considerably, further unraveling the ecology of the region. The richest fishery in North America and a unique culture that once thrived in the delta are disappearing, and with them the buffer zone that protects New Orleans from hurricanes.

And the big hurricanes will come. Kerry Immanuel, an MIT scientist and onetime greenhouse effect skeptic, researched the connection among rising levels of greenhouse gases in the atmosphere, warmer sea temperatures, and the severity of storms. As detailed in *Nature,* he's a skeptic no longer. The hard evidence on this and other parts of climate science has moved beyond the point of legitimate dispute. Carbon dioxide, the prime greenhouse gas, is at the highest level in at least the last 650,000 years. CO_2 continues to accumulate by approximately 2.5 parts per million per year, edging closer and closer to what some scientists believe is the threshold of runaway climate change. British scientist James Lovelock compares our situation to being on a boat upstream from Niagara Falls with the engines about to fail.

If this were not enough, the evidence now shows a strong likelihood that sea levels will rise more rapidly than previously thought. The third report of the Intergovernmental Panel on Climate Change (2001) predicted about a one-meter rise in the twenty-first century, but more recent evidence puts this figure at six to seven meters, the result of accelerated melting of the Greenland ice sheet and polar ice along with the thermal expansion of water.

Nine hundred miles to the northeast, Massey Energy, Arch Coal, and other companies are busy leveling the mountains of Appalachia to get at the upper seams of coal in what was one of the most diverse and relatively undisturbed forests in the United States, and one of the most diverse ecosystems anywhere.

Throughout the coalfields of West Virginia and Kentucky, they have already leveled 456 mountains across 1.5 million acres and intend to damage a good bit more. Coal is washed on-site, leaving billions of gallons of a dilute asphaltlike gruel laced with toxic flocculants and heavy metals. More than 100 slurry impoundments are located in West Virginia.

These structures rest above communities and, should they ever break, would devastate any areas below them. Two dam breaks (in Martin County, Kentucky, in October 2000, and in Kingston, Tennessee, in December 2008) permanently damaged waterways and property values of people living in the wake of ongoing disasters.

This is typical of the central Appalachian coalfields, which are largely a national sacrifice zone in which fairness, decency, and the rights of old and young alike are discarded as so much overburden on behalf of the national obsession with "cheap" electricity. For his role in trying to provide an accurate accounting of the Martin County disaster, Interior Department mine safety inspector Jack Spadaro was intimidated and bullied by the Bush administration in an effort to force him to quit his decades-long job. To see MTR from the air is an unsettling, jolting experience. In July of 2006, along with Spadaro (now retired) and corporate attorney Tom Hyde, I boarded a four-seat Cessna piloted by Hume Davenport.

Coal barges on the Kanawha River, West Virginia. Photo © Giles Ashford.

This West Virginia homestead is one of many that help define the unique cultural heritage of Appalachia. Photo © John Mullins.

Mountain Travesty

They're beheading West Virginia,
Sending her down to New Orleans.
We can make the same trip
Floating on the shallow streams,
Sluice through our downsized mountains
Mortified by flat-topped crew cuts,
Summits scalped where oak and pine once stood.
They're moving Appalachia
Peak and pinnacle
Through the slurries in the valleys
Cut between the headless hilltops,
Where she's hemorrhaging,
Her "Wild and Wonderful"
While she's stripped of the old claim
To her mountain maiden name.
Someday she'll be reclaimed
As the Appalachian plains
When they finally dislocate
Her crowning glory
Where the gulf winds' sultry blow
Warms the Mississippi delta
And Old Man River
spews his silt
Into the Gulf of Mexico.
Hey, we're sending Appalachia
Down to New Orleans
Filling swamp and marshland
With majestic mountain grandeur
Near the Louisiana bayou.
Come with me!
We can sit along the shoreline,
Sing about our heritage,
And watch the West Virginia mountains
Sink into the salty sea.

—Max Price

The ground recedes below us as we pass over Charleston and the Kanawha River lined with barges hauling coal to power plants along the Ohio River and points more distant. Quickly on the horizon to the west looms the John Amos power plant, owned by American Electric Power. This plant is one of the heaviest mercury polluters in West Virginia, as well as releasing hundreds of tons of sulfur oxides, hydrogen sulfide, and CO_2 into the environment. For a few minutes we can see the deep green of wrinkled Appalachian hills below, but very soon the first of the MTR sites appears, followed by another and then another. The pattern of ruin spreads out below us for miles, stretching to the far horizon on all points of the compass. From a mile above, trucks with twelve-foot-diameter tires and draglines that could pick up two Greyhound buses at a single bite look like Tonka toys in a sandbox.

What is left of Kayford Mountain comes into sight. It is surrounded by leveled mountains and a few still being leveled. "Overburden," the mining industry term for dismantled mountains, is dumped into valleys covering hundreds of miles of streams. Coal slurry ponds loom above houses, towns, and even elementary schools. If the earthen dams break on some dark, rainy night, those below will have little if any warning before the deluge hits.

Spadaro is our guide to the devastation. He has a knack for describing outrageous things calmly and with clinical precision. A mining engineer by profession, he spent several frustrating decades trying to enforce the laws, such as they are, against an industry with friends in high places in Charleston, Congress, and the White House. In a flat, unemotional monotone he describes what we are seeing below. Aside from the destruction of the Appalachian forest, the math is all wrong. The slopes are too steep, the impoundments too large. The angles of slope, dam, weight, and proximity of houses and towns are the geometry of tragedies to come. He points out the Marsh Fork Elementary School, situated close to a coal-loading operation and below a huge impoundment back up the hollow. In the event of a dam failure, the evacuation plan calls for the principal using a bullhorn to initiate

A coal silo looms over Marsh Fork Elementary School in Raleigh County, West Virginia. Photo © Mark Schmerling.

We learn slowly, we humans:
overburdened with lessons
taught, forgotten, taught
again in the forgetting
until the lesson becomes mere
   memory
of diminishing returns:

it was the forest that was holding
   things
together, not the rock and soil
like we once thought,
just as skin with its many layers
bears the burden of the body
with its many layers and without
which the flailed flesh weeps and
   bleeds,
sinew fails, bones part and lean
to aspects of prayer, part
and fall groveling, to dust. . . .

—*Christina E. Lovin,
lines from "Overburden"*

the evacuation of the children ahead of the fifty-foot wall of slurry that will be moving at maybe sixty miles an hour. If the official evacuation plan is accurate, they will have two minutes to get to safety, but there is no safe place for them to go.

On the circle back to Yeager Field in Charleston, Tom Hyde calls this a "tragedy." We all nod, knowing the word does not quite describe the enormity of the things we have just seen or the cold-blooded nature of it. In our one-hour flight we saw perhaps 1 percent of the destruction now metastasizing through four states. Until recently it was all but ignored by the national media.

Under the hot afternoon sun we next board a fifteen-person van and drive out to see what MTR looks like on the ground. On the way to Kayford Mountain, we take the interstate south from Charleston and exit at a place called Sharon onto winding roads that lead to mining country. Trailer parks, small evangelical churches, truck repair shops, and small, often lovingly tended houses line the road, intermixed with those abandoned long ago when underground mining jobs disappeared. The two-lane paved road turns to gravel and climbs toward the top of the hollow and Kayford Mountain. Within a mile or two the first valley fill appears. It is a green V-shaped insertion between wooded hills. Reading the signs made by water coursing down its face, Jack Spadaro notes that this one will soon fail. Valley fills are mountains turned upside down: rocky mining debris, trees illegally buried, along with what many locals believe to be more sinister objects brought in by unmarked trucks in the dead of night. He adds that some valley fills may contain as much as 500 million tons of blasted mountains and extend for as long as six miles. We ascend the slope toward Kayford, passing by the no trespassing signs that appear around the gate that leads to the mining operations.

Larry Gibson meets us at the summit, really a small peak on what was once a long ridge. The Gibson family has been on Kayford since the eighteenth century, operating a small coal mine. Larry is the proverbial David fighting Goliath, but he has no slingshot unless it is that of moral authority spoken with a fierce, inborn eloquence. Larry's land has been saved so far because he made forty acres of it into a park and has fought tooth and nail to save it from Massey Energy. Massey leveled nearly everything around him and has punched holes underneath Kayford because the mineral rights below and the ownership of the surface were long ago separated.

Larry describes what has happened, using a model of the area that comes apart more or less in the way that the mountains around him have been dismantled. As he talks he illustrates what has happened by taking the model apart piece by piece, leaving the top of Kayford rather like a knob sticking up amid the encircling devastation. So warned, we walk down the country lane to witness the advancing ruin. Fifteen of us stood for maybe half an hour on the edge of the abyss, watching giant bulldozers and trucks at work below us. Plumes of dust from the operations rise up several thousand feet. The next set of explosive charges is ready to go on an area about the size of a football field. Every day some three million pounds of explosives are used in the eleven counties south of Charleston. This is a war zone. The mountains are the enemy, profits from coal the prize, and the local residents and all those who might have otherwise lived here or would have been re-created here are the collateral damage.

Kanawha State Forest, a popular destination for hiking and mountain biking, lies between Charleston, West Virginia's capital, and both the Coal River Valley and the Twilight Mountain region, where many MTR mines operate. Photo © Jo Syz.

We try to wrap our minds around what we are seeing, but words cannot do justice to the enormity of it. One of the oldest mountain ranges on earth is being turned into gravel for a pittance, its ecologies radically simplified, forever. Perhaps as a defense mechanism from feeling too much or being overwhelmed by what we've seen, we talk about lesser things. On the late afternoon drive back to Charleston we pass by the coal-loading facilities along the Kanawha River—mile after mile of barges lined up to haul coal to hungry Ohio River power plants, the umbilical cord between mines, mountains, and us, the consumers of cheap electricity.

To permanently destroy millions of acres of Appalachia in order to extract maybe twenty years of coal is not just stupid, it is a derangement on a scale for which there are

View from the Stanley family property on Kayford Mountain. That family (of which Larry Gibson is a member) owns fifty acres on Kayford; it was the only family not to sell its land to the mining company. Photo © Jo Syz.

no adequate words and no adequate enforcement of laws to stop it. Unlike deep mining, mountaintop removal employs few workers. It is destroying the wonders of the mixed mesophytic forest of northern Appalachia once and for all, including habitat for dozens of endangered species. It contaminates groundwater with toxics and heavy metals and renders the land permanently uninhabitable and unusable. Glib talk of the economic potential of flatter places for commerce of one kind or another is just that: glib talk. The fact of the matter is that one of the most diverse and beautiful ecosystems in the world is being destroyed and rendered uninhabitable forever along with the lives and culture of the people who remain in these coalfield communities.

We justify this on the grounds of necessity and cost, but a more complete accounting of the costs of coal would also include the rising tide of damage and insurance claims attributable to climate change. Some say that if we don't burn coal the economy will collapse, and there will be no more progress; but with wind and solar power growing by 25 percent or more per year and the technology of energy efficiency advancing rapidly, we have good options that make burning coal unnecessary. Before long we will wish that we had not destroyed so much of the capacity of the Appalachian forests and soils to absorb the carbon that makes for bigger storms and more severe heat waves and droughts.

No one in a position of authority in West Virginia politics, except that noble patriarch of good sense, Ken Hechler, asks the obvious questions: How far down the Kanawha, Ohio, and Mississippi Rivers does the plume of heavy metals from coal-washing operations go into the drinking water of communities elsewhere? What other economy, based on the sustainable use of forests, nontimber products, ecotourism, and human craft skills, might flourish in these hills? What is the true cost of "cheap" coal? Why do the profits from coal mining leave the state? Why is so much of the land owned by absentee corporations like the Pocahontas Land Company? Once you subtract the permanent ecological ruin and crimes against humanity, there really isn't much to add.

Nearly a thousand miles separates the coalfields of West Virginia from New Orleans, yet they are a lot closer than that. The connection is carbon. Coal is mostly carbon, and for every ton burned, 3.6 tons of CO_2 eventually enters the atmosphere, raising global temperatures, warming oceans, creating bigger storms, melting ice, and raising sea levels. Every ton of coal extracted from the mountains is accompanied by tons of "overburden" burying steams and filling the valleys and hollows of West Virginia, Kentucky, Virginia, and Tennessee. In the land between the hills of Appalachia and the sinking Louisiana coast, tens of thousands of people living downwind from coal-fired power plants die prematurely each year from inhalation of small particles of smoke laced with heavy metals that penetrate deeply into lungs, a reminder of the interconnectedness of an energy-hungry nation.

A forest ecosystem, respected and preserved as such, can be used generation after generation without diminishment—or it can be regarded merely as an economic bonanza, cut down, and used up.

—*Wendell Berry*

The Other Side of the Light Switch

Mary Anne Hitt

Coal trains line up in Danville, Boone County, West Virginia. Photo © Mark Schmerling.

THE DISASTER UNFOLDED ON DECEMBER 22, 2008, just as families were looking forward to winding down and reuniting for the holidays. A dam failed at an East Tennessee coal plant, sending a wave of one billion gallons of toxic coal ash onto 300 acres near Harriman, Tennessee, and into the Emory, Clinch, and Tennessee Rivers, which are world famous for their freshwater biodiversity.

The spill was a hundred times larger than the *Exxon Valdez* oil spill, releasing decades' worth of ash left over from burning coal at the Tennessee Valley Authority's Kingston coal-fired power plant. The sludge was laden with toxic heavy metals known to cause cancer and a host of other serious health problems.

Other than arsenic, lead, cadmium, selenium, and mercury, what else was in that sludge? Trace the coal slurry back to its source, and it turns out it was also made up of former mountaintops, once lush, majestic peaks and ridges from West Virginia and Kentucky, now transformed into a gooey, toxic blight on the land, water, and people of my home state.

The Tennessee tragedy shone a national spotlight on the unfathomable toll that coal takes on communities. In Appalachia, where coal's journey begins, the cost paid by communities plagued by mountaintop removal mining defies description.

But take a closer look at all the stops along the way in the long journey from the mountains to your light switch, and you will see something even more profound—thousands of miraculous examples of hope, courage, and humanity. One of them is Maribeth Meaux, whom I first met at the annual Mountaintop Removal Week in Washington, hosted each year by Appalachian grassroots organizations that oppose MTR and their national partners. She was one of the hundred or so volunteers who had traveled to Washington that spring to join with coalfield residents and tirelessly walk the halls of Congress educating members and their staffs about the great tragedy taking place not far from the nation's capital. They asked them to support the Clean Water Protection Act, which would stop the dumping of mining waste into streams. Most mountaintop removal mining cannot proceed without this practice, because there is no other way to economically dispose of the mining waste.

When Maribeth returned to her home in Chicago, far from the Appalachian coalfields, she immediately started contacting parishes and religious communities in the district of Dan Lipinski, her member of Congress in the U.S. House of Representatives. Maribeth, a retired FBI agent active in the Catholic Church, coordinated workshops, film events, and legislative advocacy opportunities in her diocese, where she provided information about mountaintop removal and the Clean Water Protection Act.

Letters and calls about mountaintop removal began coming into Representative Lipinski's office, including several letters from nuns who were rallied to the cause by Sister Joellen Sbrissa of the Sisters of Saint Joseph in LaGrange, Illinois. Several months later, Representative Lipinski signed on to the bill, followed soon after by numerous members of the Illinois congressional delegation, including Representatives Rahm Emanuel, Bobby Rush, Phil Hare, and Jesse Jackson Jr.

Maribeth did not grow up in a coal camp. She does not have brown water coming out of the tap in her house, and she has not been forced to stand by and watch as her family home place or graveyard was decimated. Yet she is working

And so it has come about that finally in man all moral and spiritual values are expressed in terms of altitude. . . . The Mountain is not merely something externally sublime. It has a great historic and spiritual meaning for us. It stands for us as the ladder of life. Nay more, it is the ladder of the soul, and in a curious way the source of religion. The religion of the Mountain is in reality the religion of joy.

—Jan Christian Smuts

National Guardsmen from a unit recently returned from a year in Iraq on flood relief duty in Delbarton, Mingo County, West Virginia, June 2004. Photo © Builder Levy.

just as hard to end mountaintop removal coal mining as many of the people who live surrounded by it every day. Why?

The reasons Maribeth and thousands like her across the United States have dedicated their time, energy, and lives to the cause of ending mountaintop removal coal mining are important because they demonstrate the three threads that ultimately tie all of us to the devastation taking place in Appalachia—energy use, global warming, and injustice—and point to the need for the nation as a whole to come together and finally address this great American tragedy.

For people across the United States, it comes as a shock to learn that on the other side of their light switch lie the broken mountains and communities of West Virginia, Kentucky, Virginia, and Tennessee. Mountaintop removal coal is fueling the electricity grid across the eastern United States. Whether we live in Washington, Atlanta, Cincinnati, or New York, when millions of us turn on our coffee makers and radios in the morning, we are instantly connected to mountaintop removal and the people of the Appalachian coalfields. If you live in the eastern states, you probably receive some power from mountaintop removal coal. Even if you live in the western part of the nation, and you are not directly connected, your grid is likely fueled by western coal mined by a company like Arch Minerals that also operates mountaintop removal mines in Appalachia.

When I was working for the regional environmental organization Appalachian Voices, we developed an online tool that allows anyone to type in their zip code and see, in Google Earth, actual mountaintop removal mines feeding the grid that powers their home or business. To try it for yourself, go to www.iLoveMountains.org.

Coal-fired power plants are America's single largest source of global warming pollution. The one billion tons of coal we mine and burn in the United States each year end up adding roughly two billion tons of carbon dioxide to the atmosphere. The scientific consensus is clear—these emissions are causing global warming, and it is happening even faster than the most pessimistic scientific models predicted

The United States is also home to 25 percent of the planet's coal reserves, more than any other nation. NASA climate expert James Hansen tells us that if we burn even a significant fraction of these coal reserves, it will be impossible to avoid catastrophic climate change.

Ultimately, then, global warming starts in the Appalachian coalfields, in communities like Whitesville, Hazard, and Wise. Even if we stopped burning coal altogether in this country, U.S. coal exports have started to rise dramatically. As far as global warming is concerned, once we have mined the coal, it does not matter if it's burned in West Virginia or Western Europe—the effect on the climate is the same.

This means that the connection from mountaintop removal continues well beyond your light switch, to the California home owner who has just lost her home in an unseasonable, drought-induced wildfire, and to the Native American living in an Arctic village who has had to relocate owing to melting permafrost and rising waters. The escalating climate crisis is connecting more and more people, in increasingly far-flung regions of the world, back to mountaintop removal and the coalfields of Appalachia.

Mountaintop removal is not just a tragedy for those forced to live with coal dust and rock dust that shower down on

Beltline Lights

All the towns die in spite of us.
The coal pours out and out again
like forty years ago and forty before
and the mountains, such a large
 place,
holding so much back from us.

The mine. Such a small place. Like
constellations in the morning sky the
beltline lights shape our mythologies.

—Jason Frye

their communities, blasting that cracks the foundations of their houses, and deadly floods that rip through their once-peaceful backyards. It is not just a tragedy for our climate. Ultimately, the fact that it continues unchecked is a tragedy for our values and our democracy.

These are the mountains where our ancestors helped forge American democracy. These are the mother mountains that, like Noah's Ark, served as a refuge for countless species during ice ages, allowing plants and animals to survive and repopulate this great continent. These mountains—home to bluegrass, moonshine, and many more fine American traditions—were handed down to us as our birthright. We are now in the process, in a few short decades, of destroying this heritage for all future generations of Americans. Once these mountains are gone, they are truly gone forever.

In an era when hope and possibility have made a welcome return to the political stage, we have the opportunity to finally solve these chronic problems. By simply enforcing environmental laws already on the books, and by passing simple legislation like the Clean Water Protection Act that would close legal loopholes created by the Bush administration and restore the original intent of the Clean Water Act, we can return the rule of law to Appalachia.

We can also develop alternative forms of energy that will provide jobs with a future for the people of Appalachia. In West Virginia, locals in the Coal River Valley are organizing to build a wind farm on the iconic Coal River Mountain, as an alternative to a proposed 6,000-acre mountaintop removal mine. A 2008 study found that this wind farm would actually bring greater economic benefits to the community than the mountaintop removal mine.

Solutions like the Coal River Mountain wind project offer one possible vision and direction for the decades ahead. Down another road lie the betrayed and plundered communities of Appalachia, laid to waste by decades of coal mining and left with nothing but broken promises.

Ultimately, the Tennessee River tragedy was another reminder of the urgent need to develop truly clean, renewable

Residents of Rutherford Hollow in North Matewan, Mingo County, West Virginia, begin rebuilding their community after devastating floods. Photo © Builder Levy.

forms of energy. If we do not change course in our energy policy, those devastating reminders will keep coming.

Thankfully, we can choose a different path. This is the United States of America, where we know how to use innovation and ingenuity to build a brighter future. We put a man on the moon, and we decoded the human genome. Surely we can find better ways to turn on the lights than blowing up some of the oldest mountains in the world. Thousands of people across America, including Maribeth Meaux, have learned about our connection to mountaintop removal and are working together with the people of the coalfields to build that brighter future.

Yellowroot Mountain

Ann Pancake

Mark Cullum at an abandoned tipple near Hickory, Washington County, Pennsylvania, 1973. Photo © Builder Levy.

WHAT I SAW PUNCHED MY chest. Knocked me back on my heels. At first I saw it only as shades of dead and gray, but I pushed my eyes harder, I let come in the hurt, and then it focused into a cratered-out plain. Whole top of Yellowroot amputated by blast, and that dragline hacking into the flat part left. Monster shovel clawed the dirt and you felt it in your arm, your leg, your belly, and how lucky Grandma died, I thought. I thought that then. And past where Yellowroot had been, miles of mountain stumps, limping all the way over to what used to be horizon, and what would you call it now? The ass-end of the world. *Moonscape,* that's what many said after they'd seen it, but I saw right away this was something different. Airiness emptying me. Because a moonscape was still something made by God and this was not, this was the moon upside down. A flake of the moon's surface fallen to earth, and in that fall, it had kept its color, nickel and beige, kept its craters, its cracks. But then it landed not up, but moonside down.

My tongue moved in my mouth. It had lost all water, tasting what I saw. Then I realized I had my knee and one hand in that weird brittle grass, and I jerked my hand to my stomach and got myself up quick.

Deer won't even eat that grass. Now you know if deer won't eat it. . . . We'd come out on this raised embankment at the very edge of the mine, and I got back my balance, but the wind across that dead flat stirred the gas in my hair. Then I noticed Corey standing a few feet below me like he'd been freezetagged, his fists on his hips Jimmy Make–style, that stupid rag fluttering. There you go, Corey. There you go. *You kids won't have nothing but to clean up their mess.* I hardened my face again and scanned the killed ground until I got to where I thought the Yellowroot Creek valley fill should be. Thing was, you couldn't tell anything about size or distance up here, because, I realized right then, this was nothing. And you cannot measure nothing. What I could tell, because Cherryboy was not nothing yet, was how close they were getting to it, creeping viselike around the head of Yellowroot Hollow.

I tightened my chest and turned away. Walked down the spine of the bank a piece. A haul truck passed under us, machinery jarring in my teeth, and more blocks inside me, tumbling down. Tumbling. Now I had my back to Cherryboy. I was just staring at where Yellowroot wasn't anymore. Then I was remembering what Yellowroot had been. Yellowroot, shaped like a rabbit with its ears laid back, Grandma showed me that. It took its name from goldenseal, she said, that was the real name of yellowroot. *Yellowroot's the country name,* Grandma said. *Now yellowroot's what you use for a sore throat, gargle that, nothing better for it. Turn your mouth yellow, your throat yellow, too. Everything in these woods was put here for a reason.* Then I was hearing something else. Corey. I'd nearly forgotten about him, but it was Corey making a noise. Making a motor noise in his mouth, soft, I don't think he even knew he was doing it out loud. And then I knew Corey had learned nothing at all.

My arms flooded with wanting to knock him down, fling him off the bank, and rub his face in dead dirt. I wanted to hear him yelp and cry. But truth was, deep down I'd known all along Corey couldn't understand. I'd just had to try, but, no, that was a lie, too, why I'd really brought him. . . . The real reason I'd brought him was I was scared to see it first time by myself. And I knew I had to see it before I

An Ontological Postcard from Cumberland Falls

One thing translates into another.
Rotting shingles pried off the roof
Raise mountains at the landfill.
Windfalls from the front yard
(these rents in the maples)
Plug the gullies of our eroded
  slopes—
Those contours, this valley, in turn
Inscribed by migrating streams,
The ample ghosts of fickle water
That make orphans of the hills.
Chafed by those currents,
However muddied, however deep,
We melt, one particle at a time.
Now we are water, now silt.

—Richard Taylor

Thousands of acres of native forest near Mud River, West Virginia, have been destroyed in the course of mountaintop removal mining. Photo © Giles Ashford.

could decide. Of course Corey did not understand, and Dane understood only in a way before word, before memory, and what did Jimmy Make understand?

Understood that move-the-mountain draw, the power, the suck, the tempt. Understood anyway the wrongness of it all. Understood he could not stop it. Understood he had to go. Did he understand how Lace would choose? How I would? Would he understand why? That's just how he is, I wanted to say to her. Why can't you see that's just how he is? Go on and love him anyway. And I remembered the sleepy smell. The ginger in how he held me little, him my father and just a little older than I was now. I remembered how he'd never left, not through all those years, not even when she wouldn't marry him, not even afterwards when she did and things got worse. He never left.

The memory picture of Yellowroot faded fast. And the feeling it left behind scared me worse than the mine site did. Because what I was feeling again was nothing. The distance between me and the land had set in, complete, but this time, I didn't even have any want in me to cross it. Nothing. Just like you couldn't measure the site because it was nothing, you couldn't feel for it either, because there was nothing to feel for. Nothing stirs nothing. And it came to me for the first time: was it worse to lose the mountain or to lose the feeling that you had for it?

I still stood with Cherryboy at my back. I couldn't see Cherryboy, but I could feel it behind me the way you can feel an animal hiding close by in the woods. How Uncle Mogey always said that an animal throws off itself a hum felt not by your five senses, but by something else you carry around you. Cherryboy I could still feel like that.

This is an excerpt from the novel Strange as This Weather Has Been, *by Ann Pancake, copyright © 2007 by Ann Pancake, reprinted by permission of Counterpoint.*

I Lift My Eyes
to the Hills

John S. Rausch

*A mountaintop removal opera-
tion in Eastern Kentucky. Photo
courtesy of Mountaintop Removal
Road Show.*

BEGINNING IN 2000, MCROBERTS, A COAL TOWN nestled in the lush mountains of Eastern Kentucky, experienced five major floods in eighteen months. The mountains around the town, severely strip-mined, could scarcely hold back the water of a heavy downpour.

When we from the religious community—a Catholic sister, dedicated laypeople with Kentuckians for the Commonwealth, a Baptist minister, and I, a Catholic priest—heard about the distress of the people, we responded. We conducted a public prayer in 2002 for the restoration of creation on a mountain overlooking McRoberts. Sixty people assembled to pray, hear scripture, and sing a hymn on a moonscape devoid of vegetation. I read a letter written by the four Catholic bishops of Kentucky that said, in part, "That your Prayer on a Mountain takes place on December 10, International Human Rights Day, symbolically connects the respect for the earth with the protection of our human community."

With the exception of Saint Francis of Assisi, Jonathan Edwards, and a handful of mystics, the church has only gradually recognized the importance of creation. People of faith easily respond to the plight of people whose towns flood, chimneys crack, or drinking water turns orange, because these encroachments of industry directly violate standards of justice against people. The prophets of the Hebrew scriptures railed against injustice, and the Gospels clearly favor the downtrodden.

Over time, however, the church's awareness evolved from a strictly anthropocentric view of salvation to one that included the entire web of life. In 1975 the Catholic bishops of Appalachia wrote a pastoral letter, "This Land Is Home to Me," in which they emphasized the powerlessness of the people and the extensive absentee ownership of the land and minerals by corporations. A subtheme highlighted the erosion of the social and natural ecology.

The sheer ugliness of the destruction of the mountains by strip mining assaulted the spirit. The ever-expanding reach of the blasting and bulldozers, the abandoned high walls, and the transformation of the terrain screamed "greed," whereas we people of faith knew that only moderation and balance could serve the common good.

Turning to scripture, we knew God owned the world, as it says in Psalm 24:1, "The earth is the Lord's." We also knew that, at the conclusion of creating, God was pleased with creation. God pronounced all creation "very good" (Gen. 1:31)—God did not say creation was just "useful." Thus, creation cannot be seen in simply utilitarian terms—it has, rather, intrinsic worth.

The most challenging text came from Genesis 1:26–28, when God said to humanity: "Have dominion over the fish of the sea, the birds of the air, and all the living things that move on the earth." Many have interpreted that passage as giving humanity total freedom in controlling creation. A more critical examination of the text, however, starts with God's image in each person: "God created man in his image; in the divine image he created him; male and female he created them" (Gen. 1:27). According to the respected Old Testament scholar Walter Brueggemann, a king in the ancient Near East customarily placed statues of himself to assert his sovereignty where he could not be present. Given this custom, humanity becomes the emblem of God throughout creation. As Brueggemann writes, "The image of God in the human person is a mandate of power and responsibility. But it is

Does God offend thee? One must ask,
Another impetus cannot be seen,
To rationalize tearing off the mountaintops
To get at the coal beneath.

Love thy neighbor as thyself
Has long been the Christian way,
Many's the time the other cheek has been turned,
To keep the peace for another day.

As injustice continues throughout this land,
The laws decree we have no say,
Our cheeks are left with nowhere to turn
When the mountains are blasted away. . . .

The greedy acts of man upon the land
At all costs must be stopped,
So be not offended by the power of God
When you glance at a mountaintop.

—Matthew Burns, from
"Does God Offend Thee?"

power exercised as God exercises power." Because God is pleased and proud of creation, human "dominion" is better understood as "responsibility" or "stewardship."

Later, in Genesis 2:15, humanity is placed in the garden "to cultivate and care for it." Humanity thus has a vocation to become a co-gardener with God, that is, to share in God's work of overseeing creation.

Five years after the Prayer on a Mountain, twenty-two representatives from various Christian denominations and the Baha'i faith participated in the Mountaintop Removal Tour for Interfaith Leaders. They convened in Eastern Kentucky to see mountaintop removal (MTR) in a flyover and hear about its effects from the testimony of local people. Afterward, participants used words like "idolatry," "injustice," and "greed"—all biblical terms—to describe mountaintop removal At the conclusion of the tour, the group issued a statement based on their common faith, promising to take four actions:

> First, each of us will examine our own wasteful and extravagant lifestyle that causes the destruction of the mountains by demanding cheap energy from coal.
> Second, we will insert MTR into the growing conversation about global climate change.
> Third, we pledge voice and vote against mountaintop removal.
> Fourth, as people of faith we will make this a spiritual issue in our own lives and invite the members of our faith communities to do likewise.

The statement moved from a personal examination of lifestyle to a sharing of the common good with community. It evolved from personal wastefulness to a shared spirituality with others. For the participants, faith played an intricate role in interpreting MTR as a practice in the community and a threat to spiritual fidelity.

Mountains are prominent at key moments in the Jewish and Christian traditions. Moses receives the Ten Commandments on Mount Sinai, and Jesus ascends a mountain to teach the Beatitudes. How many times people encounter God on a mountaintop; yet the forces of commerce and economics

Dogwood blooms in central Appalachia. Photo © John Mullins.

A sign in Williamson, Mingo County, West Virginia; in the background are loaded coal cars, 1971. Photo © Builder Levy.

reduce mountains to mere inputs to production, while community and the spirit pay the price.

At the conclusion of the Prayer on a Mountain in 2002, I gave everyone a handful of wildflower seeds to take back the mountain. The wind on that overcast day blew chill, but for fifteen minutes a reverent hush came over the folks as they intentionally planted seeds in out-of-the-way crannies and on the edge of a ledge. People knew intuitively how symbolic the gesture was. Catherine Odum, a senior and lifelong resident of McRoberts, moved slowly over the ground, finding the appropriate spot for the few seeds she wanted to plant. As she stooped over in a spirit of regeneration, she said, "I'm sowing my community back."

Part Three

THE VOICES OF THE PEOPLE

In the past decade, mountaintop removal mining has infiltrated more land and more communities—with flooding, contaminated water, and residents forced from their homes as MTR gobbled up more and more land. Through it all, the people have fought back. Numerous lawsuits have been won at the federal level, only to be overturned on appeal. But as more coalfield residents speak out, as more cases are contested, and as national media coverage expands, government at every level is being compelled to take notice. No longer is MTR a hidden tragedy.

In this part, we have gathered the impassioned personal testimonies of residents from the coalfields of Kentucky, West Virginia, Virginia, and Tennessee, who have risked their lives and reputations to stand up for what they believe in and make a difference. Though they are often dubbed "environmental extremists" by the industry and its supporters, most of those involved in the anti-MTR movement are community activists, working to save their land and homes—in effect, accidental environmentalists. There is no personal gain in standing up to the coal industry; it is a very hazardous stance, often literally.

Many of these voices are those of strong Appalachian women who are fighting to protect their children and their creeks. They include Goldman Prize winners Maria Gunnoe

Maria Gunnoe on her land. Photo © Vivian Stockman; courtesy of Ohio Valley Environmental Coalition.

Page 176: On I Love Mountains Day in February 2009, more than a thousand activists ascended the steps of the Kentucky state capitol to demand an end to mountaintop removal mining. Photo © Richard X. Moore.

and Julia "Judy" Bonds, Grammy-winning singer Kathy Mattea, wind power champion Lorelei Scarbro, and the "Dustbusters," Mary Miller and Pauline Canterberry, retirees forced into activism when they discovered their golden years were being buried in coal dust. Here, too, are the haunting statements of members of Kentuckians for the Commonwealth, citizens who have banded together around the common goal of bringing a halt to the devastation. Dave Cooper recalls his efforts to create a slide show about MTR impacts and his travels with coalfield residents showing it to people around the country. And Larry Gibson powerfully describes his fight to save his family's ancestral land and graveyard on Kayford Mountain from obliteration.

These testimonies contain much pain, but they are not the words of broken people. Rather, they portray individuals who clearly recognize the root cause of their problems and are putting themselves on the line for what's right. They come from people who refuse to be silenced regardless of stereotypes about class and education, people who are using the most powerful thing they have to fight back: their stories.

This Land Will Never Be for Sale

Larry Gibson

My NAME IS LARRY GIBSON. This land here on Kayford Mountain has been in my family for over 220 years and had never been surveyed by anybody in the family. I really didn't start having violence until I surveyed my own land. I found that it had always been surveyed on behalf of the oil company, a utility company, a coal company, but never on behalf of the people, my own family. I started forcing the companies back on the boundaries where they was supposed to be and that's when the violence started.

Larry Gibson at his family's cemetery on Kayford Mountain, West Virginia. Photo © Mark Schmerling.

The first few years, I couldn't even get the law to come up there because my land sits in three counties. Then when I got to be friends with [former West Virginia congressman] Ken Hechler, only then did I start getting support from the local officials. The police, not the state troopers. But up there, it's in the wilderness, sits by itself. Most times when things happen, ain't nobody can help anyhow. It's done and over with before anybody can even be told about it, much less get ready for it.

There's people that's angry about what happens. But you got to be not only angry, you got to be willing to do something, you know? I been fighting for my place for eighteen years now. You can't go into a situation where people are gathering for the first time and saying "We've had 118 acts of violence," yet the people are just now beginning to get involved. You can't do that. You got to tell people something positive, but

A blast goes off at Kayford Mountain. Photo © Mark Schmerling.

you can't make it easy and tell them that nothing's gonna happen to them because there's always the potential.

That [coal company] fellow I met with back in '92 told me my land was worth a million dollars an acre to the coal company then. And he turns around and offers $140,000 for the whole thing. You know, it was like we didn't know the difference! He was talking to us like they were really gonna do us a favor. "We're gonna help y'all out, make a generous offer to you." And he'd just told me it was worth over a million dollars.

When he said that, I said, "The land'll never be for sale. You can have my right arm, but you'll never get the land."

So he said, "Well, you know, you're the island, and we are the ocean. You set in the middle of 187,000 acres of coal company land. You're the only thing we don't own between here and the Virginia border." I had my family members—seven of us—there for that meeting and it just didn't make no sense.

That man said, "We don't give a damn about the people up the holler. All we want is the coal and that's it."

And up to this point, they've proved their point. They don't care about the people.

The most endangered species we have in West Virginia, besides our own people that's being displaced out of the mountains and the hollers, is the deep miners. People say, "Why don't they say something?" Well, who they gonna say it to? The United Mine Workers is no longer a viable union, all they do is take money from people. They don't do anything for the people. Who you gonna go to? Up my holler when I was a boy, we had 25,000 miners. There was nothing that went out of that holler without the union's control. And if you worked for a scab outfit, you didn't tell anybody. Now there's nothing that goes out my holler that's not under company control, and if you work for a union you don't tell anybody. I see a day when the violence is gonna come back like it did on the Blair Mountain battle.

I've been through the experience of being shot at a numerous amount of times because of my stand on what I believe in. People say, "Why don't you just sell?" They've offered me seven times the amount of acreage as what I've got for my place. But the land they offered me—my people never walked on it. It's been turned over. You can't put anything on it, can't grow anything on it.

Recently I was told that we should start working with the union again. Well, it was a union site on the Princess Beverly mine right beside of me. The violence didn't start toward me heavily until [UMWA president] Cecil Roberts endorsed mountaintop removal—that was in 1999—and talked about how the attacks on coal mining by environmentalists were like the Japanese attacking Pearl Harbor.

So that's when the violence started. That's when it really escalated. I was having trouble before, but I didn't really know what I was going into.

We lost about eighty, well, close to a hundred headstones in the family cemetery, because every time the coal company would blast, they'd blast debris over into the cemetery.

I'm sitting on the bank of the Big
 Coal River
Thinking about why you left today
Talking out loud like the river can
 hear me
But the old Big Coal has nothing
 to say

It just seems in a hurry to find
 tomorrow
Somewhere yonder that's cool and
 green
Running from dark and troublesome
 waters
Till it's feeling free and it's running
 clean . . .

But I think somehow it's all
 connected
You and me and this river of time
The first sweet kiss, the loving and
 leaving
And we'll never outrun the ties
 that bind

We're just all in a hurry to find
 tomorrow
Somewhere yonder that's cool
 and green
Running from dark and troublesome
 waters
Till we're feeling free and we're
 running clean

—Billy Edd Wheeler and Johnny
 Staats, from "Big Coal River"

Larry Gibson is comforted by former West Virginia congressman Ken Hechler at Kayford Mountain. Photo © Mark Schmerling.

It would bust some of the headstones, turn some of them over. Then they'd send a crew of men over to clean them up. And then the old sandstone headstones that had carving on them, we caught them actually throwing them away, destroying them as well. And the simple reason behind that was to try to prove that we didn't have as many graves there on the ground as we had. And so if they could reclaim some of the grave sites, well, the mountain had thirty-nine seams of coal. There's a lot of wealth underneath there.

But the thing is, that cemetery has been undermined now by nine different companies we have names to, and six others that we don't, over the last 125 years. I'm just doing this because it's my right to fight for the resting place of my people, but more than likely the people are not even there anymore. And you walk through my cemetery, you can actually see where the underground mine is because the graves are dropping. We now have mine cracks developing and a big hole developing. And on the other family cemetery across the ridge we have mine cracks right through the graves that's three and four feet wide, that you can see down in and there's no casket, no body—all that's left is a headstone.

I had some people come to see me a while back. They come from Israel. And all the problems they're having in Israel right now, with the bombing and everything, and they turned and looked at me and said they feel sorry for me. And these people said, "You mean the coal company doesn't have any respect for the cemetery?" I said, "The coal company don't have respect for the living, much less the dead."

When I was a kid, our place was like a wonderland. People used to make fun of me and say I was my father's retarded son—they'd call me that, you know? But one of the things they couldn't understand was that I was always able to get close to the wild animals. I'd go out in the woods and come home with a bobcat or a squirrel or a coon. One time I was helping my dad fix a swing, hang a swing, and I had my bib overalls on. I was setting there and squirming and bouncing around. My dad asked in a kind of angry way what I was doing, and a frog jumped out of my pocket.

We never had toys. But it was a wonderland, you know? You could walk through the forest. You could hear the animals. The woods like to talk to you. You could feel a part of Mother Nature. In other words, everywhere you looked there was life. Now you put me on the same ground where I walked, and the only thing you can feel is the vibration of dynamite or heavy machinery. No life, just dust.

How was it when I was a kid? I'll put it to you this way—when they took me to Cleveland, that's the first time that I ever knew I was poor. They told me I was poor. Me? I thought I was the richest person in the world. I didn't want for anything. I'd get out in the woods, and on my way, if I was hungry I'd pick my apples. I had a pocket knife I always carried so I'd cut cucumbers up in somebody's garden. Or I'd get chased out of somebody's apple tree. I'd get berries along the way. Pawpaws. I loved pawpaws. And gooseberries.

All these things are no longer there. Now they're forcing wild boar into my area, and deer into my area, and there wasn't any kind of animal like that when I was a kid. Mostly all small game and an occasional bear. Every other year or so we'd see a bear. Now they're forcing the bears in on me. A bear needs fifty acres to feed on and now there's nothing for them.

In my childhood, I had a pigeon. I'd come out of my house and no matter where I went, he was either flying over my head or setting on my shoulder. One time I had a hawk. I named him Fred. For the longest time he was around, then all of a sudden one day he didn't show up. I had a bobcat, and I had a three-legged fox that got caught in a trap. I kept it until it got healed and then it wouldn't leave. I wouldn't trade my childhood for all the fancy fire trucks in the world that the other kids had. Nor toys.

It was a hard way, but it didn't seem so hard because it's the only way we knew. What would you walk four or five miles to school for? Because that's the only thing you knew. Now you can't get a kid to go to the front door to catch the bus. I didn't see a TV till I was thirteen. Didn't talk on a phone till I was fourteen. Now, when my kids was growing up, I'd

Ripening blackberries. Photo © iStockphoto.com/Diana Lundin.

From the rise, he looks out over his place. This is it. This is everything there is in the world—it contains everything there is to know or possess, yet everywhere people are knocking their brains out trying to find something different, something better . . . but what he has here is the main thing there is—just the way things grow and die, the way the sun comes up and goes down every day. These are the facts of life. They are so simple, they are almost impossible to grasp.

—*Bobbie Ann Mason*

threaten to take the TV off them. "How we gonna make it for a whole month without a TV, Dad?" they'd say. That's the problem today, we ain't one with the earth no more.

I don't know what the answer is as far as what's happening. Destroying all the environment, all the streams. When I was a kid, down at the bottom of the mountain, I could get crawdads, pick them up out of the water with my toes. Now nothing lives in the water. Nothing lives on the land. What they've done is irreversible. You can't bring it back.

I was asked this question when I was in Tennessee. A lady said, "We've been reading where you've been fighting for eighteen years. We'd like to know what keeps you going." I just told her I was right. You know, if you're right, you're right. There's no other answer. There's one thing I was taught at a very young age, as a boy living in the coalfields. We didn't know the United States president, but we knew the United Mine Workers' president. In other words, we was organized as young people. And that's the way I grew up. Organized. You learn to fight back and you fight back. You have to fight back.

That's the way it was, and that's the way it is for me today. And that's the way I try to reach out to people, to show them. There is a saying I've lived by all my life, "If you don't stand for something, you'll fall for anything." That's not an original statement, somebody else came up with it. But the thing is, it's true.

People need to grab a hold of what they've got, or once the coal company gets through there'll be nothing left. This ritual of taking our men to mine for coal—there's not one life worth losing for coal. We've lost thousands of men to black lung and cave-ins alike. We lose men every year. And this disaster we just had [at the Sago mine], now people are looking at it. Now people are passing laws. Every time something happens like the Buffalo Creek disaster they pass laws. But then they twist the laws and they still break the laws. Every law that's ever been written has been written in a coal miner's blood.

What I want to say now at the end of this is to encourage people to stand up against oppression and speak for theirself.

Johnny Crabtree (left) and Jim Ed Whitt preaching, Sprigg, Mingo County, West Virginia, 1970. The deep religious roots of most long-settled Appalachian families underlie the values of the movement opposing mountaintop removal. Photo © Builder Levy.

Because if they're waiting for the people that's doing it to them to speak for them, it's never gonna happen. They're gonna keep taking and taking and taking. Folks have to get in their head that the people that's doing it to them don't care about them. They have to care about theirself. They have to take control of their own destiny. Whether it's a coal company or a chemical company or what, they're not gonna do it for the people. The people have to do it for theirself.

<hr style="width:20%" />

This essay is adapted from a piece that originally appeared in Like Walking onto Another Planet, *by the Ohio Valley Environmental Coalition.*

An Open Letter

Bo Webb

A cardinal, West Virginia's state bird, on a fence post in the southern part of the state. Photo © Giles Ashford.

Dᴇᴀʀ Sᴇɴᴀᴛᴏʀ Bʏʀᴅ,

I write you today as a grandfather, and as a deep admirer of your inimitable contribution to our beloved state of West Virginia. As the son of a coal miner, I will always value your work to ensure economic investment and proper safety in our coalfields.

Soon, as you know, as the colorful peepers of red bush and the wake robins pull from the clinch of winter, I will take my granddaughter's hand and roam our Clay Branch hollows in search of ramps. This has been a 150-year tradition in my family in the Coal River Mountain range, as I am sure it was for your family along Wolf Creek.

This year, though, instead of that pungent smell of wild ramps and the blossoms of spring, my granddaughter will be exposed to the sickening haze of ammonium nitrate and diesel oil, and the aftershower of silica dust that blankets our hollow like a plague. Our ancestral mountain in the Peachtree community is being destroyed for a mountaintop removal operation.

In your wonderful book *Letter to a New President: Commonsense Lessons for Our Next Leader,* you wrote that we should never turn our backs on the lessons of our coal-mining fathers. My father, like others in my family, first started working in the mines at age eleven. But it is the grave of my

Uncle Clyde Williams, who died in the mine at Leevale here on Coal River Mountain at age seventeen, that also hovers in my mind as I walk these hills, gather herbs and berries, and hunt and fish with my grandchildren.

I want my children and grandchildren to have the right to dream and flourish as great contributors to our state in West Virginia. I don't want them to feel compelled to leave our state to look for employment or to realize their dreams. I want them to know that the rule of law protects them, their families, and our mountains.

You, more than any other person in our state, understand this. When you went to Washington, D.C., for the first time to represent West Virginia, more than 130,000 union coal miners proudly toted their lunch pails and went to their jobs in the underground mines in our state. And you, as our voice in Washington, proudly made sure their safety and security were priorities to the rest of the country. Today, only 20,000 West Virginia coal miners make up those ranks. In many respects, strip mining and mountaintop removal operations have robbed my generation and my children of a chance to maintain our great Appalachian heritage, our beloved mountains and vibrant streams, and, above all, any diverse economic development in our community.

In responding to the recent EPA decision to scrutinize mountaintop removal permits more closely, you wrote: "Every job in West Virginia matters. Everyone involved must act swiftly in concert and cooperation to remedy any problems that threaten coal jobs and the people who live in the local communities where coal is mined."

Senator Byrd, as a grandfather, I write to you: If our grandchildren are going to have any jobs and future at all in West Virginia, we must get beyond the stranglehold of mountaintop removal coal operations and find a way to bring new jobs and life to our mountain communities.

This could be your greatest legacy, among many, Senator Byrd. Your public role in cosponsoring the Appalachian Mountain Restoration Act (S. 696), to defend the health and safety of our communities and put an end to mountaintop

This is where our forefathers came and hewed the forest and carved out a living in the rivers and the mountains. Here, where the mountains meet the sky, the men and women who come from these mountains are so much like the mountains.

—Senator Robert C. Byrd,
from "A West Virginia Life"

Delisia Clark (left) and Delina Brooks, Tom Biggs Hollow in McRoberts, Letcher County, Kentucky. Photo © Builder Levy.

removal and its destruction of our local economies, would place our state back on track for responsible mining, more coal-mining employment, and would be a step toward a diversified economy that includes loans and investment in manufacturing renewable energy products, such as wind turbine and solar panels, and high-technology operations.

In your powerful *Letter to a New President*, you wrote: "What determines the quality of American democracy is the use we make of our power. We have institutions in place to help this country avoid the misuse of our power. Those institutions are Congress, the courts and public opinion. The more we cut off true debate and the exchange of ideas, and let those in power use emotion, misdirection and the manipulation of truth to whip the nation into action, the more likely we are to make dangerous mistakes in how we use our power. A representative democracy only works when the people are involved. We need them."

We need you now more than ever, Senator Byrd, to bring new jobs, and restore a new sense of democracy to the coalfields of West Virginia.

———⟨◆⟩———

Bo Webb's open letter appeared in the Charleston (WV) Gazette *on April 4, 2009, and was widely circulated on various Web sites. As of June 2009, he had not received any response from Senator Byrd.*

Above: *Moonrise over Seneca Rocks, a massive monolith of Tuscarora sandstone in the Monongahela National Forest, Pendleton County, West Virginia.* **Left:** *Ferns in spring, Pocahontas County, West Virginia. Both photos © Jim Clark.*

Below: *Red-spotted newt (eft stage), Falls of Hills Creek Scenic Area, Pocahontas County, West Virginia.* *Bottom:* *A black bear at Cranberry Glades Botanical Area, Monongahela National Forest, West Virginia.* *Right:* *Blackwater River in autumn, Blackwater Falls State Park—a prime scenic attraction in Tucker County, West Virginia. All three photos © Jim Clark.*

Left: A procession of huge coal trucks is dwarfed by the mammoth scale of just a portion of the MTR site at Kayford Mountain, West Virginia. Photo © Mark Schmerling. *Above:* A crane loads coal barges on the Kanawha River, West Virginia; industrial plants line the far shore. Photo © Giles Ashford.

Opposite: Local resident Owen Stout (left) and retired underground miner Chuck Nelson (right) stand in a stream polluted by acid mine drainage, near the head of Cabin Creek, Kanawha County, West Virginia. Photo © Mark Schmerling. Above: Julia "Judy" Bonds, codirector of Coal River Mountain Watch, outside the organization's headquarters. Photo © Mark Schmerling. Left: Larry Gibson is the founder of Keepers of the Mountain Foundation. Photo © Jo Syz.

Above: A 75-ton Caterpillar D10 bulldozer dismantles the hills and ridges of Kayford Mountain. *Right:* A tiny conifer forces its way through an expanse of graded overburden from a mountaintop removal site near Ruth, West Virginia. Both photos © Giles Ashford.

The Mountaintop Removal Road Show

Dave Cooper

HOW DO YOU ELEVATE A regional issue like mountaintop removal mining into an issue of national concern? How do you educate Americans about the source of their electricity? How do you get people all over America talking about mountaintop removal, and writing letters to their congressional representatives? These were questions that we debated during Friends of the Mountains coalition meetings at the Charleston Unitarian Universalist Church in the fall of 2002. We knew that we had an incredibly powerful and compelling issue, we just didn't know how to build a nationwide campaign against mountaintop removal.

In a coalfield community organizer's dream, the mountain people would do it all. We would teach and inspire our neighbors with quotes from Gandhi and Dr. King. Then, Appalachians would rise up, and 10,000 angry citizens of the coalfields would march on the state capitol and demand an end to the abusive coal-mining practices that devalue their homes and destroy their communities. But sadly, we knew this was unlikely to happen. With a history of oppression and mistreatment, many Appalachians do not even recognize that they are being exploited.

We decided that a good strategy was to take the story of mountaintop removal on the road to the people of America. We would show America who is paying the real price for our

A banner blocks access to a rally for the mountains in Ansted, Fayette County, West Virginia. Photo © Vivian Stockman.

Dave Cooper presents his Mountaintop Removal Road Show program. Photo © Steve Charles; courtesy of Mountaintop Removal Road Show.

nation's electricity. And we would tell them that Appalachia is not going to be a sacrifice zone for cheap energy any longer.

Our initial model for the road show concept was the successful campaign to stop oil drilling in the Arctic National Wildlife Refuge (ANWR). Lenny Kohm, campaign director of Appalachian Voices in Boone, North Carolina, and a member of the Friends of the Mountains coalition, had traveled with the Gwich'in natives of Canada for fifteen years and presented a beautiful slide show on ANWR to thousands of audiences. We tried to persuade Lenny to start up the Mountaintop Removal Road Show, but he was worn out from too many years of travel on the ANWR issue.

In the summer of 2003, I found myself a suddenly unemployed coalfield organizer with a burning interest in the mountaintop removal issue. I still maintained a strong desire to help coalfield residents like Larry Gibson and all of the folks on Coal River. So I volunteered to do some initial road show presentations until the well-funded grassroots groups that had full-time staff and money could take over and do it properly.

In July 2003, with $3,000 in seed money from the Ohio Valley Environmental Coalition, I set out with my Canon AE-1 camera to try to document the impacts of mountaintop removal on the people of the coalfields. I didn't own a laptop computer, and digital projectors at that time cost a whopping $3,500, so I decided to make an old-fashioned Kodak Carousel slide show. I found a used $75 projector for sale in St. Louis and drove six hours from my home in Lexington to pick it up. It was twenty years old, but had only been used a few times. The guy who sold it to me threw in a projector screen for no extra cost. I was off to a good start.

With the idea that my target audience for the road show presentation would be a Rotary Club luncheon somewhere in Iowa, I wanted to first establish a sense of place in my slide show, and to dispel some of the negative impressions that most Americans have about the residents of Appalachia. I photographed people who did not fit the Appalachian stereotype so often associated with the region. I drove aimlessly for days and days through McDowell, Mingo, and Wyoming

Mountaintop removal site near Whitesburg, Kentucky. Photo courtesy of Mountaintop Removal Road Show.

Counties in West Virginia. I slept in a sleeping bag in the back of my little red Saturn in vacant lots behind churches and convenience stores. If I saw someone picking blackberries along the road, I'd stop the car and ask if I could take their picture. I drove up countless mountain gravel roads to get shots of mining. I hiked up mountains. I climbed over gates marked No Trespassing. I walked on unstable valley fills. With bare feet, I stood in the middle of a stream that ran bright orange with acid mine drainage.

I am trained as a mechanical engineer and had never taken a photography class, nor did I even like public speaking. But I got a few good breaks along the way. Steve Maslowski and Chuck Wyrostock, both professional photographers, generously donated some great wildlife slides. Other breaks for my documentation were through some unfortunate circumstances in the coalfields. I was stranded in a flash flood in Wyoming County for several hours and captured some good

A coal slurry impoundment in Middlesboro, Kentucky. Photo courtesy of Mountaintop Removal Road Show.

flood shots. I managed to take some incredible photographs during the Martin County, Kentucky, sludge spill disaster in 2000. A protest against mountaintop removal in downtown Lexington, Kentucky, offered some great photo opportunities as well. The photographs that I managed to take captured a wide variety of aspects of daily life in the coalfields.

After a few weeks of taking photographs, I went home and wrote a script. I had never tried to put together a pre-sentation like this before in my life. I found an old cassette tape with some birdcalls, and a tape called *Three Songs for the Mountains,* with Mary Anne and Than Hitt singing "Green Rolling Hills." Using my home stereo and a cheap Radio Shack microphone that I attached to a door with a rubber band, I stood in my living room and recorded a somewhat coherent sound track on a cassette. After showing my draft presenta-tion to staffers at Coal River Mountain Watch, Appalachian Voices, and Kentuckians for the Commonwealth, I made a few changes. Then I called my friend Judy Vogel-Essex of Cincinnati, who had done some professional voice-over work. She agreed to record my script for free as a personal favor. We rented a recording studio in northern Kentucky and cut a professional CD featuring Appalachian music—including

Elaine Purkey's powerful song "Keepers of the Mountains"—and Judy's silky-smooth voice narrating the slide show.

It was about this time that financial anxiety arose. The recording session had been expensive, plus the costs for the many rolls of film and development. I needed to buy a good sound system for the presentation. At first, I used a boom box that I found on the curb. Plus, gas prices were eating me up. I had no income, and no idea how I was going to be able to cover my expenses on this road show. Lenny Kohm said that his ANWR road show budget had been about $2,000 per week. My entire budget was $2,000! I remember being surprised the first time a college offered me a speaking honorarium.

In the early 2000s, staff at various grassroots groups insisted that I speak only in certain targeted congressional districts: southern and eastern Illinois and Cleveland, Ohio. They also insisted that I take a coalfield resident along with me on all my road show presentations. This meant traveling four hours from Lexington, Kentucky, to West Virginia to pick up a coalfield resident, then turning around and heading all the way back to Illinois to make a few presentations. All this while paying for gas, food, and lodging for two people on a budget of basically nothing—and driving thousands of miles. It was stressful as hell.

Getting speaking gigs was hard. Initially I sent spam e-mails to hundreds of college professors, local chapters of Trout Unlimited, the Sierra Club, and the Audubon Society, and many churches. They had no idea who I was, and since I didn't have a sponsoring organization or even a Web site, I had to constantly persuade skeptical professors that I had a good presentation and was trustworthy enough to speak to their students.

But we kept going. As of the summer of 2008, I have now spoken more than 600 times in nineteen states to well over 20,000 people. I have spoken at some of America's finest colleges and universities—Duke, Notre Dame, the University of Chicago—as well as high schools, community colleges, churches, and community groups. I have overcome my fear of public speaking. In fact, the only time that I have gotten

My daddy was a miner
And my granddads too
They crawled inside the bowels
 of earth
Diggin' coal and payin' union dues
They've long since died for King Coal
Lay buried in the ground
But if they were here they'd tell you
Leave those mountains down

(chorus:)
Leave those mountains down, boys
Leave those mountains down
Don't tear up what the heavens bore
And leave those mountains down

This earth has housed my people
Our sorrow and our pain
We've climbed upon the
 mountaintops
Where we've bowed our heads
 to pray
We've seen her through some
 bad times
But none as bad as this
They're tearin' off the mountain tops
You can't put 'em back again
(chorus)

—Shirley Stewart Burns,
 from "Leave Those
 Mountains Down"

nervous recently was speaking to a group of fourth graders. Now that was scary!

Along the way I learned a lot about people. The people of the coalfields I have traveled and worked with have been some of the best companions I could have hoped for: understanding, patient, willing to drive long hours and late at night, eating in cheap diners and sleeping in some really crummy motels, helping me lug all my gear into some college auditorium or church basement, setting up displays and packing up.

I now have a Web site (www.mountainroadshow.com), a mailing list of more than 10,000 people, and some generous supporters and donors who cover my gas and travel expenses. I have met thousands of people, made some great new friends, and have brought a lot of people into the movement, especially college students in the Mountain Justice campaign. It's been the most challenging and rewarding work I have done in my entire life.

And so the Mountaintop Removal Road Show rolls on.

One Small Voice

Teri Blanton

I HAD NEVER PLANNED TO BECOME an activist. Like so many others, circumstances out of my control forced the role on me. And like so many others, it took me years to find my way through the maze of bureaucracy, the fog of laws and administrative rules, and the unsympathetic "public servants" in order to get close to the truth.

In 1982, after living in Michigan for eight years, I packed up my possessions, my two children, and returned to Day-hoit, Kentucky, where I was raised. I wanted my kids to enjoy the same kind of pleasant rural life that I had enjoyed in that small community on the banks of the Cumberland River sur-rounded by family and friends in the hills of Appalachia.

Everything changed in 1987, when we learned that a small industrial plant upstream from our community had polluted our air and our water with more than 200 semivola-tile organics and PCBs. We turned to our local government for help and found none. It was then that I learned the two most valuable lessons I would ever learn—that communi-ties are the most powerful force in our democracy, and that in order to wrestle anything like justice from the powerful, you need to be willing to put in a lot of work. We eventu-ally prevailed, but the victory we won can never make me whole, can never replace the land and water they poisoned, can never restore the health that they took from me and my

Kentucky activist Teri Blanton.
Photo © Richard X. Moore.

A jelly jar of contaminated water in Mingo County, West Virginia; residents attribute the pollution to injections of coal slurry into underground mines. Photo © Eric Falquero; courtesy of Ohio Valley Environmental Coalition.

children, or give back the lives of my friends and neighbors who are gone forever.

That was many years ago, and what I experienced in Dayhoit was but a snapshot of the destruction of Appalachia that goes on to feed the hunger of Big Coal. Countless communities in Kentucky, West Virginia, Tennessee, Ohio, and Virginia are seeing the destruction of their land and water, their health, their homes, and the future of their children to fuel an economy that benefits them very little. They live in poverty as companies rake in the profits. But people are fighting back.

If you believe what they teach you in high school government class, our leaders protect everyone's interests. In my reality, I've found that to be a pleasant little lie they tell us in the hope that we'll be quiet and stand aside. In order to make the machinations of government work for the people, communities are organizing and demanding justice from their elected officials, from the court system, and from the agencies that are charged to serve the public interest.

We often think of the three branches of government as separate beasts, but my experience has taught me that we're dealing with one creature with three heads. The legislature makes laws, the administrative agencies execute them as they see fit (often to the benefit of the very industries they're designed to regulate), and it is up to the courts to figure out if the agencies got it right. Throughout most of the process that builds our body of law, the concepts are mostly abstractions. Often it is only when these laws are put to work on the ground that we learn who wins and who loses, and how much some people can get hurt.

This suggests, of course, that activism is most effective on the local level, and this is a lesson that the environmental movement often has missed. It is certainly beneficial, even necessary, to have competent professionals in the state capitals and in Washington, D.C., to intervene in the process on behalf of the people whose lives will be affected by the decisions that are made. Unfortunately, it is often those very people who are overlooked as strategies develop, deals are made, or when one organization or another declares a victory. Then they move on to the next hot issue, leaving others in their wake to pick up the pieces and failing to nourish the roots of a movement.

Mountaintop removal mining is one of those issues, and for me and my people it is a part of our everyday lives. When Jimmy Carter signed the Surface Mining Control and Reclamation Act (SMCRA) in 1977, mountaintop removal was supposed to be an exception to the rule. Instead, this anomaly has become the rule and has destroyed tens of thousands of acres in Appalachia in the thirty years since SMCRA was enacted. As coal companies find gaping holes in the laws, agencies give their blessing, and the courts often look the other way or overturn lower-court decisions favoring plaintiffs.

Yet, one community at a time, we're fighting back through the very institutions that caused this mess in the first place. One of the greatest challenges to organizing is helping people who are directly affected by resource extraction to understand that what happens in state capitals, in the courtrooms, and in Washington touches their lives and communities. Whether they are fighting for clean water to come from their taps or protecting their homes from being blasted off their foundations, they rely on decisions made hundreds or thousands of miles away and sometimes years earlier. Politicians, judges, and public servants that draw their authority from their election by community members make those decisions. Everything is connected, and we all can play a role if we choose to embrace it.

Many times I've thought about simply walking away after being worn down by the constant struggle for simple justice. But then something will happen that brings me back, like thinking about my friends who face this adversity in their daily lives. I think of an elderly couple that lost one well after another and were terrified to talk about it for fear of the backlash from those who are protecting their livelihoods. I think of the times I sat with an old friend on his porch in a tiny green oasis surrounded by thousands of acres of barren, mined land, with the drone of the machinery all around us. I think of these things, and dozens of other scenes I've witnessed over the years, and I realize how important one voice can be, and how one voice can become hundreds, and then thousands.

Why I'm All for Mountaintop Removal

I'm from Kansas and in Kansas
the earth is flat. If something ain't
  flat,
it ain't right. You walk anywhere,
you go right from A to B. And that's
  that.
When I was a kid in Curley's
  Barbershop,
Saturday mornings, he didn't
  even ask.
It was flattop, flattop, flattop, a line
  of us
leaving the shop as God intended.
These mountains in Appalachia?
They need to be taught a thing
  or two
about plain. About who's boss.
  If God
didn't want these mountaintops
sliced off, why'd he invent the dozer
and dragline? Ask yourself that.
The earth is flat. We all know that.
No getting around it.

—Jeff Worley

In an event called Powershift, several thousand activists gathered in Washington, D.C., in March 2009 to protest climate change policy (especially the role of coal-burning power plants) and call for clean-energy development; the group included a large contingent of MTR opponents. Photo © Richard X. Moore.

This country was founded by men and women who rebelled against oppression. It's ironic that we, as a people, can somehow justify oppressing the people of Appalachia to destroy a landscape and a culture, all in the name of cheap energy. I think it is time that we take back our democracy. Organizing the communities of people whose lives have been destroyed, whose landscapes have been forever altered, one at a time, and for as long as it takes, is the only answer.

What keeps me going is the knowledge that by working hard, I can make a difference. I think of the words of Margaret Mead, who said, "Never doubt that a small group of thoughtful, committed people can change the world. Indeed, it is the only thing that ever has." I want to be one of that small group, and to help that group grow to become an overwhelming force. If my experience can help others find a way to save our homeland, I have done my job.

Homeland Security

Cathie Bird

Mʏ ᴄᴀʟʟ ᴛᴏ ᴛʜᴇ ꜰʀᴏɴᴛ lines of opposing mountaintop removal mining came from nature—trees, to be precise, which seems appropriate, since forest communities are often the first to fall to these top-down coal extraction strategies in Appalachia.

I'm not from around here in the Cumberland Mountains of Tennessee, though I have been a mountain person most of my life. I was born in the Rocky Mountains of Colorado. The first town I came home to was born of a gold-mining scam, later to become a health spa, and then a refuge for hippies, hermits, artists, retirees, and commuters. Years later I moved to Grants, a community in the San Mateo Mountains of New Mexico, where many citizens still suffer health and economic side effects of coal, copper, uranium, and gypsum mining. I lived just a few miles from the summit of Tsood-zil (Mount Taylor), one of the four sacred mountains of the Dineh (Navajo Nation).

I always felt myself to be most deeply rooted in the West. I used to tell people that it would take an act of God to get me to move east of the Mississippi. In some sense, it did. Yet in the deepest core of my being I know this Tennessee hollow is home now. I try not to be disappointed that some of my neighbors don't embrace me because I'm "not from around here."

Hiking trail in the Cumberland Mountains, Frozen Head State Park, Tennessee. Photo © iStockphoto.com/Melinda Fawver.

Even before I moved to Tennessee, I knew that coal had been mined on Braden Mountain, less than a mile from my house. I can stand on my porch and see angles and edges on Braden that don't quite match the roundness suggested by the rest of the mountain. Stretched wide and held tightly, my topographic map releases its laminated curl long enough to reveal brownish squiggles scattered along Braden's upper reaches. "Strip mines," says the map, near a large group of squiggles. A parallel track of black dashes sketches a road along the edge of some squiggles; 200 feet below that, another "unimproved" road clings to the 2,100-foot elevation contour. Near the higher track, a thin black cockeyed Y points its tail into a narrow squiggle band. "Abandoned," says the map, next to a mine tunnel symbol.

Still, I didn't appreciate the fact that I had moved to the heart of East Tennessee's coalfields until I learned from neighbors—who had just joined a group called Save Our Cumberland Mountains (SOCM)—that a coal company had filed an application with the Office of Surface Mining for a large mine on Braden Mountain. The plan called for mountaintop removal and head-of-hollow fills in two streams that flow past my house. Another company planned to mine 2,100 acres on Zeb Mountain, a few miles northeast of me. SOCM members were organizing to oppose the Zeb mine, they said, and I was invited to a meeting.

People I met there worried that operational plans at the Zeb mine included crossridge mining, a form of mountaintop mining. What I heard sounded ominous: uprooted forests, pulverized mountaintops, poisoned water, displaced wildlife, and explosive shock waves that sent boulders whizzing, cracked windows, and shattered nerves. Still, I was reluctant to get involved. Could it really be that bad? Weren't there laws to prevent this kind of stuff? Without having personally experienced these things, it was difficult to find the drive to begin such an overwhelming fight.

An idea soon burst through my indecision: if I went up on Braden, maybe nature itself would reveal what I needed to do. I didn't make it to the top but got far enough to see

The American toad, one of many amphibian species found throughout the coalfields. Photo © Vivian Stockman.

that the dashes, squiggles, and arrows had a reality beyond the symbols on my map—a life that embodied the power of humans to deface the land and disrupt the lives and homes of other species, to exploit resources without regard to nature's suffering. There among the trees, the truth that such suffering has no voice in the affairs of men abounded with profound clarity. If not for my neighbors, if not for myself, there would be no one to speak for the trees and other wild things. This thought was both inspiring and fearsome, and I resolved that MTR must never come to this mountain or to Tennessee.

With hindsight, I have found that when I take a leap into the unknown, everything I need to survive flows up from the void along with unexpected fortune. I found treasure through the voices of the people I began to meet: people from the ground zeros of MTR in West Virginia, Kentucky, and Virginia,

A bulldozer spreads coal slag into the dam that contains the Brushy Fork slurry impoundment. Photo © Mark Schmerling.

Ice-covered trees, Great Smoky Mountains National Park. Photo courtesy of National Park Service.

people who increasingly spoke of their lives near these mines in terms of war.

Standing with the trees on Braden Mountain, I connected with the feeling of being in occupied territory, invaded by a species against which there is no control, no protest, no escape. How is it any different for my coalfield friends farther up the Appalachian chain? Their words induce the same feelings, and this has been the unexpected treasure of my leap of faith into the battle—a profound knowing in mind, body, and soul that MTR represents a violent exploitation of people and nature that is fundamentally unchallenged in the United States of America, from Appalachia to Black Mesa, from the Gulf of Mexico to the arctic landscapes of Alaska.

Looking back, I find it interesting that my involvement with MTR unfolded in a post-9/11 world where the notion of homeland security was taking on new meaning for so many. The need for a secure house and homeland is primal for our species. Without it, life becomes driven by unspeakable anxiety, unbearable sorrow. A secure home should be a right for all, not a privilege for the few. But it's not enough that people and nature just *have* rights. To mean something, rights have to be upheld and respected. My experience tells me that it's a heart thing—not a head thing—that enables a person or nation to choose such a path. How do people get to that place?

Tennessee is not there yet. Zeb Mountain is pretty much wrecked, and toxic levels of selenium have shown up in some of its streams. Braden's fate, and that of the surrounding Royal Blue Wildlife Management Area and Koppers Coal Reserve, is temporarily on hold in the boardroom of the Tennessee Valley Authority.

I do not know how this story will end. I do know that stories have power. When the life story of any one of us becomes unspeakable, the power to invoke our collective, radical potential to create sustainable life on earth is disabled. Our efforts must then be aimed at helping each other find a voice, and for me that has come through standing in solidarity with other human and nonhuman beings in the coalfields.

Words are the bridge from lived experience to shared experience, and, as such, can inspire, heal, and transform. I am convinced that if we choose to speak from the heart, we can end the government-sanctioned annihilation of Appalachia by the coal industry.

I keep a mountain anchored off eastward a little way, which I ascend in my dreams both awake and asleep. Its broad base spreads over a village or two, which does not know it; neither does it know them, nor do I when I ascend it. I can see its general outline as plainly now in my mind as that of Wachusett. I do not invent in the least, but state exactly what I see. I find that I go up it when I am light-footed and earnest.

—Henry David Thoreau

A Word of Wisdom

Kathy Selvage

Miner in Kempton, West Virginia, 1939. Photo by John Vachon; courtesy of Library of Congress.

GREETINGS TO THE COMMISSIONERS:

My name is Kathy R. Selvage. I live in a small community just two miles from the town of Wise in Wise County, Virginia, located in the southwestern area of the state. I am no stranger to Wise County or coal mining. My own father took a job in the mines after the war and worked in deep mines for thirty years, and I can tell you that my own father, were he with us today, would not approve of the desecration. He would bear witness to it in his own community. I know that we cannot and should not divorce our history. In fact, we should embrace it, but it is past time to make a new history in energy production and save the land and its people in the process—a win-win proposition.

Neither am I a stranger here. I came here on October 17, 2006, to speak to you regarding the matter of a guaranteed rate of return before Dominion Power had even submitted an application to build a coal-fired power plant in our very own backyard.

I appreciate the opportunity to participate in this process; however, I do want you to understand what a sacrifice has been rendered regarding time and resources for the people of Wise County to be here today. We are people from Wise County and southwest Virginia sacrificing of ourselves for the sake of our own lands, for the sake of the health of our

Kathy Selvage and her mother on Kathy's front porch. Photo © Marian Steinert.

people, and for the sake of the state of Virginia and the planet. We stand proudly for what we believe to be just and right because our minds and conscience will not allow us to do otherwise.

No one knows what the final cost of the proposed power plant will be because there are no incentives to persuade Dominion to be as efficient as it can legitimately be. Dominion's initial estimate was $800 million, but to date that figure has more than doubled to $1.62 billion. It is not likely to stop there. But one can rest assured that wherever the price tag lands, the Virginia ratepayers will be writing the check.

Since we are speaking of costs and who pays, let us continue. The impacts to southwest Virginia and its people through the building of this plant will be many and varied, mostly detrimental. The impact will be on the land that will be doomed to nothingness, to mountains that will be laid to rest in the valleys, to the streambeds that will be buried. The burning of man-made mountains of waste coal (called gob piles) will deliver to us a toxic soup of air that we and our children shall draw hastily into our already weakened lungs. Being sentenced to another fifty years of burning coal in our midst will thus seal the fate of our people and their health; and need I remind you every time another mountain

Clinch River power plant in Bristol, Virginia. Photo © Taylor Barnhill; courtesy of Appalachian Voices.

is buried, it forever deprives us of another future economic development opportunity and seals our fate to forever live in poverty.

Not only are the costs to the health of the people too great to bear, but the costs to the planet are too great as well. Dominion has no plan greater than pretty words to control global warming pollution from this plant. They admit there is no technology to accomplish such a goal. Look around the country! These dinosaurs, outdated coal plant proposals, are falling like dominoes. Let's not make Virginia win the race to the bottom by being one of the few states that allows these polluters to build. The state of Virginia should not have this on her conscience. Over fifty proposed coal plants around the country were denied permits in 2007 because of fears of global warming, pollution, health and environmental destruction. Why should Virginia be the state that rolls out the welcome mat for this outdated technology?

I understand that we are taking a different position than our elected leaders, and I do that without personal malice, but we are concerned with their shortsightedness and think they do not adequately understand the concept of global warming and its consequences. What man has wrought, man must work to correct. Common sacrifice, conservation, and clean, renewable energy supplies for the state of Virginia are worthwhile goals for all Virginians, including those in the far southwestern corner. The message here is the same—Virginia must set a new energy policy in this global warming era—she simply cannot continue her tired, detrimental, old ways of supplying electricity needs.

There will be many opportunities for agencies and persons to intervene in this process and turn this ship around. We must bring great wisdom to this process: to save the environment of southwest Virginia, to save this state from the harmful effects of global warming, and to rise from the ashes as a bright and shining example to the world.

I know that you cannot replace the beautiful lush mountains of southwest Virginia that have been sacrificial lambs for the energy needs of this country, but I still await that one great leader who will demonstrate what Thomas Jefferson said, that "one man with courage can be a majority." I call upon Governor Kaine to examine his heart as to whether he could be that man.

———✦———

These remarks were delivered to the Virginia State Corporation Commission in Richmond, Virginia, on January 8, 2008.

I shall not leave these prisoning
  hills . . .
Being of these hills, being one with
  the fox
Stealing into the shadows, one with
  the new-born foal,
The lumbering ox drawing green
  beech logs to mill,
One with the destined feet of man
  climbing and descending,
And one with death rising to bloom
  again, I cannot go.
Being of these hills I cannot pass
  beyond.

—James Still, from "Heritage"

My Life Is on the Line

Maria Gunnoe

Maria Gunnoe on her front porch in Bob White, West Virginia. Maria's family has lived in the region since the 1800s. Photo © Jo Syz.

I'M FROM BOB WHITE ON Route 85 in Boone County, West Virginia. Mountaintop removal moved into my backyard in 2000. Since then, I've lost two access bridges, the use of my water, about five acres of land. There's thirteen landslides between me and the toe of the landfill behind me. Each time it rains these landslides move. All depending on how much rain we get, sometimes they can move as much as five feet in one day. You know that eventually they're gonna wash out, and when they do, I will have another major washout here at my home.

Since 2000, I've been flooded seven times. One time I was flooded with no rain—blue skies and just barely any clouds at all in the sky—the stream coming through my property just came up. It came up about three feet. By the time I called the DEP [West Virginia Department of Environmental Protection] and made the proper complaints and reports, the water had subsided. The DEP said there was no evidence of what had happened and therefore it was OK.

And with that, I'm going to add that the DEP doesn't allow citizens to take samples of the water that runs by their house. So I mean if I had run out there and got a sample, it would have been nothing more than my sample. The DEP is not there for the citizens, it's there for the coal companies, and it enables the coal companies. In some cases they even lie to the citizens in order to continue the work on the mountaintop removal site. I've been lied to many times. I've had five DEP agents stand and look at me and tell me an eroded mountain wasn't eroded. I have pictures and a lot of proof showing that it's eroded. It's like they were programmed to say—no matter what I said—that it was not eroded.

They just will not admit the fact that the mountains behind me are crumbling in on my home. The mountains are slipping into the hollow and, in turn, it's washing by me, and flooding the people across from me. Everyone downstream from where that mountaintop removal site is gets flooded, and their wells are contaminated. My well is contaminated. Can't drink my water. I buy on average about $250 worth of water a month, and that's on a slow month. The West Virginia American Water Company's wanting $31,000 to put water in to me. And that's only 500 feet worth of water line. I can't afford that, of course.

And the financial aspects of what these catastrophic floods has done to our lives is just unbelievable. Looking back on it, myself and my husband had real good jobs, working full-time, living life. And then this flood thing started and we was just being completely wiped out.

In response to all the floods, and to the coal company's claims that this was an "act of God" taking place in my backyard, I began organizing other people here in the neighborhood. I got to looking around, and it seemed that the people around me was being affected or were in line to be affected by this same mountaintop removal site. Doing this, I've also educated myself on mountaintop removal in the Appalachian region. And I've been working consistently for the past five years—locally I've been working for seven years—on the issue of mountaintop removal and what it's doing to our communities.

People around here are swigging down contaminated water all day long, every day. The health effects are sometimes long term. It's usually pancreatic cancer or some kind of liver disease, or kidney stones, gallstones—digestive tract problems. And then, too, people's breathing. The blasting

In 2000, a 1,200-acre MTR mine began operations at the top of Maria Gunnoe's hollow (shown here), where her family has lived since the 1950s. Photo © Jo Syz.

Maria Gunnoe with a photo of her deceased father and brother, both of whom were underground coal miners. Photo © Mark Schmerling.

is killing people—just smothering them to death through breathing all of the dust. The computers and electronics and stuff in my house stay completely packed up with black coal dirt and rock dust together. Why do they expect us to just take this? It's not gonna happen down at the state capital. I mean they're not gonna go up there and blast off the top of a mountain in the background of the capitol.

Through my organizing, I've met quite a bit of . . . I guess you could call it opposition. I've had my children get harassed. I've got a fifteen-year-old boy and an eleven-year-old girl. I have a fifteen-year-old boy that looks like a thirty-year-old man—he's very big. He's been harassed by grown men. They call him tree hugger and just generally say things to him that's not nice. My son just takes it and goes—he's a real trouper.

I've had a little bit of everything done to me. I've been accused of all kinds of stuff. I've had sand put in my gas tank—cost $1,200 to keep my truck on the road. And you know, in this kind of area, if they ground your vehicle, you're grounded! You're stopped right there, dead in your tracks. I'm twenty-five miles from the nearest town, so that really slowed me down for quite a while. Teachers in the schools make comments to my kids. It's not their place to tell my children that their water isn't poisoned by coal, when my children know they can't drink their water. I've had my tires cut, my dog shot. People spit on my truck all the time—big, gross tobacco juice spit.

One of my dogs was shot and left in the parking lot where my kids catch the school bus. This was my daughter's dog. She actually nursed this dog when he was a baby—he was fed a bottle and was a little spoiled. But this was her dog, it wasn't my dog. My aunt, luckily, worked at the post office. She called me and told me that a dog was laying over there dead, and instead of taking the kids to the bus stop, I just took them on to school. Then when I came back and confirmed that it was our dog, we were just completely devastated. He was a three-year-old baby, really. He was very close to the family. He had veered back onto the mountaintop removal site. The last time I seen him, that was the direction he was headed. When they first came in up there, they used to feed my dogs. I kind of feel like they baited him in for the kill.

Then I had a dog shot at the back of my house. It was tied at the back of my house. It's gotten to the point I can't leave my dogs untied because somebody might kill 'em. Well, I had the dog tied at the back of my house and he was shot right in the top of the head. This was within thirty feet of my bedroom window. There's a lot of trains goes by where I live at, so they could've done it while a train was going by and I wouldn't have heard it. Had it been a small-caliber gun, I wouldn't have heard it. They know that. They know how to get you. By killing off your animals, that opens them a way to get in your place without people knowing it.

Before I began doing this, let me say, I did talk to my kids about it. My children don't want to leave where they're at, and that gives us one choice. That gives us the choice of fighting to stay. And we talked about it. When all this first come up, I really felt it was in our best interest to leave, but we were unable to do so. The property's been devalued so bad that you can't get nothing out of it to move forward with your life.

Be sure to put your feet in the right place, and stand firm.

—Abraham Lincoln

And you can't hardly walk off and leave everything you've got. So that's pretty much the point that we're at now.

And I see this happening throughout the communities in southern West Virginia, and then too in Tennessee and Kentucky. And it's wrong, you know? I mean it's flat-out wrong to do people like this. If you react, the strip miners will cut you short every time. If you lash out and say, "Why are you destroying my home?" they'll look at you and say, "Well, I gotta have a job." And they will verbally attack you in front of other people in the convenience store and say things to you that's just completely and totally unnecessary. They will say things to you that really make you—considering all we go through here day to day—just want to reach out and grab 'em and shake the daylights out of 'em! I wanna say, "How can you do me like this in the name of jobs? How can you do me and my family like this and expect us to sit by and just let you do it?"

One thing about West Virginia people is we're not the kind to give up and walk away. If we was the kind to give up and walk away, we would never have settled this area years and years ago. Because this was a very rough terrain—a very rough life here. But people loved it—people like my great-grandmother, people like my grandfather before me. They loved this land, and tended this land. It's land that wasn't meant to be developed. It's a special land. God put it way up high so they'd leave it alone. I've had people to tell me that God put the coal there for us to mine. I have to disagree with that. He buried it because it's so daggone nasty!

The coal companies like to say that the mountaintop land is just useless land, and that's not true. How can they say that? That's insane to me. My family growing up—my grandfather had mountain cornfields and grew corn up in these mountains. And you know, that's our survival. The mountains are literally our survival. And now as long as you're driving through here on the paved road, you're OK, but if you get off that paved road on one side or the other, you're gonna be stopped. You're not allowed into these mountains anymore! How can they tell the mountain people that they're no longer

Nimrod Workman on School Street in Chattaroy, Mingo County, West Virginia, 1972. A retired miner who participated in the battle of Blair Mountain, Workman was also a singer-songwriter and union organizer. Photo © Builder Levy.

Henry Ooten and his wife took up temporary residence in their son and daughter-in-law's garage in Conley Hollow, Delbarton, Mingo County, West Virginia, while awaiting delivery of a new mobile home. Floodwaters in the spring of 2004 so damaged the access road that delivery was impossible. Photo © Builder Levy.

allowed in the mountains? That's not right. They're taking away everything that puts us together as a people.

And they're expecting the wrong people to sit back and take this.

We're not stupid by no means. There's a lot of very, very intelligent people here that can't read and write, but they're not stupid. They're brilliant in their own sense of the word. They have intelligence that's not taught in college. These people are the people I grew up with—the people I love. And these are people that I won't walk away from. And I would probably stand up to the biggest, strongest, most evil power in the world in order to protect them and to protect their rights to retire in their homes—to protect their rights to be who they are in the communities they're in.

The people in these communities, they feel the blasting, they see the trucks on the road running over top of their family. They see what's going on, but they don't see what it looks like from the sky. Seeing what it looks like from the sky scares you. It scares you real bad to come home to it. When it rains here, we all get flooded. And then the coal companies,

Before I Was Hungry

Before I was poor
the fish from the creek
were supper
the water from our well,
spring and creek were
clear in a drinking glass.

Before I was poor
there were no air filters
on our furnace,
you couldn't see the
air in the road in front
of our house.

Before I was poor,
I was never hungry
for the past—

The time
before the bulldozers
stripped away the natural
rights of
fishermen,
farmers.

—Walter Lane

they care so much! After five acres of my land and my life washed down the stream, the coal company engineer came into my front yard and said that this was "an act of God"!

You know, the night when this wall of water was coming down through the hollow at me, I run to the mountain. But the mountain was sliding and I couldn't go there. I couldn't get out, the streams had me and my family surrounded. I literally hit my knees, and I prayed for everything I was worth! And there was an act of God took place that night. But not the one they claimed. And that was the same claim they made after they killed 125 people in the Buffalo Creek flood. I lost family in the Buffalo Creek flood. My father was a rescuer in the Buffalo Creek flood. So that incident was very close to our family.

To see what come off that mountain, and to know what it had been like for thirty-seven years, well, it's a big eye-opener to realize what a dramatic difference the mountaintop removal makes in everything! I mean, everything around these strip sites is constantly eroding, and there's always water running in all different directions. The DEP calls that "streams meandering." They were never streams before—now they're streams!

This process, it's tearing my property all to pieces, and I have no rights over my property. The only right I have over my property is the right to pay taxes on it! I have no control over what's going on. The coal company has tore it all to pieces. It looks awful. Our place had always been pretty much hand-manicured. My father and my grandfather before me took very good care of it. We had fruit trees and just an abundance of food-producing plants right there next to where I lived at. Our land has always been tended in a way that it took care of us. Now that's no longer the case. Our soil's contaminated. A garden that we'd gardened for all the thirty-seven years that I've been there is now covered with coal slurry. You can't grow food in that.

My yard was completely washed out. My fruit trees are gone. My nut trees are gone. I woke up the next morning and looked at this massive trench in my front yard, and it took me three days to absorb it. I went from crying—sobbing—to being very mad. This was three years ago, and I'm still mad. And honestly, I'm a little madder than I was then because I realize how many tentacles this evil has. It goes all the way to Washington, D.C. And if I have to go up against it and fight for my home, I'm going against it. It's even the United States government. And that alone is pretty intimidating. But at the same time, so is that wall of water sitting back up on that mountain waiting for me.

Many residents of West Virginia's Wyoming County attribute increased flooding to mountain-top removal operations. Photo © Vivian Stockman.

I don't think I've ever run up against anything that intimidated me that bad. Keeps me up at night. Keeps my kids up at night. And that's when you know how powerful the intimidation of these waters is. When you get to the point that you ain't had ten hours of sleep in a week, and it comes time to lay down and go to sleep and it starts raining. And you don't go to sleep.

People look at you different ways. There's a lot of people here who support what I do. But there's others who drive in here every day for their jobs, and given a choice, they'd run over me in a heartbeat. They'd do anything they could to get rid of me. But I know I'm being effective, and I know I'm making a change. And with that change will come the intimidation factors. But it just doesn't work—there's nothing more intimidating than what they've already put me through. So—bring it on.

I'm setting there on my porch, which is my favorite place in the whole world, by the way—I'd rather be on my front porch than any other place in the world and I've been to a lot of places. As it stands right now, with the new permits, they're gonna blast off the mountain I look at when I look off my front porch. And I get to set and watch that happen, and I'm not supposed to react. Don't react, just set there and take it. They're gonna blast away my horizon, and I'm expected to say, "It's OK. It's for the good of all."

Am I willing to sacrifice myself and my kids, and my family and my health and my home for everybody else? No—I don't owe nobody nothing. It's all I can do to take care of my family and my place. It was all I could do before

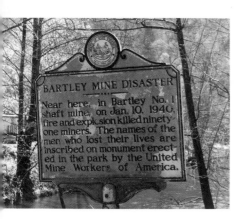

A plaque in Bartley, McDowell County, West Virginia, memorializes the Bartley Mine disaster of 1940, in which "fire and explosion killed ninety-one miners." Photo © Builder Levy.

I started fighting mountaintop removal. Now that I'm fighting mountaintop removal, it makes it nearly impossible. But at the same time, my life is on the line. My kids' lives are on the line. You don't give up on that and walk away. You don't throw up your hands and say, "Oh, it's OK, you feed me three million tons of blasting material a day. That's fine, I don't mind. It's for the betterment of all."

I can't say that there's anything out there that I'm willing to risk myself and my kids for. Nothing. No amount of money, no amount of energy, no amount of anything. If it come down to it, we could live up under a rock cliff with what the good Lord above gives us. And we could live like that, as long as we got clean water, clean air, and a healthy environment. We can take care of ourselves from there. But when they contaminate our water, our air, and our environment we're gonna die no matter what we do. That's it.

───────◆───────

Maria Gunnoe was among the 2009 winners of the Goldman Environmental Prize for her work in educating local communities about the environmental dangers of MTR mining. This essay originally appeared in Like Walking onto Another Planet *by the Ohio Valley Environmental Coalition.*

The Ripple Effect

Kathy Mattea

GROWING UP IN WEST VIRGINIA, I was blessed to spend a lot of time outdoors. My dad could tell you the name of every tree and shrub, which ones would do well, and which ones had bagworms or funguses and needed a little extra care. Years later, when my husband and I bought a chunk of land south of Nashville, my parents had to walk every inch of it, through the woods and across the fields. I can still see my mother rambling through the woods with a piece of long grass between her teeth. She was in her element.

When I was about ten, we bought a cabin up in the mountains by a river, and I learned to run a trot line, catch crawdads, dig for night crawlers, row a boat, and gig a frog (and yes, it's true—the legs do jump around in the skillet when you fry them!). There's no freer feeling than bathing in the river in a swimsuit, with a bar of Ivory soap in a nylon stocking floating at your side, and nothing makes your hair feel softer than washing it with water from the rain barrel.

I spent time up in the mountains every summer with family friends, riding the train at Cass Scenic Railroad and picking huckleberries on Spruce Knob, the highest point in West Virginia, where the wind blows so hard the branches of the trees all grow in one direction. I have hiked to the top of Seneca Rocks and ridden horses up the back trails there, to look out at the great valley below. I learned to waterski

Kathy Mattea picks a tune on the front porch of her friend Larry Gibson's home on Kayford Mountain, West Virginia. Photo © James Minchin.

Eastern hemlocks in West Virginia. Photo © Jim Clark.

on Cheat Lake, near Morgantown; later, as a student there at WVU, I hiked the Virgin Hemlocks on weekend days, away from the crush of campus life. At Scout camp in the Greenbrier Valley, I learned to spelunk with miners' helmets and carbide lamps. I have hiked and crawled a mile in, and sat in the dark and silence in the heart of the mountain, listening to the vast stillness, before starting the journey back. These mountains are not abstract for me, I know them. They are part of me.

Even today, there is a point on my journey home to West Virginia from Nashville, in Eastern Kentucky, where the hills start to rise up and the horizon closes in. The road becomes curvier, the vistas turn into little nooks and crannies nestled among the hills, and I notice something in me, deep down, relax, and let go: I am home. Tucked into those hills I feel safe and protected. It's a fundamental part of my viewpoint on the world.

So when I learned about mountaintop removal I was shocked and disheartened, to say the least. I discovered it quite by accident. I trained with Al Gore in September 2006 as part of the Climate Project to take the slide show at the core of his movie *An Inconvenient Truth* to a grassroots audience. He encouraged us to personalize the presentation with our own experiences and point of view.

I went online to look for a picture of a West Virginia strip mine, thinking maybe I could find one from the 1970s. Instead, I found a Web site called ilovemountains.org with Google Earth pictures of hundreds of mountains that are no more.

After going to see the results of this practice firsthand, I was literally speechless. My first impression was of witnessing an eco-rape not only of my beloved mountains but of the rights of the people who have lived there among them for generations. And my first instinct was to start screaming. But then a curious thing happened: I felt something in the pit of my stomach that was altogether unexpected. It was a discomfort, a tiny voice saying, "This is not helping." And I realized that I have an opportunity here, an opportunity to learn something about compassion. An opportunity to listen through my grief and anguish, to try to understand those I don't agree with.

Coal operators are doing what they're supposed to do: find and produce coal, provide jobs, and keep their industry going, for the good of all. Environmentalists and activists are doing what they're supposed to do: protect the environment, stand against injustice, and advocate for the beauty and spiritual integrity of the place they live in and love so much, for the good of all.

Everyone involved here is trying to meet a deep need to preserve a way of life that is central to how they see themselves in the world. It's a basic human need: stability, safety, and security, and I think that's why it's so hard to talk about. We're all desperate to stay grounded, to live in a life we recognize, to preserve the heart of what feeds us in this day-to-day human journey. This need is the thing we all have

My mother would get us up at four or five in the morning before gettin' us off to school. I remember her walking out to the coal house, which was just a little old house where you could keep the coal dry from the snow. She would fill up her buckets and bring the coal back and build a fire in the coal fireplaces before she would get any of us out of bed, to try and at least have one or two rooms warm for us before we got up.

—*Kentucky-born musician Patty Loveless*

in common. The conflict, as I see it, is mostly about how to meet that need.

I believe a workable solution will only come from conversation, and only if we can find a way to communicate through the desperation we all feel. It is hard to listen through great pain. This is our challenge. But everyone benefits when we can slow down, affirm our common humanity, and look for creative solutions with input from both sides. This is the legacy I dream of leaving for our children's children in Appalachia.

What do we say when laws themselves are unjust? How do we stand and give voice to the powerless? How do we hold onto hope and compassion in a seemingly hopeless situation? It's a razor's edge, for sure. But I believe that when we stand up together and say, "I can't let you do this anymore," it is a gift not just to ourselves but one that ripples in every direction.

We're Called the
Dustbusters

Pauline Canterberry and Mary Miller

W E LIVE IN THE TOWN of Sylvester in Boone County, West Virginia, the heart of the Appalachian Mountains. It is a small town of 195 people who love their community. The closeness of the neighbors along with the beauty and safety of Sylvester made it the perfect place to raise children. Right in the middle of coal country, surrounded by other coal camps, Sylvester was never owned by a land or coal company and actually was founded as an alternative to coal camp life.

In 1981, a subsidiary of Massey Energy Coal Company put an underground coal mine within 400 feet of our town, but a mountain bluff protected us from the coal dust. After this mine worked out in 1996, Massey Energy pursued a coal-processing plant permit with the West Virginia Department of Environmental Protection (DEP). This would require cutting off the bluff that protected the town and placing the processing plant on it. The airflow into the town travels east to west, across the facility, 90 percent of the time, and we realized that this permit would destroy our community.

Fifty-four Sylvester residents wrote personal letters requesting that the permit be denied. We presented a petition to the DEP with more than 75 percent of residents' signatures requesting that the DEP deny the permit. A hearing was held at the Sylvester Elementary School on November 3, 1996, to an overflowing room of citizens' objecting to this permit. The

Loose coal is loaded onto trucks and barges at the Kanawha River Terminal in Mamet, West Virginia; chemical plants line the far side of the river. Photo © Giles Ashford.

Pauline Canterberry (left) and Mary Miller on a hillside in Sylvester, West Virginia; behind them looms the court-ordered dome over the Elk Run Mining coal preparation plant. Photo © Mark Schmerling.

coal company provided no details of how it would protect the town from damage, only promises that it would not harm the community.

With no concrete plan for protection, the DEP issued the permit anyway. Just as we feared, the plant was put on the lower bluff, cutting off our naturally occurring protection. Unenclosed beltlines were installed. Huge stockpiles of coal began to accumulate. Within one month, the town was covered with black coal dust. The facility worked seven days a week, twenty-four hours a day. Coal was belted into it from as far away as the Twilight mine (about twenty-eight miles away), and up to 35,000 coal trucks a year hauled coal in and out of our town.

The presence of the plant completely changed how we lived. No longer could we socialize in our own yards. Cookouts became a thing of the past. Hanging our clothes out to dry was impossible. Coal dust blanketed everything. Our homes became covered in it. Swimming pools were polluted with it. We could no longer walk the street without coal dust blowing in our faces.

Residents began lodging complaints with the DEP. For two years, these complaints were completely ignored. A slurry impoundment began to grow behind the mountain above Sylvester. At present, it holds 2.3 billion gallons of slurry and is an imminent danger to the town if it should ever break. Still, it continues to grow.

In April 2000, a group of citizens went before the DEP. At this hearing, after seeing the evidence the citizens had gathered, Massey's subsidiary, Elk Run, agreed to install equipment to stop the dust. Their solution was a screen that did not even cover the plant. A foamer—which is meant to suppress respirable coal dust—was also installed in the plant with no success. A watering system was set up by Massey Energy's dust expert. This consisted of sprays over the stockpiles and beltlines that were to work automatically. This effort would have helped had they used the system as instructed, but instead it was used only when the DEP was coming for inspections. The reason for this was clear: while this option would have been beneficial to the community, it would have eaten into the profits of the coal company. The more you wet coal, the less value it has, and, in order to the use the watering system, the coal had to be wetted down all the time.

So, the dust continued with no letup in sight. The children would come in from playing on the school ground at Sylvester Elementary covered in coal dust. The cafeteria cooks would go into the kitchen in the mornings and have to rewash the dishes and the cooking utensils where the dust would settle on them overnight. In the end, they chose to put everything in plastic bags the night before to keep them clean. Finally, the school closed, mainly because of coal dust.

In October 2000, the citizens of Sylvester were granted a hearing before the Office of Surface Mining (OSM) to again present evidence of coal dust from Elk Run Mining. After hearing their pleas, the board of five voted unanimously that Elk Run Mining had to stop the coal dust. But just two days later, films were taken of coal dust spewing from the facility again. Elk Run had no intention of obeying the rules.

By this time, we had both become very concerned and were determined to find a solution to save our homes and town from this injustice of Massey Energy. We tried to get the West Virginia legislature to pass a bill limiting the amount of

Mary Miller holds a cloth laden with coal dust after taking samples in Sylvester. Photo © Mark Schmerling.

coal dust that could be released in the air. The bill reached the floor but was turned down. Frustrated and angry with this decision, we called a meeting with Stephanie Timmermeyer, who was then head of the Division of Air Quality for the DEP, to ask why this bill was turned down. She referred us to West Virginia State Code 22-3-13-b21, which already established such limits. Upon reading the code we were confused. It states that coal companies are supposed to protect off-site property from damage occurring because of the mining. This was clearly happening to us, and we did not understand why it was being allowed.

The DEP asked us to take dust samples and videotape Elk Run Mining Company spewing the dust. We were asked to pick six or seven spots throughout Sylvester and film the same spots every seven or eight days. For more than two years, come sleet, snow, rain, hail, or sunshine, we collected the samples faithfully. Filmed, dated, and stored them in Ziploc bags. The DEP never asked for them.

The DEP also asked us to meet with the executives of Elk Run Mining in a monthly liaison panel to see if we could work out our problems with the coal dust. This went on for two years or so with no success. Eventually the panel meetings declined into nothing but heated arguments, so when Massey requested to stop them, the DEP agreed.

Coal dust continued to rain down on our town. The one concrete result from the meetings was that several people got their homes pressure cleaned. By then, residents had begun to have problems with their furnaces and air conditioners breaking down from coal dust plugging up the motors. Still, we continued taking our dust samples and gathering evidence. One day while taking samples, we noticed a screen door covered with coal dust and decided that it would be funny to rub our faces with some of the coal dust. We continued on to our next destination, and, liking a good joke, we left our faces blackened. At one home the owner and her son came out. After staring at us for a while, she finally said, "Do you know your faces are dirty?" We had a good laugh, and her son stated, "Oh, Mom, you know they are the

A 1918 poster from the United States Fuel Administration urges citizens to "Order Coal Now." Illustration by J. C. Leyendecker; courtesy of Library of Congress.

Visiting the Site of One of the First Churches My Grandfather Pastored

The United Methodist Church in the old mining town of Caretta, McDowell County, West Virginia, seen from the Caretta Community Center. To the right of the church building are former coal company houses. Photo © Builder Levy.

My mother said later that, to the shovel operators, we must have looked like some delegation from out of town that couldn't find the picnic. Or else the funeral. Not so bad my brother and me jumping the fence, and my father, but then my mother, and all of us helping my grandfather over, and finally my grandmother deciding she wanted to see, too.

Then all of us standing together at the rim of the pit in our Sunday clothes, sun reflecting off my grandmother's black patent purse, a few trees still hanging on nearby, roots exposed, like tentacles, like the earth was shrinking under them. The smell of sulphur.

The giant bucket scoops up through the rocks and dirt, the shovel swings around, the bucket empties, and the whole thing swings back, the noise taking an extra second to reach us. I am watching the two men inside, expecting them to notice us, to wave us away because we don't belong there, but they don't. They must be used to it.

Years later, I will remember my grandfather saying that they strip away the land but all they put back is the dirt. Maybe plant a few scrub pine. "Good for nothing anymore," he says now, turning to go back to the car, "except holding the rest of the world together."

It looks almost blue in the sun, the piece of coal I have picked up to take home for a souvenir.

—Tony Crunk

'dustbusters.'" From then on, we have been known as the Sylvester Dustbusters.

We were fiercely determined that we were not going to allow our homes to be destroyed, nor were we going to move from them. In early 2000, a friend recommended that we contact the Charleston, West Virginia, law firm of Bailey and Glasser to ask what avenues we had within the law to stop Massey Energy. After our town meeting, Brian Glasser agreed to take our case, and 164 residents of Sylvester signed

Going Home to John's Creek

Dust covers our car,
beige turned gray and Effie
comes out on the porch
with a gun in her hand,

Not a criminal,
just protecting her land.
Company took her sister's
place, over on Singer's Mountain,

held the mineral rights

on some deed,
a hundred years old.
So, Effie don't know it's us,
her own kin a comin home

at two in the morning.
Reedy-Mo hops out
"Mamma, hit's jes me."
Effie lays that gun down
Starts to laugh and cry.

"Youins come on in here right now."

We drink coffee til five
and sing "I'll Fly Away"
Then lay down in the parlor
where the guest bed is.

We sleep beside
a Kimper mine
First time in ten years
and Effie, she smiles,

"G'night, y'all. G'night now."

—*Wanda Campbell*

on to a lawsuit. We were asking for comprehensive and punitive damages to our property, as well as a stop to the coal dust. We also asked that Elk Run Mining be placed under an injunction. Most of the plaintiffs had never been to court before. Many were senior citizens who only desired to live the remainder of their lives in peace.

At this time, Bob Wise was our new governor and had appointed Matthew Crum as the new director of the DEP. We invited Crum to Sylvester and showed him what we were battling. Under Crum, the inspectors began making their rounds and were actually issuing violations to Massey. In the meantime, we continued to document and film the dust invading Sylvester.

Next, Massey Energy had their dust expert install a non-patented dust-monitoring system in the town, and we monitored the system daily. Halline Thompson, a cook at the school, read it at 6:00 A.M. on her way to work. Mary Miller read it at noon, and Pauline Canterberry read it at 6:00 P.M. Massey's readings did not match up with ours, and the company soon removed the system.

On October 29, 2001, through teamwork, we recorded a film of a huge coal dust cloud as it left the preparation plant at Elk Run Mining, traveling up and over the town of Sylvester, over the school with the children playing on the playground, and going up the center street of the town. We filmed the coal dust falling on the teachers' cars parked in the school lot. We filmed the children playing under it. We recorded it as it spread out over the homes of our town. Then, we went onto the hillside and filmed it leaving the stockpiles and preparation plant. It just kept coming, covering Sylvester with coal dust. Before leaving the hillside, we asked a fellow resident to call the mine office and have Massey turn on the water sprinklers. When we got up to the preparation plant, the sprinkling system came on, and the dust died down.

When we presented this film to the DEP, they gave Elk Run Mining and Massey Energy three options: to move the plant, cover it with a dome, or close it down. They chose to cover it with a dome, which was installed at the reported

A cafeteria in Bartley Elementary School, McDowell County, West Virginia, one of several county schools that had closed or were closing in June 2005 due to declining polulation. Photo © Builder Levy.

cost of $1.4 million. Since that time, the dome has had to be replaced twice.

In the process of preparing for our lawsuit against Elk Run Mining and Massey Energy, we had our homes appraised by the top appraisal companies in West Virginia, used often by Massey Energy. We were told due to the mining facility's coal dust and conditions around Sylvester from mountaintop removal mining, our homes and property had decreased in value by 80 to 90 percent.

In December 2001 we went to court against Elk Run Mining and Massey Energy in Madison, the county seat of Boone County. Early on we were told that we could not include Massey Energy in the lawsuit, because even though Elk Run Mining was a wholly owned subsidiary of Massey, Massey was not responsible for Elk Run's violations. This is the genius of all these multiple subsidiaries. Nor were we permitted to use thirty-two violations that they had received for contaminating Sylvester's drinking water. Judge Lee Schlagel referred to it as trying to use parking tickets.

However, Schlagel determined that Elk Run released too much coal dust from its facility into Sylvester and was therefore guilty. We won comprehensive damages plus lawyer fees, trial fees, and all court costs. Elk Run was also required to decrease the number of coal trucks running through Sylvester from 35,000 to 7,000 a year. The company had to purchase a vacuum sweeper and sweep the streets with it once a week. It was told to install dust monitors in the town, though we are not satisfied with these monitors, which again are not patented. The company does not issue reports to us and will not answer our calls about the monitors.

We did get the injunction, meaning we can go back to court. We have been working with Michael Hendryx, a professor of health research from West Virginia University in Morgantown, West Virginia, on monitoring the air, especially the PM-10 particles, which enter your lungs and cause black lung. This study will be ongoing. The stockpiles of coal are still uncovered, and since the trial, the DEP has granted permits for three more.

After four years of persistence, we finally succeeded in getting a warning system installed that will alert all Boone County residents in the case of a sludge impoundment break or flooding from the barren mountains.

Another problem is that the Big Coal River, which flows through our valley, has been highly contaminated with silt and debris from mountaintop removal mining. It has been blocked and has prevented the safe flow to the river. Should another flood occur, it will be devastating to the entire area. There are also trees and logs across the river that obstruct it in many places. We have a petition with nearly 800 signatures of citizens throughout the valley who want this issue addressed. We have sent the petition to all our state and federal officials, have contacted the DNR, and brought it to the county commission for its consideration. So far, we have not been successful in our efforts to get the river rechanneled.

We are in our twelfth year of fighting for respect for ourselves, the citizens of Sylvester, and all who live in the southern coalfields of West Virginia. We realize we are not alone fighting the injustice of mountaintop removal mining, which is destroying thousands of lives.

They Think We're Throwaway People

Members of Kentuckians for the Commonwealth

A Piece of History
Archie Fields

I was born in Letcher County, Kentucky, about ten miles over from Black Mountain on the Big Cowan side. I guess where I'll start at is the time that I started going in the mountains. My daddy used to take me up there at eight years old. We went up on what they call Elk Pond and we camped for a week at a time. And all these times, if you picture the mountain, it was just like a wilderness as you go up the mountain through a road and the trees were hanging over and in the middle of the day it was like dark. But then when you got up there, you could stay up there for a week and nobody would bother you.

All this time I've been going up there it's always been a wilderness, a beautiful place. You go up there now and it looks like an atomic bomb just hit the top of the mountain and leveled all the trees down to the earth. They're cutting on both sides of the mountain—the Virginia side and the Kentucky side. They are taking it all down, and they're going to destroy the water streams on both sides of the mountain.

There are these arrowheads up there. Indian campgrounds all across the top of the mountain—plumb across from Eolia to Harlan. They sent a group up there from the University of Kentucky, and they stayed up there three months, but

Scenic trail bridge in a Kentucky forest. Photo © iStockphoto.com/ Dan Brandenburg.

they couldn't even find one arrowhead. I've dug over 2,000 of these arrowheads right up there myself in twenty-four years. But the state don't consider its Indian artifacts as any importance. The companies just get the coal out, destroy the mountain, take the streams away, make valley fills. That's the way the coal company operates. They put up a good front, kill the people's interest in the land, and then they'll come back and do what they want to it.

To me it's a piece of history. My grandfather used to cross there and go into Appalachia [Virginia] and get supplies through Black Mountain, over to Stoney, Virginia. He'd bring them across to our family store there on the Big Cowan side. They'd come from Black Mountain across Scuddle Hole Gap and down into the valley, and that's how they got the groceries from Stoney. So it's a piece of history to me, Black Mountain and Pine Mountain. And the wildlife is protected on that [Pine Mountain] so far, but if they're turned loose on that, we won't have no beauty left.

And they worry about tourism. There won't be no tourism here in Letcher County because it's gone with the strip mining and the tops of the mountains, and there's going to be nothing but a desert island. That's what it's going to be like.

Black Star Coal Company advertising clip. Photo © Dave Johnson; courtesy of Dave Johnson collection.

The Mountains Are Our Pride
Carolyn Brown

My concerns are from my heart because my parents raised me in this area. It is the area where ICG [International Coal Group] is doing the MTR. It's always been some sort of a little mining town. When they augered coal, when you had deep mines, it didn't devastate the area. It provided jobs for the people, but this mining now is something that makes me sick to my stomach when I look and see what they're doing to our mountains. These are mountains that I've run through, my daddy hunted in. The wildlife is being destroyed. It's not the same anymore.

I see the big cliffs that were set there somehow by God. Indians were in this very area that they're destroying right now. There's been artifacts such as arrowheads found in this same area. Where they're doing the mountaintop removal, it's flat now, not the natural contours of those mountains, and all the trees are gone. It's rock and dirt that you see now. Nothing will grow on that. I've seen what happens to these areas where they plant grass. In some places the grass may grow, but then the rest of it is brown.

And it's roads, you know. It's nice for four-wheeling, if you like to four-wheel, but some people like to come and just enjoy the naturalness of the mountains in the areas. There are people who travel here, that come in, that have married someone from the area, that love looking at those mountains, and they're sort of in awe, just to see those big high mountains. They protect us.

What are our children going to grow up to remember about this place? I remember it—but they're not going to be able to see that because it's going to be gone. The coal companies seem to be able to come in and pay some people a few bucks. People can buy a few four-wheelers and a new pickup truck, but the land is gone. The land is not the same, and then the money is gone, and then what are your children going to see? How are they going to grow up? Are they going to have to leave? Because all the coal sooner or later is going to be gone.

It just . . . breaks my heart. This is part of my childhood; I mean . . . it just kills me. We need to hold on to what few mountains we have left.

You know, Lexington and Louisville—they're beautiful places. They have the farmland and the grass that grows and stuff like that, but we have our mountains. And we would like to keep our mountains. And I'll tell you one thing—I'm going to be there. I own another place, but I'm selling and I'm going back to where my roots are. And I'm going to be there until they carry me out in a pine box. I don't know where they're going to put me by the time they get through there, probably in the neighborhood, but I'm going stay there one way or another.

I wanted to be here also to speak for my daddy because he's not here anymore, and I know how he felt about his

The L & N Don't Stop Here Anymore

Oh, when I was a curly-headed baby
My daddy sat me down on his knee
He said, "Son, go to school and learn
  your letters
Don't you be no dusty miner, boy,
  like me"

For I was born and raised
At the mouth of Hazard holler
Coal cars rolled and rumbled past
  my door
Now they stand in a nasty row all
  empty
And the L & N don't stop here any-
  more

I used to think my daddy was a black
  man
With scrip enough to buy the company store
But now he goes downtown with
  empty pockets
And his face is white as a February
  snow

—*Jean Ritchie*

Lee Sexton of Letcher County, Kentucky, has been playing the banjo for more than seventy years. Despite the fact that his fingers are "all smashed up" from decades of work as a miner, he is a virtuoso in the drop-thumb, or claw hammer, style. Photo © Mark Schmerling.

home and his land, and he had guts and he would stand up for what was right. I know that what I'm saying tonight—that would come from his heart also.

I thank y'all for listening to me, and I hope that this means something to a lot of you all too. That you feel some of those same things that I do about our mountains, because I know we're not supposed to be prideful people, but the mountains are our pride.

In Your Soul
Evelyn Gilbert

I'm from Eolia, which means "valley of the wind" in Cherokee. Our town, in the past, had Cherokee Indians and had a lot of artifacts. There's a lot of heritage in our community, there's a lot of pride in our community, and there's a lot of problems in our community. One of the problems recently was worked out and resolved by Carol Smith [former Letcher County judge executive].

We live at the very top of a hollow where they were going to put a [valley] fill in. We, of course, didn't want them to do that, because we knew that if they did we would be buried alive. And if the pond that was going to be 300 feet away broke, then we would be washed off the hill. We didn't know what to do or where to turn, until Kentuckians for the Commonwealth came to our help and told us what we could do and the route we should go.

It was a scary time. Our neighbors down below us, of course, were concerned also, because they knew that if we were washed away they also were going to be washed away. But some of the neighbors worked for the coal mine, and some of them lived on the property that belonged to the coal mine, and they didn't want any waves made. So they were very against us. Word came to us that we were going to be burned out if we didn't quit making so much noise.

At that point, Mr. Smith called a meeting, a joint meeting of the community, and through his work and through all that was

At the Powershift climate action demonstration in Washington, D.C., in March 2009, a contingent from the movement against mountaintop removal, including activists Teri Blanton, Sara Pennington, and Cassie Robinson; singer Kathy Mattea; and writers Wendell Berry, Terry Tempest Williams, Janisse Ray, Jason Howard, and Erik Reece. Photo courtesy of Kentuckians for the Commonwealth.

accomplished that night, our community now is on a better level. I know I sound different than everybody else because I was raised in the desert. I am a desert rat that ended up by the grace of God in the mountains. At first, when I came here, it was hard for me, because I have claustrophobia and I would feel like I was being smothered. That was in 1976 that I came here. Kentucky gets in your soul. It touches your heart, and it gets in your soul, and I've told my husband, "They're going to have to blast me out of here." Well, that's what they're trying to do! They're trying to blast me out of here. My grandson who is five told my husband, he said, "I want to go with you, Grandpa, and I want to stand up, and I want to tell whoever, whoever will listen, that they shouldn't take away our wild America." And they shouldn't.

Lives on the Line
John Roark

So, where do we start? We need to start from the beginning. When you get older, you are able to say, "I can remember when." Well, I can. I can remember when we didn't have any of this mining like we see today, the strip mining.

This was the most beautiful part of the world, in my opinion. I've traveled a little, not as much as some people. I can remember when from Ashland to Pineville, and from Pikeville to Campton, it was all forest land. Trees. The only thing you can compare it to would probably be the Smokies. You can see that one mountain range through there, but we had it in half the state. Eastern Kentucky was all that way, and then they got the bright idea that it's easier to mine the coal by taking the heavy equipment and shoving the mountains down and ripping the heart out of the country that we love so much. They've stripped, and they start this mountaintop removal, which is really nothing new. They've been doing it on a smaller scale for a long time. They're just getting more brazen at it. Then the price of coal has gone up ridiculously high. And greed—these people are after money, and the shame of it is that someone in New York City or down in Miami is reaping the benefits of the mining. They're getting the money, and they're working the people for about half of what the union scale is without benefits and all that.

Back at the home place where we live on Montgomery Creek, they'd already mined going up the hollow, which is probably seven or eight miles long, and I live up towards the head of the hollow. Before I built my new home, I lived right across from the home place, beside the creek—everyone wants down next to the creek. It had never been flooded. I built a nice home. And I had other land. I could have built anywhere, but I didn't worry about it because it had never flooded before. But, due to this mining, we got flooded while I was still building. I lost several thousand dollars' worth of building material due to this flood that was caused directly by the mining. When they strip these mountaintops off and it rains, we're all aware of what happens. There's nothing to hold it back; it all comes at once.

They're getting greedier, and they put off larger blasts. And now they're on the other side. What I'm referring to is a permit of 1,400 acres by ICG. This is the same company you see in the news with the people getting killed in West Virginia. They destroyed homes. They destroyed property.

Barn along Highway 29 in the eastern panhandle of West Virginia. Photo © Jim Clark.

An eighteen-wheel coal truck at a rail crossing in Brookside, Harlan County, Kentucky. Photo © Builder Levy.

They destroyed the roads, they stopped up the culverts and all. They blasted and the fly rock—they call it "fly rock," but some of it is pieces of rock big as your fist—come over the mountain and into a swimming pool with kids in it!

And you get the people up there, the people that are supposed to represent you and protect you, these so-called protective agencies, and they do nothing. This incident where the rock came into the swimming pool—the way they penalize this company was they shut them down for two weeks, while they were on vacation! Now that's the kind of people we got protecting us. The news media, they don't let a lot of this out, they want to keep it quiet, due to getting the low cost of energy. They may call it low cost, and it may be to some people, but if you live here, it's not low-cost energy. It's costing us a lot. Our very lives are being put on the line.

It's Where We Live
Patsy Carter

This [holding up a photograph] is—this was our daughter. She was twenty-one years old. She was killed with a coal truck. The police said the guy that was driving probably was on drugs and fell asleep at the wheel. It was a senseless death.

All this girl did was worked and went to school all her life. She lacked eleven days graduating from college. She called me every night when she got off work to say, "Mommy, I'm on my way home, do you need anything? I love you, Mommy." She didn't show up that night. She was late, and I was scared; and I got up and went to look for her, and it was a mess.

But the greed, the greed from these coal companies. The man that was driving this coal truck was on home confinement, a prison program, where he should have been checked if he was on drugs.

If they don't wreck, they get by. Nobody checks on them. They don't care if they're hauling coal. The trucks are so monstrous on our roads, it's unreal—the coal spilling off the sides. Drive up U.S. [Route] 23 towards Louisa, Kentucky, it's fifteen in a row.

Law enforcement? It's a joke. We live in Eastern Kentucky. Nobody hears us. And it's coal. It's King Coal. That's where we live.

Lucious Thompson with his granddaughters, Destiny Clark (left) and Delena Brooks, in Tom Biggs Hollow, McRoberts, Letcher County, Kentucky. Photo © Builder Levy.

What We Do to the Land, We Do to the People
Rully Urias

I'll paint a picture for you. You're sitting in your house, and you're enjoying a nice afternoon, it's a warm, sunny day out, but you can't let your daughter out because of the dust. And when she hears a blast, she drops to the ground or the floor, and she crawls to you and asks you what's going on. And you have to try and explain to a two-and-a-half-year-old, almost three, what coal mining is. There's been people come to our house, and you can hear the coal trucks barreling down the dirt road above us, and you ask my daughter, "Say, what's that noise?" and she knows what a coal truck is, just by the sound of it. Now how sad is that?

What beauty remains over there where we live at is just on my property. Everything has been gutted and bombarded. I've been on one flyover, and I've always seen pictures of it [mountaintop removal] before, but I've never seen it first-hand from above. And it nauseated me; it made me sick. I don't ever get sick and it made me sick to see the butchered, scarred land.

And they say reclamation is as good or better as God made it. It's not. What we do to the land, we do to the people. My land's sick, and I'm sick. We're fighting two battles. I'm fighting one with my health and one to keep my land intact, so I can have something left to leave for my little girl. I don't come from a rich family, but we do have a little land left. I want to be able to make sure that she always has a place to call home if she ever ventures off and comes back.

Throwaway People
Sam Gilbert

I've lived in these mountains all my life. My grandparents, great-grandparents, were of Cherokee descent. I can go back to the beginning of time in these mountains. To see greed take over from everything else . . . and I wonder how many souls have been bought with this money. I wonder. And then I wonder how many souls have died from the impact of this.

Now these people that worries about these little checks that they get right now reminds me of one time a long time ago I went to an old guy that lived in Letcher County, Clarence Huff, and tried to buy a squirrel dog off of him. He said, "Son, if I sell that dog, I'll spend the money, and then I won't have no money or no dog either."

That's the same way it is with these checks that the coal companies buy you temporarily off with. One day you wake up, you ain't got no job and you ain't got no money . . . and you still don't have your dog either!

What they consider us to be is throwaway people. Just like the American Indian was, back there in the time when the ones that they couldn't drive off the Plains, they put on a reservation and starved them to death.

The people of the watersheds may themselves be a permanent economic resource, but only and precisely to the extent that they take good care of what they have. If Kentuckians, upstream and down, ever fulfill their responsibilities to the precious things they have been given—the forests, the soils, and the streams—they will do so because they will have accepted a truth that . . . the forests, the soils, and the streams are worth far more than the coal for which they are now being destroyed.

—*Wendell Berry*

A young underground miner at Wolf Creek Colliery, Lovely, Martin County, Kentucky, 1971. Photo © Builder Levy.

When I first moved on Eolia, it was a nice quiet community, and everybody stuck together. Everybody was close, honest. And then this coal company came in, which coal companies have been known to bust communities, run people off, made them sell their property, and then made them sign away their First Amendment rights by doing so. Now I'm not going to sign away my First Amendment rights for no damn body. I may die there because of these coal companies, but I'll keep my rights.

And I'm an ex–strip miner. When I stripped, we didn't do this. They didn't do these mountaintop removals. We put the wall back behind us. Just kept bringing the trucks around, putting it back behind us, and reclaiming it, but it still left a scar.

Now, they take all that fill off and put it in the hollow. They don't put it around behind them. Then they jump up, get the next seam, and do the same thing. They put a high-wall miner in on that bottom seam and come around through there, and it goes in 800 to indefinite [feet], and they take all the coal out under that mountain—leaving that land unreclaimed. And they've permitted every hollow, everything around through there.

I went up there last week and took some people up. I hadn't been up there in a while and I was surprised. A mountain goat couldn't walk up that mountain! Nothing on it but that grass mixture that they plant. And then when they plant trees, they'll put burr pines every six foot and they grow about as high as this ceiling—just got a lot of limbs on them. No benefit. They don't make timber or anything. The government won't make them put anything back that's of any benefit. There's a dust bowl up there now that you can't see a truck driving in front of you.

And, again, why is this allowed?

━◆━

This was adapted from a collection of oral histories put together by Kentuckians for the Commonwealth, a grassroots organization that has been on the front lines of the fight against mountaintop removal.

A Sense of Place, a Sense of Self

Janet Keating

WHEN I THINK ABOUT A sense of place, what comes to mind is mountains, rivers, and forests, my life experiences, generations of family and friends, the Appalachian culture that spawned me—its politics and history. While all those things undoubtedly helped me develop a sense of place, my deepest connections are with nature and the land.

Hardly any other place on earth can boast the rich biodiversity found in West Virginia. The hardwood forests alone are home to more than eighty species of trees. And that is only the beginning. A walk in the woods in early spring offers a profusion of wildflowers—delicate quaker-ladies, spring beauties, and trillium—carpeting the rich, moist forest floor. The melodious sounds of the wood thrush echo in the valley. Deeper in the forest, an ovenbird adamantly calls, "Teacher, teacher, teacher!" Our unique forests support numerous species of wood warblers, neotropical migrants that nest throughout the state or rest here during spring and fall migration, though populations are declining due to habitat destruction. A moss-covered sandstone rock provides a front-row seat for pondering the beauty before me. All my senses are heightened. No compasses or maps are necessary. I know where I am—at home in Appalachia.

In West Virginia, nature is so abundant and accessible, providing me not only with a sense of place but also with a

A fisherman enjoys the New River, West Virginia. Photo courtesy of Appalachian Voices.

A split rail fence along the Highland Scenic Highway in rural West Virginia on a foggy morning. Photo © Jim Clark.

sense of self. As a child, I counted myself luckiest when my parents farmed me out with aunts and uncles who had homes in the country, where my freedom to explore knew almost no boundaries. My favorite place to visit was Aunt Florence's dairy farm. The instant we arrived, off I would dash—to a hillside, meadow, or creek to explore the rich, natural treasure trove that lay before me. Whether I was watching the birth of newborn kittens or mourning the loss of a baby bird found featherless and cold on the ground, nature provided me with ample opportunity to feed my curiosity about life and taught me about the inevitability of death as well as the bounty just a hand's grasp away.

My father's love of fishing and his willingness to let me tag along when he fished on a lake or on the Ohio River fostered in me an enduring love for the outdoors. We would set out in the predawn hours, sometimes with early-morning fog shrouding the other shore from view. My fishing gear was always the simplest—just a pole with a short line rigged with a small red-and-white bobber and tiny hook for catching sunfish or bluegills. Though I didn't mind handling and catching live bait, I flatly refused to kill and impale worms on a hook. Dad indulged me on that matter, but he took his fishing seriously; whatever he caught, he killed, cleaned, and cooked. I learned about the web of life firsthand—worms in the earth were food for the fish that became food for our dinner table and me.

But life in these sheltered hills and hollows goes far beyond practical matters like food for the table. There's the significant matter of spiritual development. The majority of folks here find peace of mind as regular churchgoers. I have no argument with their method, but my church has no walls. I'm convinced that stargazing is akin to soul-searching. We're lucky in West Virginia to still have access to the stars on a clear night—especially away from city lights. Awed by the moon and stars, comets, and eclipses, I feel a deep connection to generations of my ancestors who watched the same night sky season after season. The infinite cosmos and its mysteries help me keep my life in perspective. Though I'm just a speck on this vast blue dot, the same spirit that enlivens all of life enlivens me   I'm of neither greater nor lesser value than all that we know as life here and perhaps beyond.

Thousands of tired, nerve-shaken, over-civilized people are beginning to find out that going to the mountain is going home; that wildness is necessity; that mountain parks and reservations are useful not only as fountains of timber and irrigating rivers, but as fountains of life.

—*John Muir*

Economic Exile

Regina Hendrix

Chelyan Bridge spans the Kanawha River in Kanawha County, West Virginia, 1968. Photographer unknown; courtesy of Library of Congress.

I WAS BORN IN CHARLESTON, WEST Virginia, in 1936 and grew up in the Kanawha Valley. During the 1950s, I was forced to leave for economic reasons. At that time, Charleston was home to more than 80,000 people, and job opportunities were mainly in the coal and chemical industries. These two industries owned our whole governing structure.

When I returned to the Kanawha Valley in 1999, the population had dropped to 53,000. The coal industry still maintained control of our economy and our statehouse, while most of the chemical industry had found greener pastures overseas in the form of cheap labor and lax environmental regulations.

During my forty-five-year economic exile from West Virginia, I always wanted to return to live in the hills of the place I called home. These rocks and mountains, verdant green mountains and wild rivers, are forever imprinted in my mind. So, shortly after my retirement in 1998, it was an easy decision to return home to live in Charleston. I found an apartment near the capitol building and settled in. This was not as easy as it sounds, partly because of West Virginia's punitive taxes. During his time as governor, Joe Manchin began a "Come Home to West Virginia" campaign, encouraging exiled West Virginians to return home, but many state policies make this difficult.

Determined to stay in my home state, I faced up to the economic realities, stashed my possessions, and began my golden years. One day I was looking out my window, and I saw an Uncle Sam figure on Greenbrier Street, a main thoroughfare that runs adjacent to the capitol complex. He was mounted on stilts and was headed towards the capitol. It was obvious he was preparing for a rally, and I decided to follow him to see what was going on. At the capitol I encountered a scene that was to become all too familiar to me in the years to come. People were rallying to stop mountaintop removal, and they were saying some really unbelievable things about the destruction and dislocation caused by this practice. I thought they must be exaggerating, but I accepted their invitation to go on a flyover to look at the MTR sites.

I was anticipating a little sightseeing excursion in the mountains, but mere words cannot describe the extent of the destruction and defilement of our mountains that I witnessed

Pettry Bottom, part of the Edwight MTR site, cleared of timber in preparation for mining, Raleigh County, West Virginia. Photo © Denny Tyler.

Passkey to Time

I live for the time
when I will be nothing
more than a memory—
a distant face like
the man in the moon

I am no appalachian
like a doctor
living in a townhouse
or a brick chateau
high on Medicaid Mtn.
with county water
A.D.D. agency sewer
due to being on the
gov. aid pipeline.

I am a creeker

I remember the day
of chasing chickens in the barnyard
for Sunday dinner
and counting crows in the cornfield
for Granddad's shotgun

Society has taken away the
divine rights of the mtn. farmer
leaving half naked mountains
naked women on satellite t.v.—
replacements for our birthright—
a view of Pine Mountain
fully dressed in her Spring Clothes.

—Walter Lane

that day. Most of these MTR sites cannot be seen from the highways, but the companies cannot hide them from the air. When I returned from the flight, there were tears in my eyes. I grieved the loss of hundreds of square miles of mountains and more than 1,000 miles of destroyed streams.

While at the capitol rally I joined the Ohio Valley Environmental Coalition (OVEC) and rejoined the Sierra Club. Some years back I had hiked with the Sierra Club in the Shenandoah Mountains and had become a member in the Washington metropolitan area. After the flyover I was reborn as an activist with both of these organizations. OVEC had already dedicated itself to stopping mountaintop removal, but at the time the national Sierra Club seemed unaware of what was happening in West Virginia and other central Appalachian states where MTR takes place. After education efforts and many pleas, the Sierra Club entered the fight against MTR in a very visible and crucial way, joining the lawsuits on valley fills and assigning an environmental justice staffer to our region. The West Virginia chapter of the Sierra Club has become a part of an informal coalition called Friends of the Mountains.

I have thought many times of returning to the eastern seaboard, where my granddaughters and other relatives remain. I always hoped that some of my siblings would come back to West Virginia to retire, but over the years they, along with many other expatriates, have been scared away by the environmental destruction we wreak on ourselves, as well as by the cumbersome state tax system. My desire to stay in these West Virginia hills leads me to be optimistic that we are making progress in efforts to stop mountaintop removal, promote renewable energy, and rescue our political system from the coal interests. So I remain in West Virginia and will continue to fight as long as this injustice remains—and as long as there are others like me who want better for our children and grandchildren than a one-resource economy and a devastated environment.

In Care of Creation

Julia "Judy" Bonds

THE APPALACHIANS ARE AMONG THE oldest mountains on earth and the first mountains God created. A picture from a flyover of these mountains shows the fingerprints of God's creative hands. The gaps in the range looks as if God's very hands reached down to form and mold those beautiful and lush mountains.

Mountaintop removal is not only an environmental disaster and a human rights issue but also a moral and spiritual sin. How very sad God must be at the destructive deeds that his children are taking part in. I imagine that it must make him turn his eyes away; watching us destroy the very place he gave us to live in, worship in, and raise our children in.

Here in central Appalachia, religion plays a huge part in our lives. Unfortunately, coalfield churches have been "possessed" and used by the coal industry for many years, dating back to the beginning of the company towns. The industry's intent was to oppress, control, and silence us mountaineers, to keep our people from speaking out, and to encourage us to betray our own people, our own interests, and even the Creator. This tactic is still going on today and has been used by oppressive corporations and governments in other areas. There must be an instruction book straight from hell, hidden somewhere in their evil lairs.

My faith in God keeps me sane and moving in the right direction for our children and grandchildren. Our children

Judy Bonds outside her home in Raleigh County, West Virginia. Bonds, whose family has lived in the Coal River Valley for generations, won the Goldman Environmental Prize in 2003. Photo © Jo Syz.

Early spring sunlight on the Seneca Rocks formation in Monongahela National Forest, Pendleton County, West Virginia. Photo © Jim Clark.

and our souls depend upon what we decide to do today. From my backyard, I can feel the ancient energy of the Appalachian Mountains. The energy in these mountains from God restores my soul. The mountain streams sing a song of love and peace from the Creator. Both beckon me to come closer and hear God's natural message, much better and truer than an interpretation from man. The aroma of the forest God created fills me with such joy that I cannot express it. My first memories are of the smell of the rich black earth as my father and grandfather turned the spring garden. The apostle Paul says that the creation shows us God's creativity, beauty, and power. Look, you will see that all creation is pointed upward to God. The Appalachian Mountains are the perfect example of this. The mountains cause us to lift up our eyes to God. The Book of Psalms is full of mountains, and scripture is explicit about how God expects us to care for the creation, *all* of creation.

In Genesis, we are told that God put man in the garden to "dress it and keep it," not to destroy it. The Bible tells us that God knows every creature that he created, and furthermore, they "belong to him." Some coal minions say that God gave man dominion over the earth and animals and that man is placed above them. To their dismay, I agree with them. Their argument proves our point. God holds us accountable for the care of the earth and animals. Man's attempted justification for his destruction is defenseless. God put us in charge of the care of the animals and the creation.

God gave us dominion and charge over our children as well; do we think that God wants us to abuse them? So, then, why would we think that God would condone our abuse of his other creations? Many of us have not been very good stewards of his creation. In fact, we are even poisoning our own unborn children to ensure easy lifestyles for some people. Mercury from coal is present in one of every five women's wombs, and it can cause low IQs, mental retardation, attention deficit disorder, and behavioral problems in our babies.

The workers on a mountaintop removal site destroy animals in the permitted area. Then the animals' entire habitat is destroyed by blasting and stripping; only God knows if it will ever be livable again. First is the clear-cutting of trees, with animals running everywhere for their lives. Then comes the blasting of the mountains and the bulldozing of the earth, often as the animals and their young hide in their dens. A friend of mine described the horrific screams of a mommy bear as a man on a giant bulldozer covered up her cubs in the den where they waited. He said that he would never forget her screams as long as he lives. Another instance of such unwarranted abuse happened as workers on a mountaintop removal site were getting ready for a blast. They drilled holes and filled them with explosives, set up the blast, and moved back to the safe area. Then they noticed a black bear nearing the charges. They delayed the blast until the bear was over the explosives and then detonated it, blowing up the bear. I don't understand what would make people do this to helpless animals.

Maybe it is because they make a living (or make their own death) by destroying so much, and therefore they become immune to it. It is shameful that these men would accept this and try to justify such evil deeds in order to make a living. They blast their neighbors' homes and poison their neighbors' wells using the same excuse. Greedy, corrupt politicians

Mountaintop removal mining, by destroying homeplaces, is also destroying ancestral ground, sacred ground, where generations after generations have lived, gone to church, married, made and birthed babies, taken family meals, slept in peace, died and been buried. The sanctity and sacredness of all life and the natural environment created by God should not be destroyed in the name of corporate profit.

—*Catholic Committee of Appalachia, 1998*

Concerned citizens, including activist leaders Larry Gibson and Judy Bonds, demonstrate against mountaintop removal at a Massey Energy shareholders' meeting in May 2004, Charleston, West Virginia. Detail of photo © Builder Levy.

are owned by coal money, so they encourage and pass laws that allow this to happen. These puppet politicians are supposed to protect the people. Our politicians could bring other jobs to our area, but they refuse to do so in order to do the bidding of the coal industry and keep this region a mono-economy. May God forgive them.

The coal industry and their workers say that they have lawful permits to destroy the mountains. The government, not God, gives out these permits. The coal industry often thinks it is God. I have heard greedy people try to justify strip mining by saying that they "put it back better than it was before." Blasphemy. They dare think that they do a better job than God?

At a public hearing, I heard a strip-mining so-called preacher testify that he saw the Grand Canyon while on vacation. He said his workplace looked just like the Grand Canyon, considered a wonder of the world. He proudly exclaimed that miners created the same thing here in West Virginia. The gasps from the audience at the blasphemy he spouted were loud and clear. This is a prime example of the audacity, vanity, and pride that the coal barons fill their employees with. Woe to the shepherd that leads his sheep down the evil path.

When the greed of coal minions causes death and destruction in disasters such as Buffalo Creek, the industry and their puppet politicians dare blame it on God. In 1972, a reply from a Buffalo Creek survivor answered this better than any "expert" could. As the coal company officials stated that the Buffalo Creek disaster was an "act of God," a survivor sat straight up and replied, "I didn't see Jesus a driving that slate truck up there on that mountain." That statement must've brought a big smile to God's face. I wonder if God is tired of being blamed for the greedy, evil acts of the coal industry. Buffalo Creek, other coal disasters, and mountaintop removal are "acts of greed." These are but a few examples of why Jesus said to avoid greed above all.

Willfully destroying the earth, the creation, is a sin for which we will all be judged. We must remember that, as if our souls depend upon it, because they do.

To Harness the Wind

Lorelei Scarbro

I AM A COMMUNITY ORGANIZER FOR Coal River Mountain Watch, and my primary focus right now is the Coal River Wind Project. I live in Rock Creek, West Virginia, which is just one of several communities soon to be destroyed if the governor of the Mountain State does not honor his word on supporting renewable energy. At risk are Rock Creek, Dry Creek, Horse Creek, Clear Fork, Dorothy, Sycamore Hollow, and many, many more. And make no mistake about it, when the air is contaminated on Coal River and the water destroyed by a valley fill or chemicals from the processing of coal, it doesn't matter where you live on this planet—it will eventually be a part of your life.

The reason we are here today is because we offer the alternative they say we never have. We offer hope for the generations to come. We are proposing the largest wind farm on the East Coast. The benefits of this are numerous: revenue for the county and state; increased spending in the surrounding communities to help our local economy grow; green jobs and an increase of underground coal-mining jobs; renewable energy that will benefit us all. Southern West Virginia has been devastated by generations of a mono-economy, and the powers that be need to be willing to change that. All you need to do to see the results of this is to drive through any dying coal town throughout Appalachia.

Water droplet on fern frond, West Virginia. Photo © Jim Clark.

A reclamation site and valley fills at a mountaintop removal mine in West Virginia, seen from the air. Photo © Vivian Stockman.

We are here today to lay this at the feet of Governor Joe Manchin. As the head of the executive branch of the government in this state, he is responsible. We are aware of the fact that there is a ninety-man shortage in the Department of Environmental Protection. Our position is, if you can't police it, don't permit it. We are tired of doing their job for them. Last week, the governor was willing to allow the top of Coal River Mountain to begin to be blown apart. Only because we had a researcher poring over permits did we find that the coal company had not taken the necessary steps to legally proceed. This particular company has a history of operating outside the law in our backyards and in the state of West Virginia. The governor needs to put an end to that.

Some people may ask, "Why this mountain?" The fact

of the matter is that nearly 500 mountains throughout Appalachia have been decapitated by mountaintop removal, and thus the wind feasibility and the possibility of building an industrial-scale wind farm are lost. Postmined land would prove to be unstable. We need to start rebuilding our wild, wonderful West Virginia—this project would save a mountain and help us preserve Appalachian culture and the history that remains in these hills.

When I was a little girl growing up in Lincoln County, West Virginia, I remember my daddy going into the woods with his gun over his shoulder, and whatever he came back with was what we had to eat for dinner, along with whatever we harvested from our garden. We need to continue the practices of harvesting ginseng, ramps, berries, nuts, and other sources of food that are found in these hills. Hunting and fishing provide a source of food but also are an important part of this way of life. Many people harvest ginseng in the fall, which is selling for around $1,000 a pound, and that is the money they use to buy Christmas gifts for their family.

There are those of us who love living in a city or a town, and there are those of us who are not comfortable when the horizon stretches out too far in front of us. I am, of course, among the latter. This wind farm would preserve this mountain and all that is there for many generations to come. This mountain, this earth, is not ours. It is just borrowed for the time that we are here. As you look into the faces of your children, grandchildren, brother, or sister, know this: We need to leave this place better than we found it. The Coal River Wind Project is our answer as to how we do that.

This is the text of a speech given at the Pro–Wind Farm Rally in Charleston, West Virginia, September 16, 2008.

I'll walk where my own nature would
  be leading,
It vexes me to choose another guide;
Where the grey flocks in the ferny
  glens are feeding,
Where the wild wind blows on the
  mountain side.
What have these lonely mountains
  worth revealing?
More glory and more grief than I
  can tell;
The earth that wakes one human
  heart to feeling
Can centre both the worlds of
  Heaven and Hell

—*Emily Bronte*

Meeting Governor Manchin

Mary Ellen Lough

Mae Phillips and her grand-daughter Jeanie, Kildav, Harlan County, Kentucky, 1974. Photo © Builder Levy.

ONE OF MY MOST POIGNANT memories is of visiting my Aunt Sarah's farm in the hills of Pendleton County as a child. Not much changed over the years in her farmhouse. I remember her warm wood cookstove and the narrow, low-ceilinged upstairs where we sisters nestled under handmade quilts passed down from generations. We would roll up our pant legs and walk with my dad up the creek to the waterfall. I thought there was no more beautiful place on earth. It was not until much later, after moving from the mountains, that I realized how much of my family history is there, how my blood is not so far removed from those rolling hills. My heart has not stopped aching for West Virginia since.

My sister lives in Grant County, the next county over from the farm. She had first made me aware of mountaintop removal through her activism, blogging, and untiring sharing of information on the subject. At the time, I had been living overseas for three years and had become more and more distraught at the disparity between the urban life I was living and the destruction of those solid mountains I loved so much. It was in this faraway place that I realized that the land I cared most about—the sturdy mountains that had brought me peace and surety—was being systematically depleted and exploited for the purposes of excess energy that America can live without.

This profound love of land and home eventually brought my family and me back to live in West Virginia. It was this same love of the land that made my sister call Governor Manchin's office several times a day to ask him to issue a stay of execution on the destruction of Coal River Mountain, even though her calls were never answered. So it seemed providential that the day after I arrived at her home for a visit, the governor would in fact be in town for the dedication of a refurbished town depot in Grant County. We were both ready to shake his hand and get in whatever words we could, since he was impossible to reach any other way.

My sister had readied her pamphlets and was hoping for, at most, a brief, two-sentence exchange before he moved on, expecting to be in a long line of hand shakers. We had discussed what the best sound bite would be and had decided on "Please put an end to mountaintop removal and issue a stay of execution on Cold River Mountain." Then we would hand him a pamphlet, and the deed would be done.

We arrived early with my four young children in tow and found out that the governor would be arriving by helicopter in just a half hour. It was a very dramatic entrance. We were some of the first in line, and he approached us with a politician's smile and outstretched hand. Amy shook his hand and

People working to halt MTR activities on Coal River Mountain hope to prevent a future in which the landscape resembles that of Kayford Mountain, shown here. Photo © Mark Schmerling.

gave him the leaflet while I stood in the background with my children.

"As one of your constituents, I would like to ask you to end the travesty of mountaintop removal and issue a stay of execution on Coal River Mountain," she said.

The statement was answered by an easy, smooth smile. "Well, now you don't have to worry about that around here. It doesn't affect your county."

I was taken aback by his charm. His first statement, his easy smile, and his fatherly tender tone made me feel like a Jedi mind trick was being played on me. I forgot what it was I wanted to say so badly, but Amy kept her bearings. She continued, "Actually, it does. A 500-acre site was just permitted for surface mining at the corner of our county."

"Oh really?" he said. "Well, I hadn't heard anything about that." His Jedi confidence seemed to waver for a moment. "Anyway, that's just contour mining, right?"

"We all live downstream, and we all share water," my sister replied. "It affects us all."

The smile returned, and his answer was a quick diversion. "Well, there are already so many regulations. It is all being handled very carefully. And are these your children?"

"No, they're mine," I said, stepping out from the background. The opportunity had fallen to me. "And I want there to be mountains left for my children. Please put an end to mountaintop removal."

Four pairs of the biggest, most beautiful and uncorrupted brown eyes stared up intensely at the governor. He could have patted my children's heads and walked away at that point, but with elections coming up and a crowd of voters watching him, he turned up the charm instead.

"Well, there are just so many safeguards and regulations in place for that. National, state, local—it's so heavily over-seen that you don't need to worry about it. It's all about balance. We just need balance."

Jedi mind tricks again. I found myself wanting to believe him, but I didn't. I said, "If they were enforced, but they're not because of corruption, and there needs to be an end to the corruption and more protection for the mountains and the people of West Virginia."

"And especially a stay of execution at the Coal River Mountain site," my sister added.

"We would love to see windmills put up there," I said.

"Oh," he laughed, seemingly relieved to have a new tactic to rely on, "but then the environmentalists complain about the windmills. You wouldn't believe all the stuff I hear." I noticed a reassured shift in his countenance. Now he had a more solid platform to stand on—the one that puts all environmentalists in a category of too difficult to please and best dismissed.

And with this, Governor Manchin began to move on, but not before facing the crowd and saying loud enough for the voting constituency gathered around to hear, "But, yes, I agree, we need a green package, and I am working on that. It's all about balance."

Green package? Balance? We had not mentioned a green package. It seemed he wanted the crowd to have the impression that he had been having a friendly, agreeable dialogue with concerned constituents, in which we primarily agreed and were satisfied. But I'm afraid what the governor calls balance means nothing more than capitulation to Big Coal's terms.

Several times during our conversation and afterward during his speech, I found myself unwillingly liking him. The

Spitting in the Leaves

In Spanishburg there are boys in tight jeans,
mud on their cowboy boots and they wear huge hats
with feathers, skunk feathers they tell me.
They do not want to be in school, but are.
Some teachers cared enough to hold them. Unlike
their thin disheveled cousins, the boys on Matoaka's
Main Street in October who loll against parking meters
and spit into the leaves. Because of them, someone
will think we need a war, will think the best solution
would be for them to take their hats and feathers,
their good country manners and drag them off somewhere,
to Vietnam, to El Salvador. And they'll go.
They'll go from West Virginia, from hills and back roads
that twist like politics through trees, and they'll fight,
not because they know what for but because what they know
is how to fight. What they know is feathers,
their strong skinny arms, their spitting in the leaves.

—Maggie Anderson

way he speaks is so down-to-earth, with confidence in us small-town people with our quaint and hardworking ways. And I think he relies on his charm and our visceral reaction to it.

We left the interaction glad for a chance to have added our voices to the many other demanding change, and we were grateful that our presence there, with my children, had disquieted him for at least a moment. But we were not heard; we were only passed over as quickly and smoothly as possible. Still, that does not mean we'll be quiet.

Yes We Can

Jason Howard

THERE'S NOTHING LIKE WASHINGTON, D.C., in the mornings. As the sun rises above the Anacostia River, traveling up East Capitol Street and shimmering through the old beech trees lining the sidewalks, it bathes the Capitol dome in a glow that forces even the most jaded Washington insider to marvel at its brilliance, sometimes pausing as if to acknowledge a head of state passing by in a motorcade. Shades of pinks and blues and whites collide in a spectacle above the Mall. It's a restorative sight, one that reminds Americans that something good can happen here, after all.

And so it was on the morning of Inauguration Day 2009.

I'd made a nine-hour pilgrimage from my native Appalachia to witness history. As a former six-year resident of Washington, I'd been to many gatherings and events. I'd swallowed my partisan pride and attended George W. Bush's first inaugural—I couldn't bring myself to go to the second— as well as Ronald Reagan's funeral procession. I'd been to Fourth of July celebrations on the Mall, concerts at the Lincoln Memorial, marches for various causes.

This was different. It was a family reunion. We were gathering to celebrate one of our own, a brother who had challenged us to realize the Dream, a son who had made us proud again, a father who had reassured us during tough times.

Underground coal miner Toby Moore at an Eastern Coal Company operation in Pike County, Kentucky, 1970. Photo © Builder Levy.

I thought about these things as I walked down Maryland Avenue toward the Capitol, winding my way through lines of ticket holders behind the Senate office buildings, being routed through the Third Street tunnel, which runs under the Mall. Exiting into the sunlight, the throngs moved at a snail's pace to the public viewing spaces that remained open. What should have been a twenty-five-minute walk took more than an hour and a half, ample time to reflect on the change I had traveled from Eastern Kentucky to witness. For the first time in years, I was full of hope not just for America but also for Appalachia: Barack Obama had publicly criticized mountaintop removal on a few occasions during the presidential campaign.

"Strip mining is an environmental disaster," he told the group Appalachian Voices. "We have to find more environmentally sound ways of mining coal than simply blowing the tops off mountains."

An imperfect promise full of political wiggle room, yes—especially given Obama's troubling history as a supporter of clean coal technology. But this was something that didn't seem like an idle campaign pledge. After all, it's not necessarily a popular position to take when asking for the votes of Appalachians, many of whom still believe that to criticize the coal industry is to speak against the miners themselves.

Reaching the Washington Monument, I found a spot of ground on the knoll that faces the Capitol. As the area filled to capacity, people began introducing themselves and conversing easily. We exchanged the stories behind our respective pilgrimages to D.C. as we struggled to stay warm in the frigid weather. When the Marine Corps Band struck up "Stars and Stripes Forever," we willed our stiff legs to march along to the beat. We let out cheers as we watched the arrival of various dignitaries on the Jumbotrons that lined the Mall.

I was in full sympathy with the seven-year-old boy standing next to me who tugged at his mother's coat: "When will Barack Obama get here?"

"Any minute now," she said with a smile.

She was right. We watched in anticipation as he strode out

An American flag overlooks the destruction wreaked by mountaintop removal at Kayford Mountain, West Virginia. Photo © Nick Regalado; courtesy of Coal River Mountain Watch.

onto the platform. Our view obscured by the press stand and the expanse of the Mall itself, we relied on the big screens for our images as he greeted the various dignitaries. When it finally came his turn to take the oath of office, a silence spread over the length of the Mall. Before he could finish his last word, a roar went up from the crowd that surely rattled the Statue of Freedom atop her perch on the Capitol dome. It was our shout of thanksgiving after wandering in the wilderness for eight long years. Eight years of mountains blasted, streams buried, water polluted. Eight years of futile appeals to the White House and the Environmental Protection Agency. Eight years of despair.

As President Obama began his inaugural address, my mind wandered across the Potomac into Virginia, down through the Shenandoah Valley, across Clinch Mountain in Tennessee, and up into the craggy hills of my native Kentucky. And I felt relieved.

Hope is sometimes a scarce commodity in the hills and hollers of Appalachia. Parents who send their children to Marsh Fork Elementary School in West Virginia can't muster much optimism when a 2.8-billion-gallon slurry pond sits on a mountain above the school. The few remaining folks living on Island Creek in Eastern Kentucky find it difficult to see their glass as half full, especially when the water is orange.

But standing 500 miles away on the Mall, the roar of the flags surrounding the Washington Monument loud in my ears, a hope like I've never known began to swell in my belly. It moistened my eyes and quickened my pulse. As I looked around at the millions of my kinfolk gathered there with me, I said a prayer for our mountains and our people: "Yes we can."

Our remnants of wilderness will yield bigger values to the nation's character and health than they will to its pocketbook, and to destroy them will be to admit that the latter are the only values that interest us.

—*Aldo Leopold*

Acknowledgments

THE PEOPLE OF THE APPALACHIAN coalfields have offered their truths with courage and honesty in this book, their voices as rugged as the mountains that run through their homeland. It has been our privilege to present their stories here. Our first thanks must go to them, as well as to our families and all the families of the coalfields.

The book benefited from the generous contributions of numerous scholars, activists, journalists, and community members who unselfishly gave of their time and expertise; we are fortunate to include their insights in these pages. The extraordinary and powerful photographs were donated by their talented creators, as were the poems, song lyrics, and other sidebar texts, and we offer our thanks to all these contributors. We also offer very special thanks to Dick Fauss, Bryan Ward, Joe Geiger, the staff at the West Virginia State Archives, and book designer Harry Choron and literary agent/book producer Sandy Choron.

This book is a companion to the documentary film *Coal Country*. Writer and director Phylis Geller deserves the credit for telling these stories in the film, which came to life through the work of Jordan Freeman, who lived and filmed in the coalfields for two years, providing a complex understanding of the issues as well as excellent cinematography; Sam Green,

Opposite: Country road, Pocohontas County, West Virginia. Photo © Jim Clark.

who edited the film and whose wisdom helped us tell the story; and Charlie Barnett, our brilliant composer.

Shirley Stewart Burns continues to be inspired and motivated by people she has known and by others through their work. She especially wishes to thank the following for their inspiration and support: Jesus, Matthew Burns, Neely and Cora Stewart, her Stewart and McKinney kin and ancestors, Christina Bailey, Maya Nye, Mary Miller and Pauline Canterberry, Carlos Gore, Jim Clark, Ron Lewis, all of Ron's Angels, as well as Harry Caudill, Homer Morris, Merle Haggard, Governor William C. Marland, Pete Seeger, Hazel Dickens, Mother Jones, and each and every individual working to bring the travesty of mountaintop removal to an end.

Mari-Lynn Evans wishes to acknowledge especially the support of Phylis Geller, Adam Lewis and the Adam Lewis Foundation, the Sierra Club, Kathy Mattea, Jean Ritchie, Earthjustice, the Park Foundation, Appalachian Voices, David Orr, Sam Green, Charlie Barnett, Vivian Stockman, Jordan Freeman, Joe Lovett, Nick and Nina Clooney, Sarah Dupont, Michael Shnayerson, Fred Pollock, Marvin Evans, the Currence family, Zack Evans, Cindy Bailey, Eddie Morris, Larry Gibson, Ashley Judd, Adrienne Bramhall, Aaron Isherwood, Owen Bailey, Oliver Bernstein, Mary Anne Hitt, Bruce Niles, Bill McCabe, Bill Price, Jason Wilber, Andy Mahler, Steve Schmidt, Glynis Board, Mike Youngren, Steve Fesenmaier, Tom and Catherine Ball, Bernice and Kathy Selvage, Joan Mulhern, Jared Saylor, Randall Maggard, Julia "Judy" Bonds, Elisa Young, William D. and LaVon Mick Currence, Pauline Cantenberry, Mary Miller, Chuck Nelson, Ken Hechler, Bo Webb, Teri Blanton, Matt Noerpel, and the Steele family.

Silas House became involved in this fight because of the many heroes who inspired him to stand up for what he believes in. Among those he wishes to thank are Wendell Berry, Ollie "the Widow" Combs, Dan Gibson, Judy Hensley, Florence King, Mike Mullins, members of the Reel World String Band, Jean Ritchie, Eleanor Roosevelt, Lee Smith, Patty Wallace, Nellie Woolum, and the hundreds of schoolchildren across Appalachia who are speaking out against mountaintop removal. He also thanks Donna Conley, Cheyenne House, Olivia House, Jason Howard, Denton Loving, Eleshia Sloan, and Neela Vaswani for various acts of kindness.

We owe a special debt of gratitude to the community groups that have been so integral to informing both the book and the documentary film: Appalachian Voices, Coal River Mountain Watch, Kentuckians for the Commonwealth, Ohio Valley Environmental Coalition, Save Our Cumberland Mountains, and the Southern Appalachian Mountain Stewards. We are truly humbled by the generosity of so many who shared their time and talent to create this book. We are forever grateful for your passion, your inspiration, and your absolute belief that we can make our world a better place. In the end, it is the work of numerous people, all striving to convey the understanding that, whether we realize it or not, we all live in coal country.

Credits

Information Resources

The FOLLOWING LIST OF BOOKS, articles, films, organizations, and online resources is far from exhaustive, but it will provide interested readers with more background on the places and issues discussed and depicted in this book.

Books

Abramson, Rudy, and Jean Haskell, eds. *Encyclopedia of Appalachia*. Knoxville: University of Tennessee Press, 2006.

Berman, Morris. *Dark Ages America: The Final Phase of Empire*. New York: Norton, 2006.

Biggers, Jeff. The *United States of Appalachia: How Southern Mountaineers Brought Independence, Culture, and Entertainment to America*. Emeryville, CA: Shoemaker and Hoard, 2006.

Burns, Shirley Stewart. *Bringing Down the Mountains: The Impact of Mountaintop Removal on Southern West Virginia Communities*. Morgantown: West Virginia University Press, 2007.

Corbin, David. *Life, Work, and Rebellion in the Coal Fields: The Southern West Virginia Miners, 1880–1922*. Urbana: University of Illinois Press, 1981.

Davis, Donald. *Where There Are Mountains: An Environmental History of the Southern Appalachians*. Athens: University of Georgia Press, 2000.

Depta, Victor. *Azrael on the Mountain*. Ashland, KY: Blair Mountain Press, 2002.

Dix, Keith. *What's a Coal Miner to Do? The Mechanization of Coal Mining.* Pittsburgh: University of Pittsburgh Press, 1988.

Dreiser, Theodore, et al. *Harlan Miners Speak: Report on Terrorism in the Kentucky Coalfields.* Lexington: University Press of Kentucky, 2008 (reprint).

Eller, Ronald. *Miners, Millhands, and Mountaineers: Industrialization of the Appalachian South, 1880–1930.* Knoxville: University of Tennessee Press, 1982.

Evans, Mari-Lynn, Robert Santelli, and Holly George Warren, eds. *The Appalachians: America's First and Last Frontier.* New York: Random House, 2004.

Fisher, Stephen. *Fighting Back in Appalachia: Traditions of Resistance and Change.* Philadelphia: Temple University Press, 1993.

Freese, Barbara. *Coal: A Human History.* Cambridge, MA: Perseus Books Group, 2003.

Gaventa, John. *Power and Powerlessness: Quiescence and Rebellion in an Appalachian Valley.* Urbana: University of Illinois Press, 1980.

Goodell, Jeff. *Big Coal: The Dirty Secret behind America's Energy Future.* Boston: Houghton Mifflin, 2007.

Green, Chris, ed. *Coal: A Poetry Anthology.* Ashland, KY: Blair Mountain Press, 2006.

House, Silas, and Jason Howard, eds. *Something's Rising: Appalachians Fighting Mountaintop Removal.* Lexington: University Press of Kentucky, 2009.

Johansen, Kristin, Bobbie Ann Mason, and Mary Ann Taylor-Hall, eds. *Missing Mountains: We Went to the Mountaintop but It Wasn't There.* Nicholasville, KY: Wind, 2005.

Kennedy, Robert, Jr. *Crimes against Nature: How George W. Bush and His Corporate Pals Are Plundering the Country and Hijacking Our Democracy.* New York: HarperCollins, 2004.

Loeb, Penny. *Moving Mountains: How One Woman and Her Community Won Justice from Big Coal.* Lexington: University Press of Kentucky, 2007.

Montrie, Chad. *To Save the Land and the People: A History of Opposition to Surface Coal Mining in Appalachia.* Chapel Hill: University of North Carolina Press, 2003.

Morris, Homer. *The Plight of the Bituminous Coal Miner.* Philadelphia: University of Pennsylvania Press, 1934.

Pancake, Ann. *Strange as This Weather Has Been: A Novel.* Emeryville, CA: Shoemaker and Hoard, 2007.

Reece, Erik. *Lost Mountain: A Year in the Vanishing Wilderness.* New York: Riverhead Books, 2007.

Shifflett, Crandall. *Coal Towns: Life, Work, and Culture in Company Towns of Southern Appalachia, 1880–1960.* Knoxville: University of Tennessee Press, 1991.

Shnayerson, Michael. *Coal River.* New York: Farrar, Straus and Giroux, 2008.

Smith, Barbara Ellen. *Digging Our Own Graves: Coal Miners and the Struggle over Black Lung Disease.* Philadelphia: Temple University Press, 1987.

Squillace, Mark. *Strip Mining Handbook: A Coalfield Citizens' Guide to Using the Law to Fight Back against the Ravages of Strip Mining and Underground Mining.* Washington, DC: Environmental Policy Institute and Friends of the Earth, 1990.

Stacks, John F. *Stripping.* San Francisco: Sierra Club, 1972.

Articles

Abramson, Rudy. "A Judge in Coal Country." *Alicia Patterson Foundation Reporter,* 2003, available from www.aliciapatterson.org/APF2003/Abramson/Abramson.html.

———. "New Coal Isn't Old Coal." *Alicia Patterson Foundation Reporter,* 2001, available from www.aliciapatterson.org/APF2001/Abramson/Abramson.html.

Anderson, George M. "Of Many Things." *America,* February 3, 2003.

Babich, Phillip. "Dirty Business." *Salon,* November 13, 2003, available from www.salon.com/tech/feature/2003/11/13/slurry_coverup/index_np.html.

Bingham, Clara. "Under Mined." *Washington Monthly,* January/February 2005.

Bowe, Rebecca. "In Defense of Mountains." *E/The Environmental Magazine,* January/February 2006.

Chamblin, H. Douglas, Petra Wood, and John Edwards. "Allegheny Woodrat *(Neotoma magister)* Use of Rock Drainage Channels on Reclaimed Mines in Southern West Virginia." *American Midland Naturalist,* April 2004.

Clarke, Kevin. "And Every Mountain Brought Low." *U.S. Catholic,* September 1999.

Gabriel, Margaret. "Appalachian Catholics Tackle Divisive Mining Issue." *National Catholic Reporter,* July 30, 2004.

Galuszka, Peter. "Strip-mining on Steroids." *Business Week,* November 17, 1997.

Goodell, Jeff. "You Fight for What You've Got, Even if It's Only Worth a Dime." *O, the Oprah Magazine,* July 2006.

Hattam, Jennifer. "Dethroning King Coal." *Sierra,* November/December 2003.

Kiger, Patrick J. "Unnatural Wonders." *Mother Jones,* July/August 2006.

Loeb, Penny. "Coal Activists Stir Up Dust in West Virginia." *U.S. News & World Report,* October 13, 1997.

———. "Shear Madness." *U.S. News & World Report,* August 11, 1997.

Mitchell, John G. "When Mountains Move." *National Geographic,* March 2006.

Nichols, John. "A Novelist Runs for Governor." *Progressive,* November 2000.

Paulson, Amanda. "In Coal Country, Heat Rises over Latest Method of Mining." *Christian Science Monitor,* January 3, 2006.

Reece, Erik. "Death of a Mountain." *Harper's,* April 2005.

———. "Moving Mountains: The Battle for Justice Comes to the Coalfields of Appalachia." *Orion,* January/February 2006.

Shnayerson, Michael. "The Rape of Appalachia." *Vanity Fair,* May 2006.

Sleight-Brennan, Sandra. "Appalachia's Vanishing Mountains." *Contemporary Review,* October 2002.

Vollers, Maryanne. "Razing Appalachia." *Mother Jones,* July/August 1999.

Ward, Ken. "Mountaintop Removal." *IRE Journal,* July/August 2001.

———. "Using Documents to Report on Mountaintop Mining." *Nieman Reports,* Summer 2004.

Warren, Carol E. "Power Down in Solidarity with All Creation." *National Catholic Reporter,* February 12, 1999.

Williams, Scott. "Mine Wars. *Christian Century*, May 31, 2005.

Williams, Ted. "Mountain Madness." *Audubon,* May/June 2001.

Wood, Petra, Scott Bosworth, and Randy Dettmers. "Cerulean Warbler Abundance and Occurrence Relative to Large-Scale Edge and Habitat Characteristics." *Condor,* February 2006.

Films

All Shaken Up. Produced and directed by Bob Gate and Penny Loeb, 32 minutes. Omni Productions, 1998.

The Appalachians. Mari-Lynn Evans, executive producer; written and produced by Phylis Geller, 180 minutes. Evening Star Productions, 2005, http://www.sierraclub.org/scp/appalachians.aspx.

Black Diamonds. Produced and directed by Catherine Pancake, 90 minutes. Bullfrog Films, 2005.

The Buffalo Creek Flood: An Act of Man. Directed by Mimi Pickering, 40 minutes. Appalshop, 1975.

Buffalo Creek Revisited. Directed by Mimi Pickering, 31 minutes. Appalshop, 1984.

Burning the Future: Coal in America. Directed by David Novack, 89 minutes. American Coal Productions, 2008.

Coal Bucket Outlaw. Directed by Tom Hansell, 26.40 minutes. Appalshop, 2002.

Coal Country. Mary-Lynn Evans, executive producer; written and produced by Phylis Geller, 90 minutes. Evening Star Productions, 2009, www.coal countrythemovie.com.

In Memory of the Land and People. Produced by Bob Gates, 50 minutes. Omni Productions, 1977, reissued 2007.

The Mountain Mourning Collection. Produced by B. J. Gudmundsson. Patchwork Films, undated, www.christiansforthemountains.org/resources.

Mountain Top Removal. Directed by Michael C. O'Connell, 74 minutes. Haw River Films, 2007.

Moving Mountains. Directed by Virginia B. Moore, 30 minutes. 2006.

Mucked. Produced by Bob Gates, 52 minutes. Omni Productions, 2003.

Razing Appalachia. Directed by Sasha Waters, 54 minutes. Bullfrog Films, 2003.

Rise Up! West Virginia. Directed by B. J. Gundmundsson, 73 minutes. Patchwork Films, 2007.

Sludge. Directed by Robert Salyers, 40 minutes. Appalshop, 2005.

Citizens' Groups and Web Sites

Appalachian Center for the Economy and the Environment. www.appalachian-center.org/index.html.

Appalachian Voices. www.appvoices.org, www.ilovemountains.org.

Christians for the Mountains. www.christiansforthemountains.org.

Citizens Coal Council. www.citizenscoalcouncil.org/.

Coal Impoundment Project. www.coalimpoundment.org.

Coal Moratorium. www.cmnow.org.

Coal River Mountain Watch. www.crmw.net.

Coal Swarm. www.coalswarm.org.

Depopulation Plan as Proposed by Industry Lawyer. www.crmw.net/tools/Handouts%20&%20Flyers/Depopulation_Plan_Full.pdf.

End MTR. www.endmtr.com.

The Final Programmatic Environmental Impact Statement on Mountaintop Removal and Valley Fills. www.epa.gov/region03/mtntop/index.htm.

Greenpeace Report, "False Hope." www.greenpeace.org/international/press/reports/false-hope

I Love Mountains. www.ilovemountains.org.

Keeper of the Mountains. www.mountainkeeper.org.

Kentuckians for the Commonwealth. www.kftc.org.

League of Conservation Voters. www.lcv.org.

Mine Impoundment Project: Mine Impoundment Location and Warning System. www.coalimpoundment.com.

Mountain Justice Summer. www.mountainjusticesummer.org/.

MoveOn. www.moveon.org.

Ohio Valley Environmental Coalition. www.ohvec.org.

Save Our Cumberland Mountains. www.socm.org.

700 Mountains. www.700mountains.org/.

Sierra Club. www.sierraclub.org.

Southern Appalachian Mountain Stewards. www.samsva.org.

SouthWings. www.southwings.org.

Stop Mountaintop Removal. www.stopmountaintopremoval.org.

Tending the Commons: Folklife and Landscape in Southern West Virginia. www.memory.loc.gov/ammem/collections/tending/.

Teri Blanton. www.teriblanton.org.

West Virginia Coalfield Communities. www.wvcoalfield.com.

West Virginia Highlands Conservancy. www.wvhighlands.org/.

West Virginia Rivers Coalition. www.wvrivers.org.

About the Contributors

Giles Ashford is a painter and photographer whose work can be seen regularly at shows in Manhattan and online at www.ashford7.com. He has used his fine art photography to chronicle mountaintop removal in West Virginia, as well as environmental activism. Born in Australia, he currently lives in New York City.

Shannon Elizabeth Bell is a PhD candidate in the sociology department at the University of Oregon. She spent five years working in the coalfields of West Virginia, organizing around public health and community development issues through her position at Cabin Creek Health Center. Bell's dissertation research focuses on the social impacts of the coal industry on rural communities and on the grassroots environmental justice movement that has risen up to hold the industry accountable for the injustices it inflicts on these communities.

Wendell Berry is an award-winning poet, essayist, farmer, and novelist who was born in Newcastle, Kentucky, and currently makes his home on a farm in Port Royal, Kentucky. The author of more than thirty books, he has taught at New York University and the University of Kentucky.

Jeff Biggers has worked as a writer, educator, radio correspondent, and community organizer across the United States and in Europe, India, and Mexico. His award-winning stories have appeared on National Public Radio and Public Radio International and in scores of travel, literary, and music magazines, as well as national and foreign newspapers. Biggers has been a commentator on NPR's *Morning Edition* and for Pacific News Service national syndication and is a frequent contributor to the Huffington Post. He is the author of *In the Sierra Madre* and *The United States of Appalachia*.

Cathie Bird is a citizen-scientist and psychotherapist in private practice in Pioneer, Tennessee. She currently chairs the Strip-mine Issues Committee of Save Our Cumberland Mountains and serves on that organization's Anti-racism Transition Team.

Teri Blanton is a longtime environmental activist working to protect Kentucky citizens from the ravages of coal mining and to open up the political process to local residents. Originally from Harlan County, Kentucky, she currently resides in Berea, Kentucky.

Julia "Judy" Bonds is a co-director of Coal River Mountain Watch. A lifelong resident of southern West Virginia, she has been fighting for social and environmental justice for the Appalachian coalfields since 1998. In 2003, Bonds was the North American winner of the coveted Goldman Environmental Prize. She also received the Earthmover Award in *Geo* magazine and was included on *Organic Style* magazine's Environmental Power list. She has been featured in *National Geographic*, the first "green" issue of *Vanity Fair*, *People*, and an issue of *O, the Oprah Magazine*, which focused on tough West Virginia women.

Carolyn Brown lives in Montgomery Creek (also known as Robertstown), Kentucky, surrounded by the mountains in which she played as a child. Her connections to this land are strong and deep.

Matthew Burns, a native of Pendleton County, West Virginia, is an avid family historian and amateur storyteller and photographer. He grew up listening to old family stories, which he vividly recounts on www.appalachianlifestyles.blogspot.com.

Shirley Stewart Burns, PhD. See biography on page 294.

Pauline Canterberry lives in Sylvester, West Virginia. The widow of an underground coal miner, she began taking samples to document the coal dust raining down on her community from the coal preparation plant located just outside the town. Along with Mary Miller, she became widely known as one of the "Dustbusters."

Patsy Carter lives in Martin County, Kentucky. Her daughter, Dorlis, was struck and killed by a coal truck. Carter hopes that telling her story will convey the truth that mountaintop removal and mining issues do not end with the extraction of coal.

Jim Clark (www.jimclarkphotography.com) is a contributing editor for *Outdoor Photographer* and the author-photographer of three books, including *West Virginia: The Allegheny Highlands* and *Mountain Memories: An Appalachian Sense of Place*. A native and resident of War, West Virginia, Clark travels the country speaking to organizations about photography, nature, and his beloved home state of West Virginia. The documentary *Mountain Memories* profiled Clark's life and career.

Nick Clooney is a journalist, author, television personality, and activist from Maysville, Kentucky. He has won several awards, including the

Kentucky Broadcaster's Association Distinguished Kentuckian Award, and he is a member of both the Kentucky Journalism Hall of Fame and the Ohio Television Hall of Fame. He and his wife, Nina, are the proud parents of two children—a daughter, Ada, and a son, George.

Dave Cooper is a resident of Lexington, Kentucky. After twenty years of working as a mechanical engineer in various industries, he quit his job shortly after seeing a mountaintop removal mine on Kayford Mountain, West Virginia. Since 2003, he has been on a national speaking tour to educate communities across America about mountaintop removal.

Mari-Lynn Evans. See biography on page 294.

Archie Fields was born and raised in Letcher County, Kentucky. He is an avid outdoorsman, and his family has enjoyed the mountains for generations.

Denise Giardina grew up in a coal camp in McDowell County, West Virginia. She is the author of six novels, including *Storming Heaven* and *The Unquiet Earth,* which are set in the southern West Virginia coalfields. Giardina is also a featured columnist for several publications, including the *Nation* and the *Village Voice.* She has received creative writing fellowships from the National Endowment for the Arts, as well as the Hillsdale Prize for Fiction from the Fellowship of Southern Writers for her contributions to southern literature. A resident of Charleston, West Virginia, she teaches at West Virginia State University and is an ordained deacon in the Episcopal Church.

Larry Gibson is known to many in Appalachia as the Keeper of the Mountains. He maintains the Stanley Heirs Park at Kayford Mountain, West Virginia, where he has been fighting for more than a decade to protect his ancestral land from a mountaintop removal site looming all around it. Gibson has been featured on CNN and, in 2007, was named one of CNN's Heroes. He has spoken all across America about the devastation of mountaintop removal.

Evelyn Gilbert and her husband, Sam, a native of the area, have had their lives disrupted by a mining operation near their home in Eolia, Kentucky. She hopes to help preserve their home and the mountains for the sake of their grandchildren.

Sam Gilbert, a retired coal miner and Vietnam veteran, was born and raised in Letcher County, Kentucky. He has been forced out of a peaceful retirement by the effects of the Kentucky River Coal Company mine near his property, and he is fighting to prevent the mountains and streams he enjoyed as a boy from being turned into valley fills.

Jeff Goodell is the author of *Big Coal: The Dirty Secret behind America's Energy Future.* His work has appeared in many publications, including the *New York Times Magazine,* the *New Republic,* the *Washington Post, Rolling Stone,* and *Wired.* He lives in Sunnyvale, California.

Maria Gunnoe, a resident of Bob White, West Virginia, is a community outreach and issue organizer for the Ohio Valley Environmental Coalition. In 2009, she was named the North American winner of the coveted Goldman Environmental Prize; in 2008, she was selected as a Sierra Club Law Program Hero; and in 2007, she was the recipient of Rainforest Action Network's World Rainforest Award for her efforts to create a sustainable world. She has also received the Joe Calloway Award for Civic Courage, created by the Shafeek Nader Trust for the Community, based in Washington, D.C. Gunnoe is featured in several documentaries, including *Mourning Mountains, Burning the Future: Coal in America,* and *Mountain Top Removal.* She has also been featured in numerous publications, including the *Washington Post,* the *Boston Globe,* and *O, the Oprah Magazine.*

Ken Hechler, PhD, graduated from Swarthmore College and earned an MA and PhD from Columbia University. He taught political science at Columbia, Princeton, and Marshall Universities. Hechler was a speechwriter for President Harry Truman, served in the U.S. Congress for eighteen years as a representative from West Virginia, and was elected to four terms as West Virginia's secretary of state. He has written six books, including the World War II bestseller *The Bridge at Remagen,* which was produced as a major motion picture. He currently lives in Charleston, West Virginia.

Regina Hendrix was born and raised in the Kanawha Valley of West Virginia. After a forty-five-year economic exile from the region, she returned in 1999 and, after witnessing the environmental degradation caused by chemicals and coal, became an activist with the Sierra Club and the Ohio Valley Environmental Coalition.

Michael Hendryx, PhD, is director of the West Virginia Rural Health Research Center and an associate professor in the Department of Community Medicine at West Virginia University in Morgantown. He conducts research on population health outcomes in Appalachian coal-mining areas.

John Hennen, PhD, is a professor of history at Morehead State University in Morehead, Kentucky, specializing in Appalachian labor history. He is working on a history of Local 1199, the National Union of Hospital and Health Care Employees, in West Virginia, Kentucky, and Ohio from 1970 to 1989.

Mary Anne Hitt is deputy director of the Sierra Club's National Coal Campaign. Previously she served as the executive director of Appalachian Voices, a nonprofit organization that brings people together to solve the environmental problems having the greatest impact on the central and southern Appalachian Mountains.

Silas House. See biography on page 294.

Jason Howard is a writer, editor, and musician from Eastern Kentucky. He is the coauthor with Silas House of *Something's Rising* and the editor of *We All Live Downstream: Writings about Mountaintop Removal.* A graduate of George Washington University in political science, Howard is a former senior editor and staff writer for *Equal Justice* magazine, based in Washington, D.C. His works have appeared in such publications as *Paste, Kentucky Living,* and the *Louisville Review. He lives in Berea, Kentucky.*

Jon Blair Hunter was born and raised in West Virginia and currently lives in Morgantown. An army veteran who holds a master's degree in social work, he has worked as a community organizer in West Virginia for more than thirty years, assisting low-income communities and senior citizens; he also helped organize the state's Coalition on Legislation for the Elderly. In 1996, he was elected to the West Virginia Senate, where served as the chair of the Military Committee and the Energy, Industry and Mining Committee; he voluntarily ended his term in 2008.

Ashley Judd is an eighth-generation Eastern Kentuckian and a critically acclaimed, award-winning actress. She has served as a board member for Population Services International, as a global ambassador for YouthAids (since 2001), and as a spokesperson for Defenders of Wildlife (for whom she also serves as a board member) and the Sierra Club, advocating in particular against aerial wolf hunting and mountaintop removal coal mining. Judd resides in Tennessee and Scotland with her husband, international auto racing driver Dario Franchitti.

Janet Keating, a West Virginia native, is the executive director of the Ohio Valley Environmental Coalition, located in Huntington, West Virginia. She has worked for many years to help preserve and protect the environment, especially the West Virginia mountains.

Robert F. Kennedy Jr. earned his reputation as a resolute defender of the environment with a series of successful legal actions over the course of twenty-five years as an environmental advocate and litigator. He was named one of *Time* magazine's "Heroes for the Planet" for his success in leading the group Riverkeeper's successful fight to restore the Hudson River, an achievement that helped spawn more than 170 Waterkeeper organizations across the globe. Kennedy serves as senior attorney for the Natural Resources Defense Council, chief prosecuting attorney for the Hudson Riverkeeper, and chairman of Waterkeeper Alliance. A clinical professor and supervising attorney at Pace University School of Law's Environmental Litigation Clinic, he is also the co-host of *Ring of Fire* on Air America Radio.

Builder Levy (www.builderlevy.com) has been a photographer for more than forty years. His images have appeared in more than 170 exhibitions worldwide and have been published in numerous collections, including *Images of Appalachian Coalfields, Life of the Appalachian Coal Miner,* and *Builder Levy: Photographer.* He has received a National Endowment for the Arts Fellowship for Photography, as well as an Alicia Patterson Foundation Fellowship. He lives in New York City.

Penny Loeb was the first journalist to give mountaintop removal national exposure, in an article for *U.S. News & World Report* in 1997. A graduate of the University of Missouri School of Journalism, she has been a journalist for thirty years and has received many awards and honors, including being a finalist for the Pulitzer Prize. Loeb is the author of *Moving Mountains: How One Woman and Her Community won Justice from Big Coal,* published in 2007.

Mary Ellen Lough is a home-schooling mother of four, as well as a traveler, musician, and part-time writer whose home is in the Blue Ridge Mountains of North Carolina. She and her husband have worked internationally in the movement for fair trade, and she has become active in the struggle against the devastation caused by mountaintop removal.

George Ella Lyon, originally from the mountains of Kentucky, is the author of "Where I'm From," a poem used as a model by teachers around the world. Her recent books include *Don't You Remember?* (a memoir); *Sleepsong and My Friend, the Starfinder* (both picture books); and *With a Hammer for My Heart* (a novel). A peace activist, Lyon is also a member of Public Outcry, an anti–mountaintop removal band.

Kathy Mattea is a Grammy Award–winning entertainer, twice named female vocalist of the year by the Country Music Association. In her long history of working for social justice, Mattea has brought public attention to several environmental issues, including global warming and the destructive mining practices in her native Appalachia. This work and her music are joined in her latest CD, *Coal,* featuring songs from "her place and her people." Originally from Cross Lanes, West Virginia, she now resides in Tennessee.

Bryan McNeil, PhD, is an assistant professor of anthropology at American University in Washington, D.C. His book, *Mountaintop Removal: New Directions in Activism,* will be published by the University of Illinois Press in 2009.

Mary Miller lives in Sylvester, West Virginia. She began collecting samples to document the coal dust raining down on her community from the coal preparation plant located just outside the town. Along with Pauline Canterberry, she became widely known as one of the "Dustbusters."

Richard X. Moore is a native of Michigan, where he attended Grand Valley State University before earning an MS in resource development from Michigan State University. He worked for nonprofit conservation groups in Michigan, Minnesota, and Montana before settling in Berea, Kentucky, where he currently resides. His photographic interests include environmental portraiture, still lifes, and landscapes rendered both digitally and on traditional film. He especially enjoys documenting the hidden, often-overlooked beauty of the natural world.

John Mullins is a sixth-generation West Virginian from the town of Oak Hill. His interests include landscape photography, colonial American history, and Appalachian culture.

David W. Orr, PhD, is the Paul Sears Distinguished Professor of Environmental Studies and Politics at Oberlin College and special assistant to the president of the college, as well as the James Marsh Professor at the University of Vermont. He is the author of six books, including *The Transforming Climate: Leadership in the Age of Consequences* (2009), and coeditor of three others. Orr is active in efforts to stop mountaintop removal in Appalachia and to develop a new economy based on ecological restoration and wind energy.

Ann Pancake, PhD, grew up in Romney and Summersville, West Virginia. Her first novel, *Strange as This Weather Has Been*, features a southern West Virginia family devastated by mountaintop removal mining. Based on interviews and real events, the novel was one of *Kirkus Reviews*' Top Ten Fiction Books of 2007; it won the Weatherford Award in 2007 and was a finalist for the Orion Book Award in 2008. Pancake holds a doctorate in English literature from the University of Washington and teaches in the low-residency MFA program at Pacific Lutheran University.

John S. Rausch, a Glenmary priest living in Stanton, Kentucky, directs the Catholic Committee of Appalachia. His monthly syndicated column, "Faith and the Marketplace," appears in twenty Catholic diocesan newspapers. He received the 2007 Teacher of Peace award from Pax Christi, U.S.A.

Erik Reece teaches writing at the University of Kentucky in Lexington. His work has appeared in *Harper's, Orion,* and *The Oxford American,* among other publications. He is the author of *Lost Mountain* and *An American Gospel: On Family, History, and the Kingdom of God.* Reece was the recipient of the Sierra Club's David R. Brower Award, and his *Harper's* story on which *Lost Mountain* is based won the Columbia University School of Journalism's John B. Oakes Award for Distinguished Environmental Journalism in 2005.

John Roark lives in Montgomery Creek, Kentucky, where his property and life have been much affected by mountaintop removal. He is concerned about the dangers a community faces when mining is conducted near family homes and about the failure of state agencies to protect community members.

Lorelei Scarbro, a resident of Rock Creek, West Virginia, is an activist with Coal River Mountain Watch. She has been instrumental in the struggle to promote the Coal River Wind Project, a clean-energy project that is an alternative to mountaintop removal in the Coal River Valley. Lorelei's land, home, family cemetery, and surrounding environment all face the threat of future mountaintop removal.

Mark Schmerling (www.schmerlingdocumentary.com) is a professional photographer who has been documenting the effects of mountaintop removal since 2005 in images that capture its true costs to Appalachia's land and culture. His work is featured in Shirley Stewart Burns's *Bringing Down the Mountains* and has been displayed by the Sierra Club and the Ohio Valley Environmental Coalition. He works with the Sierra Club Clean Water Campaign, which supports legislation to help end mountaintop removal. Schmerling lives in Bryn Athyn, Pennsylvania.

Kathy Selvage is vice president of Southern Appalachian Stewards, an organization formed by local residents of southwest Virginia, including retired coal miners, to protect their communities from the impacts of mountaintop removal coal mining. She lives near Wise, Virginia.

Michael Shnayerson is a longtime contributing editor to *Vanity Fair,* with nearly 100 feature articles to his credit. These include reporting for the magazine on the environmental ills arising from policy changes in the Bush administration's Interior Department. Haunted by the tragedy of Appalachian mountaintop removal coal mining, he went on to write the book *Coal River: How a Few Brave Americans Took on a Powerful Company—and the Federal Government—to Save the Land They Love* (2008). Shnayerson lives on the east end of Long Island, New York.

Jack Spadaro, a mining engineer for more than three decades, is a former superintendent of the National Mine Safety and Health Academy. Motivated by the Buffalo Creek disaster of 1972, he made a vow to protect the people and environment of Appalachia against life-threatening hazards caused by mining operations. Now a vocal opponent of mountaintop removal, Spadaro lives in Lincoln County, West Virginia.

Marian Steinert studied at the Rochester Institute of Technology and the Savannah College of Art and Design, and has taught at Kent State University and the University of Akron. Her photographs can be found in collections across the United States and were featured in *The Appalachians,* the companion book to the film of the same name.

Vivian Stockman works for the Ohio Valley Environmental Coalition, based in Huntington, West Virginia. Her photos of the movement to end mountaintop removal have been published in newspapers, magazines, and books, and have appeared in documentaries and on Web sites. Her publication credits include the *New York Times, the Washington Monthly, Orion, World Watch* magazine, *E/The Environmental Magazine, French Geo,* and dozens more.

Jo Syz is a UK-based photographer who documents humans' impact on their environment. His photographic series *Coal River Mountain* records communities and landscapes affected by mountaintop removal coal mining in the Appalachian Mountains of West Virginia. Syz graduated from the Royal College of Art, London, in 2004. His work has recently been shown at Exit Art in New York and the 198 Gallery in London; it has also been published in *The Independent, The Guardian, The Observer, Psychologies* magazine, *Hotshoe International,* and the *Artists Newsletter.*

Denny Tyler, a native of Bolt, West Virginia, is an avid outdoorsman and amateur photographer who is also known as the Backwoods Drifter. In recent years, he has become an outspoken opponent of mountaintop removal, and, in 2008, he created the Web site www.endmtr.com, where visitors may view his photographs, read his blog, and voice their own opinions on the practice.

Rully Urias lives in the small community called Island Creek of Phyllis, in Pike County, Kentucky, on the land his family settled in 1825. Though a mountaintop removal site now encroaches upon their home, and all the neighbors have sold out, he and his family refuse to leave.

Bo Webb is a native West Virginian who comes from a long line of coal miners, including his father, grandfather, and uncles. A Vietnam veteran, Webb sold his business in 2000 to devote himself full-time to the fight against mountaintop removal. He currently resides in Naoma, West Virginia.

About the Editors

Shirley Stewart Burns is the author of *Bringing Down the Mountains: The Impact of Mountaintop Removal on Southern West Virginia Communities,* the first academic book on the subject. She holds a PhD in history with an Appalachian emphasis and served as an editor for the Family and Communities section of the *Encyclopedia of Appalachia.* A native of southern West Virginia, Burns is the daughter, granddaughter, great-granddaughter, and sister of underground coal miners. She now lives in Charleston, West Virginia.

Mari-Lynn Evans is the CEO of Evening Star Productions and the executive producer of many award-winning national television and video programs, including the three-part public television documentary series *The Appalachians.* She spent three years making the documentary film *Coal Country* and coediting this companion book. Evans grew up in Bulltown, West Virginia, and currently makes her home in Akron, Ohio.

Silas House is the author of the novels *Clay's Quilt, A Parchment of Leaves,* and *The Coal Tattoo* and of the nonfiction book (with Jason Howard) *Something's Rising: Appalachians Fighting Mountaintop Removal.* His work has received many awards, including two Kentucky Novel of the Year Awards, the Award for Special Achievement from the Fellowship of Southern Writers, the Appalachian Book of the Year, and the Chaffin Award. House lives in Eastern Kentucky, where he was born and raised. Visit his Web site: www.silashouse.net.